**Investor Relations and
Financial Communication**

Investor Relations and Financial Communication

Creating Value Through Trust and Understanding

Alexander V. Laskin,
Quinnipiac University
Hamden, Connecticut

WILEY Blackwell

Registered Office
John Wiley & Sons, Inc., 111 River Street, Hoboken, NJ 07030, USA

Editorial Office
The Atrium, Southern Gate, Chichester, West Sussex, PO19 8SQ, UK

For details of our global editorial offices, customer services, and more information about Wiley products visit us at www.wiley.com.

Library of Congress Cataloging-in-Publication Data
Names: Laskin, Alexander V., author.
Title: Investor relations and financial communication : creating value through trust and understanding / Alexander V. Laskin.
Description: Hoboken, NJ : John Wiley & Sons, 2022. | Includes bibliographical references and index.
Identifiers: LCCN 2021024481 (print) | LCCN 2021024482 (ebook) | ISBN 9781119780458 (paperback) | ISBN 9781119780489 (pdf) | ISBN 9781119780472 (epub) | ISBN 9781119780496 (obook)
Subjects: LCSH: Corporations--Investor relations. | Financial services industry--Communication systems. | Corporations--Finance.
Classification: LCC HD2744 .L267 2022 (print) | LCC HD2744 (ebook) | DDC 659.2/85--dc23
LC record available at https://lccn.loc.gov/2021024481
LC ebook record available at https://lccn.loc.gov/2021024482

Cover image: © Nikada/Getty
Cover design by Wiley

Set in 9.5/12pt STIXTwoText by Integra Software Services, Pondicherry, India

SKY10031047_110121

Contents

Part I   Profession   *1*

1   Introduction to Investor Relations and Financial Communication   *3*

2   Investor Relations and Financial Communication Industry   *24*

3   Stockholders and Stakeholders   *39*

Part II   Disclosure   *61*

4   Communicating Financial Information   *63*

5   Communicating Nonfinancial Information   *81*

Part III   Context   *93*

6   Legal and Regulatory Environment of Investor Relations and
Financial Communication   *95*

7   Corporate Governance, Environmental Sustainability, and
Social Responsibility   *107*

8   Shareholder Activism and Crisis Management   *121*

Part IV   Work   *133*

9   Main Activities and Publications in Investor Relations and
Financial Communication   *135*

10   Going Public and Going Private   *155*

11   Measurement and Evaluation of Investor Relations and
Financial Communication   *169*

Part V   Transformation   *179*

12   Globalization of the Financial Markets and Regional Distinctions   *181*

13   The Future of Investor Relations and Financial Communication   *189*

Bibliography   *200*
Index   *211*

Part I

Profession

1

Introduction to Investor Relations and Financial Communication

Definition

Many people rely on the stock markets and entrust their future to the efficiency of the investment system. Think about it: in the United States alone pension and retirement saving accounts constitute about US$20 trillion in assets, with most of those assets being equities and bonds. Efficient markets require information in order to function properly – corporations disclose important details related to their operations and finances to ensure all market participants, from professional investors managing billions of dollars to a retired teacher in Iowa with a few hundred dollars invested, have the same access to the information they need to make an informed decision about their investments. Investor relations professionals are on mile one of this information highway, enabling timely and comprehensive disclosure in order to help all investors better understand the company's business and its value, and help investors better understand what they can expect from their investments in the future. In other words, the goal of investor relations becomes not just disclosure of information but educating investors and managing their expectations related to the accurate, or fair, value of the corporations.

The largest professional organization for investor relations, the National Investor Relations Institute (NIRI), proposes the following definition of investor relations: "a strategic management responsibility that integrates finance, communication, marketing and securities law compliance to enable the most effective two-way communication between a company, the financial community, and other constituencies, which ultimately contributes to a company's securities achieving fair valuation."

The key part of this definition is the fair valuation – this is what all investor relations activities should be targeted at according to the NIRI's definition. This focus on fairness is important. It means investor relations professionals, who are often referred to as IROs (investor relations officers), should be eager to disclose negative information as much as positive; information that can pull the stock price down as much as information that can push the stock price up. Indeed, if IROs focus only on positive updates and trying to hide or diminish the impact of negative developments, they may contribute to a phenomenon called *overvaluation*, which is when stock price is priced above its fair market level. The danger of overvaluation lies in overcorrection: if and when all information finally becomes available, market participants may overreact to the

Investor Relations and Financial Communication: Creating Value Through Trust and Understanding, First Edition. Alexander V. Laskin.
© 2022 John Wiley & Sons, Inc. Published 2022 by John Wiley & Sons, Inc.

negative news as it would typically come as a surprise, as a leak, or as a discovery by a third party such as a business journalist or a financial analyst, and may send the stock price below even what would be the fair price. In addition, these events tend to undermine the credibility of the company, its management, and its investor relations department, compromising all future disclosures and putting the relationships between the company and the financial stakeholders at risk.

The concept of fair market valuation is based on the efficient market hypothesis, which defines an efficient market as "a market in which prices always 'fully reflect' available information" (Fama, 1970, p. 383). Such a market is in equilibrium: all securities are fairly priced, according to their risks and returns. No investors can consistently outperform, or beat, the market, and thus there is no reason to constantly buy and sell shares of companies trying to outperform the average market return. The efficient market hypothesis, however, requires key assumptions to be met: all relevant information about the company and its performance is publicly available, all market participants have equal access to such information on a timely basis, and all investors are rational and capable of evaluating the information available to them.

Thus, investor relations, a function charged with providing information about the company to shareholders, financial analysts, and other market participants, is at the very foundation of the efficient markets. In fact, investor relations becomes a key activity not just for a particular company but for the whole modern economy. The survival of modern capitalism depends on how well IROs perform their task in ensuring equal access to information for various financial market participants. IROs are tasked with ensuring that the key assumptions of the efficient market hypothesis are met through extensive and timely disclosure of all relevant information pertaining to the company and its securities.

It is not enough for IROs just to disclose the information, however, for the share price to arrive at its fair value. Disclosure in itself may not be enough for a successful investor relations program. The efficient market hypothesis requires not just access to information but also understanding of the information and developing reasonable expectations based on such information. It is possible for somebody to have access to accurate information but still make incorrect conclusions based on it or have unreasonable expectations based on that information. A big part of an IRO's job is similar to the job of a teacher: IROs must educate investors, shareholders, financial analysts, business journalists, and others on what this information actually means for the company – what the implications of the information are for the future of the company.

Today's businesses are complex structures making money on advanced technological developments, intangible reputational assets, and unique processes they develop over multiple years. For example, it may not be sufficient for the investor relations department of a pharmaceutical company to disclose information about the discovery of a novel chemical compound – for many in the investment community this information may not mean much. Instead, it may be important to explain what the potential of that chemical compound is – maybe it can lead to a new type of medication that will completely revolutionize how certain types of health conditions are treated. Without such in-depth knowledge of this discovery, it may be impossible to know how this compound may make extraordinary profits for the company in the future. Yet, it is important not to oversell and to talk about the challenges as well – how much time it may take before this discovery can become a marketable product, what are the potential roadblocks along the way, and what are the chances of success or failure. Again, people in the financial community, outside of the company, may not have a good understanding of all these details even if they have been disclosed to them. They require more than just an information dump; they require explanation and guidance in order to understand how this discovery can affect the business and value of the company. Thus, it is impossible for anybody to arrive at the fair value of a company without some help from the investor relations professionals doing their job of disclosing the information and educating the investment community.

When the definition talks about fair value, it talks about the fair value of the company's *securities*. So, what are securities? In the simplest terms, securities are tradable financial instruments. There are generally two types of securities: equity and debt. Equity securities represent an ownership in a corporation stock. These are usually called shares of stock. People can buy shares in many publicly traded companies – for example, Microsoft, Tesla, or Snap – each share has a price that fluctuates based on all the information available about the company and the resultant supply and demand for the shares of this company. If somebody were to buy every single share of, for example, Tesla, they would own the whole company. Owning shares of companies makes you a shareholder – you become eligible to participate in shareholder meetings and vote on various issues around how the company is run, including the election of the Board of Directors. The more shares you have, the more votes you have. Not all shares are the same and not all give the same rights and privileges; in addition, corporations may introduce their own unique type of equity securities as well.

Debt securities do not represent ownership in a company – instead, it is just a debt, a loan that must be repaid. As a result, debt holders do not get to vote on issues related to how a company is run, but they get their money back as the loans are paid back by the borrower and usually with interest. Both of these types of securities, equity and debt, may be traded; for example, if a debt holder does not want to wait till the loan is due for repayment, they may sell their debt securities on the secondary market to somebody else.

The same is true for equity. However, shares do not have any repayment or expiration date – once you buy a share of a company, you have a share in the ownership of this company forever. If you decide at some point that you would rather part with your shares, you can sell them on the secondary market to somebody else. Although the corporation that originally issued those securities does not typically participate in these transactions on the secondary market, it has a big effect on the price of its securities. Consider somebody who bought a share of Apple stock in 1990 when the shares were traded on a secondary market for about 30 cents. Today, the same share is worth about US$120. Investing a few thousand dollars in Apple stock 30 years ago would have made a significant contribution to the investor's retirement account balance today. This increase in value is also good for a corporation: if a company decided to raise additional funds and sell more securities, it would be evaluated based on its current price not based on the 30-cent value from 30 years ago – it makes it easier for corporations to finance big projects.

NIRI's definition of investor relations also talks about the way the fair value is built – specifically, it talks about *two-way communication*. What makes communication "two-way"? When the company sends out a news release or posts information on its website, it communicates in a one-way fashion – from the company to the outside world. There is nothing wrong with one-way communication – it is an appropriate communication technique in many situations, but it has its drawbacks, and it does not work all the time. For example, the company may be disclosing torrents of information about cost-cutting measures and new business development ideas, but without feedback from shareholders the company cannot know if shareholders actually understand how these new business ideas affect the company's business model. This feedback becomes the return loop in the communication process and the communication becomes two-way communication.

In other words, in two-way communications both parties have a chance to speak and to be heard, and the information travels both ways – from the company to the stakeholders and from the stakeholders to the company. This puts an extra responsibility on the IROs – they are responsible not just for disclosure, or sending the messages out, but also for listening. IROs must be not only the mouthpieces of their organizations, but also their ears and eyes. Two-way communication is an essential part of investor relations if the goal of investor relations is educating investors and others in the financial community on the value of the company – education calls for two-way communication and dialogue. Investors must have the opportunity to ask questions and ask for clarifications in order to improve their understanding; in fact, IROs should welcome these investor inquiries as they help IROs understand where investors stand and what their expectations of the company are.

But there is more to two-way communication than enhanced understanding. Ultimately, investors are the owners of the corporation and the company's management has a fiduciary duty to them, a duty to act in the best interest of the investors. Part of this process is for IROs to listen to investors and then to communicate the messages from the investors to the company's management. Indeed, if the company's management works for the shareholders, the management should know what shareholders think of their performance. It is the responsibility of IROs to collect this information and communicate it to the company's management. As a result, investor relations departments must focus on building two-way communication channels to enable dialogue between corporations and a financial community.

The definition of investor relations talks about various skills that IROs must possess in order to do their jobs successfully: finance, communication, marketing, and securities law compliance. In fact, it may sound like four different professionals should be doing this job! Indeed, as an IRO you have to be knowledgeable in all these four areas – you need to be an expert communicator, after all, two-way communication is a foundation of the profession as we have just learned. But the topic of the communication often revolves around financial content – IROs' communications are often financial communications – meaning communications about sales, profits, expenses, earnings before interest, taxes, depreciation, and amortization (EBIDTA), earnings per share (EPS), rate of return, and other financial terms. It may be challenging even for the best communicators to talk about subjects they know nothing about. So, understanding of accounting and financial concepts in investor relations is important. In addition, all these communications are occurring in a highly regulated environment – there are many rules on what information must be communicated, when it must be communicated, and what channels must be used to communicate it. There are rules against selective disclosure and against trading on privileged information. All these rules require IROs to be knowledgeable about laws and regulations governing the securities markets and make IROs agents of enforcement of these regulations. Investor relations is also part marketing. Investor relations professionals are expected to engage in and build relationships with the financial community – identify investors who may be a proper target for the company's stock, increase the coverage of the company by the financial analysts, and even promote stock to retail shareholders.

As a result, it is quite common for IROs to have multiple educational degrees. A study that analyzed educational backgrounds of IROs at Fortune-500 companies found that almost 60% of IROs had a second, graduate-level degree. It is not uncommon that if an IRO's first degree is communication-based, they would earn a second degree in finance or accounting to complement their communications expertise; in some cases, maybe even a law degree. If an IRO has an undergraduate finance or accounting degree, however, then they may complement it with graduate studies in communication or marketing. In addition, NIRI has a variety of professional development opportunities available for its members to enhance their knowledge and skills.

The two remaining terms in the definition of investor relations are "strategic" and "management." The strategic part of investor relations refers to the proactive nature of the profession. Investor relations is not just reacting in response to the outside world – to the request for information from shareholders, for example. Instead, IROs set goals and objectives, and develop a plan for how to reach these goals. For some companies, IROs may set a goal to increase the financial analyst coverage of the company stock and they would work proactively to identify financial analysts who cover similar companies or companies in the same industry and reach out to them to generate interest. In another case, IROs may set a goal of influencing the company's shareholders mix – for example, they may try to increase the number of retail shareholders, and would develop a plan for how to achieve this target.

Of course, these investor relations goals and objectives must benefit the company as a whole – all these decisions are rooted in the overall corporate strategic vision. This makes it essential for IROs to be part of the top management and to have a seat at the proverbial table where the top-level discussions are happening. This is where the term "management" comes from. IROs are part of the top management team of a company. It would be virtually impossible to be successful as an IRO without having access to the executive *C-suite*, also called the *dominant coalition* – people who run the company. It is important for IROs to be well versed in short- and long-term corporate strategy in order to be able to educate investors on the short- and long-term corporate value. It is also important for IROs to be able to relay investor feedback to the C-suite directly and in a timely fashion. All this makes access to the C-suite a must. There is also another way to look at the concept of management responsibility in the definition of investor relations. The term management also means a certain autonomy and ability to control its own domain. IROs are recognized as having an expertise in the investor relations tasks and thus they have a certain autonomy over managing these tasks. They have an autonomy over how to better communicate with financial analysts or how to better relay negative news to the market, for example. This expertise is recognized and appreciated. This autonomy is not absolute – almost every task in a corporate world is done within a team. The same is true for many investor relations processes – the legal team, treasury, accounting, marketing, public relations, and other departments often get involved – but each is recognized as having their unique perspective and their unique expertise.

This is the meaning of NIRI's definition of investor relations. It is, of course, not the only professional organization and it is not the only definition. For example, *IR Society*, the professional organization for investor relations in the UK, has a slightly different definition: "Investor relations is the communication of information and insight between a company and the investment community. This process enables a full appreciation of the company's business activities, strategy and prospects and allows the market to make an informed judgement about the fair value and appropriate ownership of a company." It is easy to see the parallels between these definitions – fair value is the key goal in both of these definitions. And this fair value is achieved through full appreciation or understanding of the company and what it does. The main process, the main activity of investor relations is communication between a company and the investment community. So, both definitions, although they use different words, basically talk about the same concepts.

These definitions are not set in stone – they evolve with changes in society. For example, several books on investor relations from the 1990s define investor relations as aimed at increasing the share price instead of aimed at fair value. Even the definition of investor relations that NIRI used in the 1990s calls it a marketing function aimed at creating a positive impact on the company's value. Thus, to better understand the profession it is important to take a glance at its history.

History

Financial communication, as a function of communicating financial information, has existed since the emergence of finance – if there was money, it was important to communicate about it. In fact, one of the oldest surviving documents of human civilization, The Code of Hammurabi, a Babylonian code of laws of ancient Mesopotamia, dating back to about 1745 BCE, has references to such key concepts of financial communication as minimum wage, interest rates, contractual obligations, and inheritance rules.

Investor relations, however, developed later as it is inextricably connected with the separation of ownership and management. In the past, when blacksmiths or other craftsmen conducted their business they did not need to communicate their financial information or build relationships with investors because they financed themselves. They were investors, managers, and employees of their enterprises. As the industries progressed, they started hiring more employees, but the original investors were typically the managers themselves. There was still no separation between ownership and management.

At some point, instead of one manager, it became more common to see a family – fathers, sons, uncles, mothers, daughters, aunts, and so on – as investors and managers of family businesses, which started to replace singular craftsmen. But still family relations were used instead of investor relations in such family enterprises. Finally, the demands of the human enterprises became larger than one person or even one family could satisfy. It required pulling resources together from many different individuals. It was the time for many people to come together and contribute a share of resources to the overall organization – hence the birth of a shareholding company.

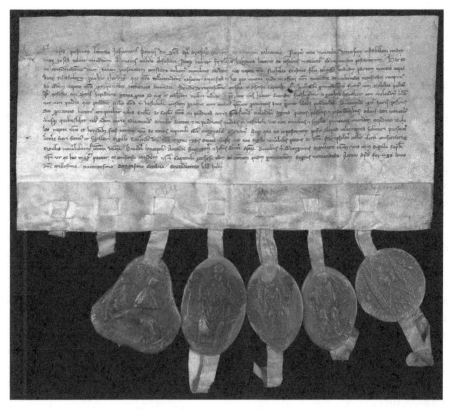

Figure 1.1 The oldest share: Stora Kopparberg original share, June 16, 1288. Source: Archives of Sweden.

It is fitting that the first shareholding company is alleged to be a mining operation. Extracting resources from the earth is a massive undertaking that indeed requires efforts and resources of many people to come together. The copper mine in the Swedish town of Falun is believed to have been operational since the year 1000 based on archeological studies in the area (Rydberg, 1979). However, the first official document of the Stora Kopparberg Bergslags Aktiebolag, a corporation responsible for mining the Falun mine, dates back to June 16, 1288, when 12.5% of Stora Kopparberg shares were sold (Figure 1.1). Thus, we can say that the history of shareholding companies dates back to the thirteenth century.

In 1347, as the largest copper supplier in Europe, the company was granted a charter by King Magnus Eriksson "setting up a corporation of master miners" (Anon., 1963, p. 98). The company is still in operation today with 2019 sales of over €10.1 billion. It is still a shareholding company with shares traded at the Stockholm and Helsinki stock exchanges. It employs about 26,000 people in 30 countries and its focus has shifted from copper to "renewable solutions in packaging, biomaterials, wooden constructions and paper on global markets" (Stora Enso, n.d.).

Although Stora Kopparberg is the first example of a shareholding corporation, initially it was not a publicly traded company. In other words, not anyone could purchase a share in Stora Kopparberg. In fact, the shares were reserved for either professional miners or noble people of the area – people whose contributions were essential for the mine to operate. On the other hand, the first publicly traded company, where shares could be purchased by anybody who was willing to pay the price, is believed to be the Dutch East India Company. The company, founded in 1602 for the primary purpose of trading between Asia and Europe, is claimed to be not just the first publicly traded company, but also the first multinational corporation. The first publicly traded company also required the first stock exchange: "The Amsterdam bourse was founded in September 1602 within six months of the company's formation [Dutch East India Company] and was an integral component to its success" (Chambers, 2006, p. 1).

The revolutionary idea of opening company ownership to the people allowed the company to bring in more than 6 million guilders, with share price jumping about 15% in initial trading, and a subsequent increase of 300% over the next 20 years. As a result, the Dutch East India Company was able to finance its growth to unprecedented heights: "50,000 civilian employees, with a private army of 40 warships, 20,000 sailors and 10,000 soldiers and a mind blowing dividend flow... With a market for its stocks and bonds, the Dutch East India Company became probably the most powerful business in the history of the world" (Chambers, 2006, p. 1).

In the United States, investments in the securities of companies became popular at the end of the nineteenth and beginning of the twentieth centuries. Macey and Miller (1991) explain this development as being a result of a variety of factors happening at the same time:

> The growth of large industries such as railroads and heavy manufacturing stimulated unprecedented demands for capital. At the same time, increases in wealth among the middle classes created a new source of capital that could be tapped effectively by means of public securities issuance. Developments in transportation and communication technology made widespread promotion and distribution of securities practicable. Realizing the potential purchasing power of the rising middle class, bond issuers began to offer securities in denominations of $100 instead of the traditional denominations of $1,000 or even $10,000. A surge of new investment followed.
>
> *(pp. 352–353)*

In addition to traditional blue chips, shares in large and well-known corporations, many speculative securities appeared that promised get-rich-quick opportunities: gold mines or oil companies – usually something distant and at the very early stages of development. "The speculative securities in the early 1900s were typically equity securities issued by mining and petroleum companies, land development schemes (such as irrigation and tract housing projects), and patent development promotions" (Macey & Miller, 1991, p. 353). Many investors lost money in these schemes. The securities markets at the time had a severe informational problem – it was difficult, if not impossible, to verify the claims made about the securities, especially if the shares were part of a distant gold mine in the Wild West.

These speculative securities were also promoted and sold outside of normal distribution channels – often by door-to-door salesmen and in other face-to-face solicitations.

The securities salesmen were also among the first ones to utilize mailing lists – which traditional brokers referred to as "sucker lists" – where securities were hyped beyond any measure: "one-third of which [letter] is devoted to an extravagant flattery of the intelligence of the recipient, and the remaining two-thirds to the extolling of the excellent merits of the Gold Hammer Mines and Tunnel Company, from the investment standpoint; after which this most valuable stock is offered at the amazingly low price of seven and one-half cents a share" (as cited in Macey & Miller, 1991, p. 354).

As a result, thousands and millions of dollars were lost to fraud: "pure fake" and "near fake" enterprises. Other enterprises may have been legitimate and not an outright fraud, but too overhyped, too risky, and too speculative. The end result for investors was the same – loss of money. Investors could not rely on the truthfulness of statements made in connection with securities transactions and that put the whole securities market in jeopardy. A banking journal at the start of the twentieth century wrote, "So many people have lost their money on 'fake' investments that they seem to be incapable of distinguishing the false from the genuine, and hence are distrustful of all" (as cited in Macey & Miller, 1991, p. 394).

These developments required Kansas in 1911 to enact legislation to protect its citizens from these con artists. As Kansas Banking Commissioner J. N. Dolley explained, these fakers were duping unwitting investors by selling worthless interests in fly-by-night companies and gold mines along the back roads of Kansas. Yet, no actual assets backed up these securities; nothing but the blue skies of Kansas (Gelber, 2013). The first actual usage of the term *blue sky* dates back to June 5, 1895, when an article in the Colorado newspaper, the *Castle Rock Journal*, said: "When a promoter by artful persuasion succeeds in getting money for something which has no value except in the mind of the credulous purchaser he is said to have been selling 'blue sky'" (Gelber, 2013). As a result, these types of securities were called blue sky and hot air securities (Wooldridge, 1906), and later just blue sky securities.

Soon after Kansas, other states followed with their own regulations and, as a result, a network of comprehensive securities legislations developed at the state level. These state laws are commonly referred to as blue sky laws:

> The name that is given to the law indicates the evil at which it is aimed, that is, to use the language of a cited case, "speculative schemes which have no more basis than so many feet of 'blue sky'"; or, as stated by counsel in another case, "to stop the sale of stock in fly-by-night concerns, visionary oil wells, distant gold mines and other like fraudulent exploitations."
>
> *(Hall v. Geiger-Jones Co., 1917, p. 539)*

These laws created the first requirements for disclosure and securities registration. The issuers were required to file periodic reports of financial conditions of the company; before selling the securities in a state, the company was required to provide a business plan and a copy of the securities offered for sale. The state had the right to ban the company from doing business in the state if it did not "promise a fair return on the stocks, bonds or other securities" (as cited in Macey & Miller, 1991, p. 361).

So, as a result, the first type of securities regulations that could have started the development of investor relations and financial communication in the United States, blue sky laws, were created as

> a means to thwart the schemes of a class of people who were denigrated repeatedly as fly-by-night operators, fraudulent promoters, robbers, cancers, vultures, swindlers, grafters, crooks, gold-brick men, fakirs, parasites, confidence men, bunco artists, get-rich-quick Wallingfords, and so on. Against this class of bad operators was counterpoised a class of victims, usually portrayed as innocent, weak minded, vacillating, foolish, or guileless, and usually cast in the roles of widows, orphans, farmers, little idiots or working people.
>
> *(Macey & Miller, 1991, p. 389)*

The legislation was needed not just for their protection, however. In fact, "if consumers could not discover accurate information about the quality of securities offered for sale, a loss of confidence in securities markets generally might result" (p. 394). It was needed for the protection of society as a whole. "The functioning of capital markets in facilitating capital formation would be severely impaired, to the detriment of issuers, buyers, and the economy at large" (Macey & Miller, 1991, p. 390).

Blue sky laws were not universally praised, however. Some issuers had concerns regarding how these laws could affect their ability to raise capital and the extra burden the regulations imposed on them. But probably the biggest opponent of blue sky laws was the Investment Bankers Association (IBA). IBA saw these laws as an attempt to keep money within state borders and prevent, or at least impede, inter-state security trade – and perhaps not without reason. One of the local Louisianan financial professionals was quoted as saying: "the sooner we learn the lesson of keeping our money at home and patronizing home industry, instead of putting it into the hands of the New York Stock Exchange speculators and gamblers, the better it will be for our State and the South" (as cited in Macey & Miller, 1991, p. 361).

World War I and the Great Depression slowed down the development of financial markets as well as investor relations and financial communications. However, the most important federal regulations appeared at that time, in large part in response to the stock market crash of 1929 – the Securities Act of 1933 and the Securities Exchange Act of 1934. These laws paved the way for professionalization of investor relations and continue to influence the practice of financial communications today.

The history of the professional period of investor relations and financial communication begins after the end of the World War II. The professional period saw the creation of professional associations, the appearance of the titles of investor relations officers, vice-presidents, and specialists, the arrival of big and small financial communication agencies, and the advent of stand-alone corporate investor relations departments. This period can be divided into three historical eras: the *communication era*, when investor relations and the financial communication landscape were dominated by people with communication backgrounds; the *financial era*, when the pendulum swung the other way and the field became dominated by professionals with financial and accounting degrees; and, finally, the current era, the *synergy era*, where the industry is looking for the balance between communication and financial fields of expertise.

Communication Era

The communication era of investor relations was characterized by the domination of strategic communication, public relations, marketing, and other communication professionals in performing the duties of IROs. Thus, this era is labeled the *communication* era.

The earliest mention of the investor relations function is traced back to Ralph Cordiner, a chairman of General Electric, who in 1953 created a department in charge of all shareholder communications. The first consulting agencies also began offering investor relations services. Most of the investor relations work focused on putting the word about organizations out and on attracting attention to the stock – perhaps not that different from the exploits of P. T. Barnum. Silver (2004) recalls that in its early years, investor relations was often associated "with the so-called dog and pony shows for sell-side analysts and retail investors, usually held at the offices of securities brokerages" (p. 70).

These developments were a response to the post-World War II economic boom that generated wealth for private Americans and at the same time encouraged business growth in order to satisfy the constantly growing needs of consumers. The corporations needed money to grow and develop; people needed a way to invest surplus income. In this situation, the meeting of the two worlds was inevitable.

Among the first corporations to strategically target private shareholders–consumers were car companies, such as Ford, GM, and Chrysler. It was no surprise that car companies figured out that if you give at least one share to a person who buys a car that person would never buy a competitor's vehicle from that point on, and vice versa! Product marketing, as a result, merged with stock marketing. Increasing the demand for stock became an important part of the corporate agenda: "Occupants of the executive suites were quick to see, that all of this demand for stock was helping to push prices up and up. This helped immensely to finance growth, enhance empires" (Morrill, 1995). The companies accustomed to competing on the product market brought similar tactics to their competition on the financial markets. Thus, the investor relations function was charged with the task of grabbing investors' attention and selling them the company in fierce competition with other corporations.

This was, however, a new experience for many corporations, a competition they were not prepared for. And, thus, most corporations looked outside for help. Unfortunately for them, investor relations agencies did not exist yet. In this vacuum of investor relations expertise, someone had to fill the void. Morrill (2007) explains that in this situation management turned to the recognized experts in communication – public relations and marketing: investor relations was often viewed as an extension of the public relations function.

In the 1950s, however, public relations was not a well-established practice itself. Only the largest companies had internal public relations staff and the functions and roles of public relations were quite limited. Cutlip (1994) suggests that in the first half of the twentieth century many viewed public relations as a simple adjunct to advertising to stimulate better sales. In addition, the end of World War II and the booming economy left little time for public relations, which was sliding to the bottom of the priority list. In fact, "many companies were undergoing radical change, often in the form of mergers and acquisitions, with new businesses and new executive personnel appearing on the scene. In these fluid situations, public relations often fell to the person nearest at hand" (Morrill, 1995). In other words, when corporations turned to public relations to manage investor relations, public relations was not yet ready to take on this challenge.

As a result, the new and not-well-established public relations function was suddenly charged with the additional duties of the investor relations job – a job for which most practitioners on the corporate or agency sides were not qualified. So, they approached this new task in the same way they approached other public relations tasks – relying on press agentry and publicity:

> In concrete terms, shareholder relations became transformed into publicity, promotion and pageants... The annual reports suddenly blossomed as a 48-page, glossy sales brochure for the company's products. The financial were there, mandatorily, but the sell was in the sizzle, not the steak... The annual meeting became a huge, gala free-for-all. A large eastern railroad put together a special train for stockholders and carried them first class to a company-owned hotel in the southern Appalachians for the meeting... An international telecommunications company held a large gathering under two large tents in central New Jersey. A bountiful lunch was served, and there were several open bars. Members of the press were delivered in limousines from New York and returned the same way. Products were richly displayed. The chairman, himself a noted gourmet and bon vivant, addressed the gathering. Reactions were enthusiastic – but absolutely nothing of substance was done... Companies made gifts or gift boxes of products available to shareholders, sometimes free. Liquor companies also provided their products under advantageous purchase agreements... The way companies treated their shareholders resembled more entertaining a blind date [rather] than developing a relationship.
>
> *(Morrill, 1995)*

In addition, public relations practitioners who suddenly found themselves in charge of investor relations often "had little or no understanding of finance or of financial markets" (Morrill, 1995); they did not understand how the markets work and who the players are. The public relations practitioners were not ready to manage investor relations:

> Punctilious attention to financial details was not one of their strong units. The story was. They were skilled in using the media, and the brokerage community, to propagate stories about their clients best calculated to arouse investor attention. Often they did not really understand more than the bare rudiments of what they were trying to sell... The trend to producing, peddling and promoting half-truths and untruths, even if cloaked in hedged language, was increasing at an accelerating rate – a sort of monkey see, monkey do syndrome.
>
> *(Morrill, 1995)*

Laskin (2010a) concludes "public relations was set up to fail in investor relations – it just came too early" (p. 11).

The variety of new private shareholders was also quite a new experience for many corporations in the 1950s and created another incentive (along with the need to compete for capital) for the formation of investor relations departments. The new shareholders owned very small amount of stocks, and had very little understanding of business and finance, but the sense of ownership among them was great. These new shareholders were proud to own just one or two shares of a corporation and craved information, yet because of their large numbers, it was difficult to communicate with all of them directly. The financial intermediaries who transmit large amounts of financial information today were not well developed in the 1950s. The private shareholders often owned the stock directly instead of through pension or mutual funds and had to be the direct targets of early investor relations communications.

In addition, the management did not want to take the private shareholders seriously or invest any effort in communicating with them. So, managers were looking for a way to communicate with these shareholders from a distance, to give them information without meeting with them in person, ideally without any chance for shareholders to respond or ask questions. Public relations was ready to oblige: "many have engaged public relations counsel, or similarly styled agencies who issue press releases" (Morrill, 1995). Today, hardly anyone would equate investor relations with media relations. Laskin (2009) claims that media relations is among the lowest priority tasks for today's IROs. In the 1950s, however, press communications were a significant part of the investor relations job.

The corporations also did not have any interest in listening to their shareholders – the focus was on a one-way stream of information from the company to the financial publics. No feedback was received or analyzed. No dialogue was promoted. Nobody was listening.

As a result of this history, public relations became almost a derogatory term in investor relations. This was also a reason investor relations professionals started trying to actively distinguish themselves from public relations, and disassociate themselves from public relations education, professional associations, and consulting agencies. Cutlip et al. (2000) observe, "As press agents grew in number and their exploits became more outrageous – albeit successful, more often than not – it was natural that they would arouse the hostility and suspicion of editors and inevitable that the practice and its practitioners would become tainted. This stigma remains as part of the heritage of public relations" (p. 107).

This stigma remains strong in the financial world: "The word public relations became increasingly a pejorative in Wall Street" (Morrill, 1995). Financial publics lost any credibility they might have had in public relations practitioners, their ethics, integrity, or simply capabilities of handling investor relations. Investor relations engaged in significant efforts to distinguish itself from any public relations background. If initially joining the Public Relations Society of America (PRSA), a professional association for public relations practitioners, was considered, in the 1960s investor relations practitioners began talks about the need to create their own professional organization where the public relations "chaff" would not be allowed.

The association of investor relations practitioners, the Investor Relations Association (IRA), later NIRI, came about in 1967. It kept its promise and made every effort to differentiate its members from public relations practitioners by conducting strict background checks on all the applicants: "Our aim is to separate ourselves from the so-called financial public relations consultants, who operate on the fringe of stock touting, and who are fouling the nest" (Morrill, 1995).

Thus, in its earliest days investor relations began as a subset of public relations. However, it began at a time when public relations itself was rarely more than a press agentry. Lack of financial expertise, lack of ethics, and lack of strategic vision hurt investor relations at its early stages and moved the function away from public relations departments. Much of the public relations and communication expertise was voluntarily cut off and disregarded as unnecessary or even harmful in favor of financial and accounting expertise.

Financial Era

The 1970s saw the shift from individual retail investors to institutional investors.

On one side, the enormous growth of investment activities in the 1950s and 1960s put pressure on the financial market infrastructure. The growth in individual investors was exponential in the years after World War II: from 4.5 million people in 1952 to over 20 million people in 1965, which represented every sixth adult in the United States. Chatlos (1984) explains:

> As the trading and brokerage system creaked and strained under the increasing load of activity imposed on it, Wall Street's response was less than prudent. Profitable success after success as "the only game in town" proved to be a harsh taskmaster to the system. When problems emerged because sale activities were extended beyond the back offices' ability to handle the resulting volume, the immediate response was arrogant quick fixes rather than anticipatory long-term business planning.
>
> *(p. 87)*

When it became painfully obvious that the system could not handle any more transactions, the response was a monopolistic one. Banks stopped taking on any new clients. Brokers became particular in choosing who to work with or whom to drop from the client list. The processing times were long, and the services were not friendly.

Another problem was the track record. The market was growing in leaps and bounds after World War II and shareholders (especially individual shareholders) expected it to continue like this forever. The expectations became too high for the reality to deliver. In other words, "success bred a level of expectations that could not be fulfilled" (Chatlos, 1984, p. 87). The system was destroying itself: the system built on volume of transactions could not handle that volume anymore, and the investors were ready to quit:

> Customers were less than happy and did what might have been expected. They walked away. They did not sell their shares. They just walked away. For a system geared to the retail trade – and in many respects it remains so today – it was a devastating blow. The system was geared to volume, couldn't plan for high volume, and suddenly had very little volume. Again, as could have been expected, broker failures and bankruptcy-avoiding mergers followed. It was a grim sight and the individual shareholder moved further away from the system.
>
> *(Chatlos, 1984, p. 87)*

Professional investors began replacing retail investors. Consolidation was the name of the game. It was time to take all these retail investors with just a few thousand dollars and pull them together in investment funds. Although mutual funds existed for years, they really became popular only in the 1970s as more and more investors entrusted their cash to the fund managers. The first ever index fund available for individual investors, First Index Investment Trust (Vanguard 500), was launched in 1976 by the Vanguard Group as a response to the changing market demands.

This, however, meant a change for investor relations – instead of retail shareholders they would now face professional investors. Instead of less than knowledgeable individuals, overqualified stock analysts became the main contacts for the IROs The whole expertise previously geared toward private retail shareholders was becoming less and less relevant. Communications through mass media to reach large crowds of retail shareholders or conducting majestic special events to put the company's name out there were not appropriate anymore: "Because of the legal fiduciary responsibilities to their clients, these institutions have demanded detailed and timely strategic and financial information" (Higgins, 2000, p. 24). They could not be satisfied by gift baskets or tours of company headquarters – they demanded detailed information on the company's financial performance.

Financial analysts, however, were not valued highly in the corporate world; in fact, they were often regarded as "pests or worse" (Morrill, 1995). Yet, educated and knowledgeable analysts demanded lots of information on the company's finances, strategy, sales, research and development, and so on. Investor relations practitioners with no or little knowledge of finance were not capable of providing such information and often could not even speak the same language as the analysts did.

In addition, financial analysts themselves were not accustomed to dealing with investor relations people. In fact, analysts were around long before the 1970s. In 1945 the New York Analysts Society already had 700 members and the number was growing fast. IROs, however, did not communicate with the analysts before the 1970s as they were mostly occupied with the retail shareholders, the dominant market force at the time. The job of communicating with analysts often fell to the *chief financial officer* (CFO), or somebody in the treasury department. As a result, when the 1970s brought the shift from retail to institutional ownership, many of institutional analysts already had their pre-established contacts at the corporations – most often in the finance department. Many analysts were not even aware that they needed to communicate with the investor relations people. They tended to go to the same source they used to go to earlier – a person in the treasury or finance department. Retail investor and professional investor communications were completely separated. Even today, because of this history, at some US corporations there are two separate departments: the *investor relations department*, aimed at professional institutional shareholders; and the *shareholder relations department*, aimed at individual retail shareholders.

The role of mass-mediated communications in investor relations suddenly lost its importance. Public relations practitioners were losing their grip on investor relations, while the financial departments were engaging in talks with analysts and institutional investors more and more often. It was not a one-day switch, but a slow transition over the years that eventually brought investor relations from the public relations office to the office of the CFO.

Typical CEOs, however, were still actively trying to avoid the financial gurus of Wall Street in the same way as they had been trying to avoid private shareholders earlier. Executives were used to being the only ones running the show and they did not plan on sharing their powers with either undereducated private shareholders or overeducated financial analysts. However, private shareholders were easy to deal with and could be kept at bay by using mass media and giving them occasional hand-outs. Management succeeded in creating "a nice warm feeling" in shareholders and keeping them "happy and calm" by avoiding "telling them anything that wasn't legally required" (Morrill, 1995). The financial analysts, however, were far more difficult to please.

Financial analysts were not satisfied by the small amount of substantial information the companies were disclosing. They asked questions, sometimes questions "that management had not asked itself, or for various reasons did not want to answer" (Morrill, 1995). Moreover, institutional investors had power over the companies they owned stock in and perhaps even more power over the companies they did not invest in. Large institutional players could sweep all the company's shares off the market, pushing the price up, just to unload them several days later causing the stock value to plummet. Chatlos (1984, p. 88) recalls, "The new institutions had so much money to invest that there literally was not enough time to observe the prudent ground rules. The new method was to dump the shares when a sell decision was made and to buy as quickly as possible when that decision was made. This had a severe impact on market price volatility." If earlier private shareholders at least smoothed out this volatility, in the 1970s with individuals off the market the price was in the hands of the financial analysts. A single word from the company might have changed the price of stock enormously. The management decided they would rather avoid meeting with analysts altogether for fear of saying something wrong.

As a result, the investor relations profession in the 1970s experienced a notable change. Investor relations moved away from the public relations of the 1950s and 1960s. First, there was no demand any more for mass-mediated communications to myriad private shareholders, who moved off the market. Second, institutional investors demanded other communication channels than mass media. In addition, earlier public relations-based investor relations practices had left a bad taste in the mouths of Wall Street professionals, and financial analysts rarely wanted to communicate with this breed of investor relations professionals. Institutional investors and analysts tried to talk with managers of the company directly. The management, however, avoided any direct contact, choosing instead to communicate through the corporate secretaries or forward the calls to the CFO's office or the treasury department.

In response to these changing demands, a new type of investor relations professional was emerging. Management often saw former financial analysts as being ideal IROs because they were expected to easily find a common language with the company's financial analysts and professional investors. Wall Street-based firms started offering investor relations services, too. These firms were often an outgrowth of investment banks and thus had strong connections with and deep understanding of the financial markets.

These changes in the investor relations landscape had a strong effect on the investor relations function itself. Powerful and knowledgeable institutional investors evaluated every action the company took and were not afraid to ask questions and provide criticism if they did not believe the action was in the best interests of shareholders. Higgins (2000) describes the new institutional investors:

> They have successfully sought an activist role in corporate governance, focusing their institutional power on company's performance, the proper role of the board of directors, and executive compensation... The overall impact of the institutionalization of U.S. equity markets has been to make the job of the investor relations executive infinitely more challenging and complex.

(pp. 24–25)

From provider of information investor relations professionals had to turn into defenders of managers' decisions – if investors had criticisms of company actions, investor relations were expected to provide counter-arguments to explain and protect the company's executives. IR meetings started to become argumentative and, at times, confrontational. Proactive investor relations practices called for anticipating shareholders' reactions and preparing to respond to them in advance. Financial analysts-turned-IROs prepared their own analysis to counter-act anything that other financial analysts may throw at them. Shareholder research became a necessity. Some IROs simply did not allow negative questions to be asked at conferences and annual meetings, tightly controlling the communication channels. Top executives wanted to stay away from all of this as far as possible.

The focus of investor relations, in addition to protecting the top management, was often on persuasion and making the sell. Marcus and Wallace (1997) explain that investor relations became "the process by which we inform and persuade investors of the value inherent in the securities we offer as means to capitalize business" (p. xi). Ryan and Jacobs (2005), financial analysts turned investor relations consultants, suggest the investor relations contribution is helping the management to "to package their story for institutional buyers or sell-side analysts" (p. 69).

In conclusion, this financial era of investor relations history was focused on professional investors and financial analysts. For the tasks of defending the corporation in front of them, CEOs were hiring former financial analysts and former professional investors who became the new breed of investor relations professionals. They lacked the public relations knowledge and skills, but they understood the numbers and knew the rules of Wall Street. CEOs needed to have somebody between themselves and the professional investment community and decided to give it a try. Investor relations at that time was often viewed as a marketing activity with a goal of having a positive impact on a company's value. This led to a constant struggle for an overevaluation and pushing a share price up by any means necessary.

The collapse was inevitable. The chain of corporate scandals at the start of the twenty-first century brought down even companies that were once thought to be among the leaders of their fields – Enron, Tyco, WorldCom, Arthur Andersen, and others. CEOs started realizing that investor relations is more than just a financial function and started looking for communication expertise again – the pendulum was swinging back. Yet this communication expertise in investor relations was not easy to find any more.

Synergy Era

The beginning of the twenty-first century brought in the new era of investor relations that requires expertise in both areas – communication and finance – to be present and co-exist in the investor relations programs. Today's IROs need to gain proficiency in both areas through dual degrees, graduate degrees, and professional training.

A *Harvard Business Review* article predicted this synergy era in investor relations:

> Aside from those companies that assign to the investor relations function who-ever happens to be available (one major corporation, for example, gave investor relations duties to a retired chemist), many organizations make one of two com-mon errors:
>
> 1. Some companies will decide that investor relations are properly a part of public relations. They are unaware that many security analysts feel uncom-fortable when talking with public relations people because, rightly or wrongly, analysts are generally suspicious of being "snowed."
> 2. Other companies assume that the best candidate for the investor relations function is found in the treasurer's or controller's department. Security ana-lysts, the reason, are figure-happy, and who is better qualified to throw around statistics than the man who has lived with them? Such reasoning is unsound, and if it accomplishes nothing else, it serves to demonstrate that the chief executive of the company has not got the message of what investor relations is all about. A moment's reflection will reveal that knowledge of the figure does not, per se, establish ability to communicate that knowledge effectively.
>
> The solution to be found lies somewhere between these two extremes. The best candidate for the investor relations post will have had experience in both public relations and the financial phases of a company's operations.
>
> *(Savage, 1972, pp. 126–127)*

The synergy era requires IROs to be experts in both communications and finance, as well as to have knowledge about securities laws and marketing. The new investor rela-tions professionals are not mere advocates of management – they listen to investors and analysts and bring the feedback back to the company. Shareholder research and collection of feedback from the financial community become of vital importance. Chatlos (1974) suggests that the goal of investor relations is "reaching and hearing from a diverse audience" (p. 3). Investor relations professionals are responsible for the important task of researching "who the shareholders were, what they perceived their needs to be and how best to communicate with them – and for them to communicate with management" (Morrill, 1995).

In today's investment market, the responsibilities of IROs to the investment com-munity at large are growing. "Investor relations officers should heed marketplace rumblings about earnings measurers and understand exactly what analysts and inves-tors of the company want, but may not be getting, from financial disclosures," Allen writes (2002, p. 210). Investor relations today is based on a dialogue rather than mono-logue – two-way communications become a key strategy in communicating with investors.

This feedback serves both the management of the company and the shareholders. Shareholders should have a chance to persuade management to adopt the sharehold-ers' propositions in the same way as the management should have a chance to per-suade the shareholders to accept the company's course of action. In this two-way communication model, IROs become loyal to both their employers and to the shareholders. The goal of investor relations is to have the interests of shareholders and managements aligned. Indeed, serving investors is the exact work that corporations' management requires from the IROs. Lou Thompson, the former president of NIRI, explains,

> The role of investor relations is to minimize investor risk by assuring that the company is providing information that is clear and understandable through means that achieve full and fair disclosure. The lower the perceived risk in investing in a company, the lower the company's cost of capital. There is a true bottom line benefit of full and fair disclosure.
>
> *(as cited in Allen, 2002, p. 209)*

In other words, the more IROs serve the investment community, the better it is for the organization because it decreases investor's risk and thus decreases the cost of capital for the company. Two-way communications appear to be at the very heart of the investor relations profession.

The previous eras saw IROs as technicians following management's directions or responding to shareholders' requests. Rao and Sivakumar (1999) observed that IROs were mostly consumed by technical rather than strategic activities: "an exclusive emphasis on intended technical activities deflects attention from the symbolic nature of investor relations departments and the institutional sources of organizational structure" (p. 30). Investor relations today is becoming a management responsibility with respected autonomy and decision-making power within the corporate structure. IROs are engaging in a growing number of proactive communications through conference calls, roadshows, conference participations, websites, social media, and so on.

As with the previous eras, the shift to the synergy era was caused by changes in the economy. The shocking corporate failures of the early twenty-first century, including the collapse of dotcoms and accounting scandals at the largest companies, put the whole model of corporate America to the test. The collapse of Enron became the wake-up call for the practice of investor relations, which now has to assume more responsibilities than ever before. Suddenly, the unprecedented growth in the stock market was replaced by recession. The competition for capital became more intense. Investor relations became one of the key activities that could make or break a corporation; CEOs saw that investor relations is not one of the auxiliary functions, but an activity that can create a competitive advantage.

The scandals also led to new and stiffer regulations from the Securities and Exchange Commission and Congress, with passage of the Sarbanes–Oxley Act in 2002, aimed at improving corporate governance and making managers and boards of directors more accountable. The Act expanded the scope of required disclosures and changed the disclosure procedures. But despite the expanded disclosure, investor relations must go beyond publications of obligatory disclosure documents. Investor relations is about understanding; investor relations' task is to help investors understand the company and its business model. The goal is not as high a valuation as possible, but rather a fair value of the stock price. Finding the right investors, building trust and relationships with them, and developing long-term ownership patterns to combat volatility are the new goals for the professionals.

The history of investor relations shows that this is an integrated function. It is most successful when it is not limited to just one expertise. A successful IRO is more than a financial analyst in residence or a publicist in residence – either way, lots of value is being left at the table. Investor relations is a profession in its own right that requires its own set of skills and expertise. At the very least, it combines both communication and financial skill sets. And this is the foundation of the current, third, synergy era of investor relations development.

In conclusion, the shift to the synergy era of investor relations was caused by many changes in the economy, technology, regulations, increased shareholders' attention to the role of corporations in the society, and many other factors. These changes placed new demands on the investor relations professionals and required investor relations function to adapt. *CBS MarketWatch* suggests, "Markets do not run on money; they run on trust" (Minow, 2002). To respond to these challenges, investor relations has to move away from being a technical reactive function, and become recognized as its own profession that combines the expertise of communication, finance, and law to proactively devise sophisticated research-based two-way symmetrical programs to facilitate dialogue between the company and the financial community with the purpose of enhancing mutual understanding, managing expectations, and building and maintaining relationships.

Key Terms

Amsterdam bourse
The Code of Hammurabi
Blue chips
Blue sky laws
Blue sky securities
CEO
CFO
Chief executive officer
Chief financial officer
Communication era
C-suite
Debt
Disclosure
Dominant coalition
Dutch East India Company
Efficient market hypothesis
Equilibrium
Equity
Eras of investor relations
Fair value
Falun mine
Fiduciary duty
Financial era
Financial communication
Hot air securities, see Blue sky securities

Investor relations
Investor relations officer
Investor Relations Association
Investor Relations Department
IRA
IRO
IR Society
Management
Mutual fund
National Investor Relations Institute
NIRI
One-way communication
Overcorrection
Overvaluation
Professional period
PRSA
Public company
Publicly traded company
Public Relations Society of America
Securities
Share
Shareholder Relations Department
Shareholding company
Stock
Stora Kopparberg
strategic
sucker list
Synergy era
Two-way communication
Vanguard 500

Questions and Activities

1 Define the concept of the fair market value. Why do you think it is considered an ultimate goal of investor relations?
2 Analyze the definition of investor relations. What would you add to or delete from the definition?
3 Explain what the efficient market hypothesis is. Why do you think investor relations is an integral part of the efficient markets?
4 Describe key periods in the investor relations history. What connections can you identify between this history and the modern practice of investor relations?
5 Research investor relations history in another country. Prepare a report comparing the investor relations history in the country you analyzed with the investor relations history in the United States.

2

Investor Relations and Financial Communication Industry

Investor Relations Officers

First of all, it is important to note that investor relations is a relatively small profession. The leading professional association for the industry, the National Investor Relations Institute (NIRI) has only 3,300 members. Furthermore, some of the members are academics and service providers rather than investor relations officers (IROs). As a result, the number of actual IROs in NIRI is under 3,000 members. However, these 3,000 members represent 1,600 publicly traded companies with more than US$9 trillion in stock market capitalization. Not every investor relations professional is a member of NIRI – some are members of other professional organizations such as the Public Relations Society of America (PRSA), which has a dedicated financial communications section, and some are members of the International Association of Business Communicators (IABC). In addition to investor relations, there are professional organizations for financial communicators working in other industries; for example, the Association of Fundraising Professionals (AFP) unites about 30,000 members working in the field of philanthropy and fundraising.

Even taking all this into account, investor relations and financial communication is a relatively small professional area. One of the key reasons is that not every company needs investor relations. Investor relations is required for the publicly traded companies – in other words, the companies in which shares of stock are available for people to buy and sell. These companies are called *public companies* because their stock is available to the public as opposed to private companies where the ownership is private. Public companies are also called *publicly traded companies*, *publicly held companies*, or *publicly listed companies*. Although the estimates vary slightly, the World Bank calculated that there are only about 4,100 public companies in the United States. This actually correlates well with 3,000 investor relations members of NIRI. The World Bank also estimates that globally there are about 43,000 public companies.

The shares of public companies are traded on *stock exchanges* or on the *over-the-counter* (OTC) markets. The New York Stock Exchange (NYSE) trades shares of 2,800 companies and Nasdaq lists about 3,300 companies. These numbers include US companies as well as foreign corporations that want to be listed in the United States. It is also possible to have dual listings – where a company can be listed at NYSE and Nasdaq, or at an exchange in its home country and at an exchange abroad. For example, BHP, one of the largest Australian corporations, is listed domestically at the Australian Securities Exchange, and at the London Stock Exchange in the UK. Carnival, a cruise line operator, is listed at both the London Stock Exchange and at NYSE.

All these public corporations are governed by a specific set of laws and regulations focused on helping investors make an informed decision about buying and selling the company stock. In order to satisfy these requirements, these companies employ investor relations professionals. Many large corporations would have a standalone dedicated investor relations department. These departments may have from just one IRO to 20 or more. The reporting structures vary widely – the investor relations department may report directly to the *chief executive officer* (CEO), or the department may report to the *chief financial officer* (CFO), *chief communications officer* (CCO), *chief operations officer* (COO), or even the head of Human Resources (HR).

At smaller companies, there may be no dedicated investor relations department. In this case, the investor relations function is commonly performed by the office of the CFO or the treasury department. In other cases, investor relations may reside in the corporate communication/public relations department. Since investor relations relies on both financial and communication expertise, if assigned to the CFO or to the CCO, the investor relations function must work closely across the corporate silos with departments that can supplement their missing knowledge and skills. It is also not uncommon for such investor relations programs to rely on investor relations agencies and consultants to, once again, make up for the missing skill set.

The person responsible for leading the investor relations department typically has a title of *vice president of investor relations*, in some cases, *senior vice president* or *executive vice president*. In large investor relations departments, there are also positions of *director* or *senior director* or *associate director* of investor relations. In those cases where the investor relations function does not have a dedicated department, the function is usually led by the *director of investor relations*. At the lowest level of the corporate chart, investor relations departments and programs employ professionals with titles like *manager of investor relations, investor relations specialist*, or *investor relations analyst*.

The average salary for a vice president of investor relations who is leading an investor relations department is over US$290,000. Mid-level investor relations roles pay on average US$201,000, and the manager/specialist/analysts jobs pay about US$140,000. According to a NIRI/Korn Ferry 2019 salary survey, the average IRO's paycheck also varies depending on the industry and location. IROs working for consumer goods companies make on average US$284,375, while IROs in the life sciences industry make on average only US$226,974. The highest IROs salaries are in the northeast (US$267,824), and the lowest in the South (US$242,130).

Salary is not the only compensation that investor relations professionals receive. It is also common to collect some kind of performance bonuses: these bonuses average to about 30% of the IRO salary. It is also common to receive equity as part of the compensation – this may be stock options, restricted stock, or other types. The equity component on average varies from a quarter to a half of the base salary. All this makes investor relations a well-compensated profession. In fact, quite a few studies call investor relations the highest paid specialization in corporate communication.

The most common activity of investor relations professionals is providing information to the investors, shareholders, financial analysts, and regulatory agencies. In fact, investor relations professionals are responsible for assembling and filing key periodic reporting documents – *quarterly reports* (Form 10-Q) and *annual reports* (Form 10-K). These disclosure reports are required documents with specific guidelines for what must be included in them and when and how they must be filed. As a result, producing these reports is a complex and collaborative task. Although IROs take the lead, many other departments within the organization contribute as well. Working on these reports is almost a never-ending process – as soon as one quarterly report is submitted the work starts on the next quarterly report.

In addition to the periodic reporting, investor relations programs are responsible for nonperiodic filings, *current reports* (Form 8-K). If a company experiences a significant event that can influence its fair value, it is a responsibility of the IROs to notify investors about this event. IROs cannot wait for the next quarterly or annual report for such disclosure; in fact, in many cases, companies have only four days to inform the market about the new developments. In some cases, it may even be less than four days. Such events that can influence the company's fair value and that companies must notify investors about are called material corporate events. Once again, IROs would work closely with the corporate legal counsel and other departments to prepare and file those reports.

In addition to the periodic and nonperiodic disclosures initiated by the company, it is also common for IROs to spend a significant amount of time responding to investors', prospective investors', and financial analysts' queries. Since investor relations is built upon two-way communications, IROs must be available to and accessible by the investment community. IROs are the point of contact for those who are looking to better understand the company and have questions about its business model. Thus, IROs respond to email, phone calls, website communications, and other queries from the investors. As a result, disclosure is a mixture of proactive and reactive communications and is perhaps the most common activity for the investor relations professionals.

Related to disclosure is the IRO's outreach to the investment community. It is common for IROs to organize and participate in *one-on-one meeting* with investors, where a current or prospective investor would have the chance to sit down with the IRO, CFO, CEO, and other top managers of the company in order to develop a really good understanding of the company. Such meetings are especially valuable for investors or financial analysts new to evaluating a particular stock. IROs also organize meetings with groups of investors, participate in investor conferences, and perform roadshows – large-scale events where top managers of the company visit its largest investors to provide updates on the company's business.

All these efforts are part of building and maintaining relationships with the members of the investment community. Shareholders invest in anticipation of future returns and if there is no trust in the management team, the promise of the future returns does not mean much. Trust and relationships serve as the foundation for all the information being disclosed.

Sharing a wealth of information about a company and helping investors and analysts better understand a company's fair value requires investor relations professionals to be exceedingly knowledgeable about the company, and also to have good working relationships with almost every single department throughout the organization. If a company's *research and development department* (R&D) is on the verge of a technological breakthrough, it is important for the IRO to understand the details of this technology, and to understand how it may affect the future of the company and the industry in general. If one of the company's factories is investing resources in buying new equipment, it is important for the IRO to understand why these investments are needed and how they might affect the company's business in the future. If the marketing department lowers the price of the company's best-selling product, the IRO should know and be able to explain what is behind this decision.

For example, if Tesla's R&D comes up with a new "tabless" battery design, Tesla's IRO should know what it actually means, what kind of technology is behind it, and how it is likely to affect future car design, production, and user experience. Only then, can IRO appropriately educate the company's investors on all these details to help them properly understand how this new technology can influence the fair value of Tesla. As a result, a big part of an IRO's job is learning about the company, meeting with key people at the company, being present at important meetings, traveling to various plants, facilities, and branches, and simply being in the know.

Finally, as previously mentioned, investor relations is a two-way communication function. The management team of the company makes IROs responsible for keeping them informed about the company's shareholders and what they think about the company. The company's management wants to know who the company's shareholders are, how much stock they own, who is buying and who is selling the stock, what are the trading prices and volume, and what the reasons are behind the trades. IROs conduct shareholder research and monitor changes in the stock trading and ownership patterns. IROs may prepare reports for the management team indicating this information and provide additional details on large institutional shareholders. IROs also collect financial analysts' and business journalists' reports about the company competitors, and the industry, and provide that information to the management of the company. IROs are also responsible for collecting and, if needed, communicating any other feedback from the investment community to the company's management. IROs are also involved in corporate governance issues, facilitating relationships and communication between the Board of Directors and the executive team.

Other Jobs in Financial Communication

Investor relations is limited to the corporate sector of the economy – only corporations have investors. There are no investors in government or not-for-profit organizations. It is impossible to become a shareholder in the Department of Education, for example, or own stock in the Red Cross. It does not mean, however, that there is no financial communication and no financial communicators in the governmental and not-for-profit organizations. In fact, some of these government or not-for-profit organizations produce significant amounts of financial information.

For example, most countries around the world have some type of *central bank* authority, a governmental agency with supervisory and regulatory powers responsible for the country's banking system and monetary policy. Many of the communications coming from the central banks focus on financial information. In the United States, since 1913, the *Federal Reserve System*, or simply the Fed, has served as the central bank authority. A year after Congress created the Fed, the Federal Reserve delivered its first annual report and has been providing these reports ever since. In addition to annual reports, the communicators at the Federal Reserve produce a large volume of publications, including publications of the Board of Governors of the Federal Reserve System, publications of District Federal Reserve Banks, statements and speeches of the Federal Reserve, economic data publications, and various statistical releases. The Fed is responsible for collecting, analyzing, and communicating such important data as the federal debt, gross domestic product, consumer price index, industrial production, and many more (Figure 2.1). Similar to investor relations professionals, financial communicators at the Fed must go beyond just putting the information out there into the void: they need to ensure their audiences understand the information, what the information means, and frame it in the appropriate economic, political, and social contexts. In other words, they have the function of explaining the information and educating their audiences. Former chairman of the Federal Reserve System, Ben Bernanke said, "Perhaps most important, as public servants whose decisions affect the lives of every citizen, central bankers have a responsibility to provide the public as much explanation of those decisions as possible, as long as doing so does not compromise the decision-making process itself."

Of course, many other departments in the federal government are also responsible for communicating financial information – the Department of Treasury, Internal Revenue Services, Securities and Exchange Commission, and many more. The same is also true at the state and local levels. For example, in the State of Florida, the Florida Department of Revenue communicates large volumes of financial information about money collected as taxes and distribution of tax money. Similarly, the Florida Department of Lottery provides information about money collection and spending from the lotteries. Since money is the lifeblood of the modern economy, even the agencies that do not necessarily focus their work on financial matters communicate financial information from time to time. For example, law enforcement agencies may talk about money laundering or counterfeit bills, while various health departments may talk about costs of vaccinations. And almost every government agency talks about their budget needs and priorities when it is time to ask for money from the legislature. It is also beneficial for government agencies to have a high-quality financial communication strategy targeted at the general public in order to show the importance of the work the agency is doing and to pressure the lawmakers to expand the budget of the agency or at least to avoid potential budget cuts. As a result, expert financial communicators are needed in every part of the government.

Not-for-profit organizations also communicate a great deal of financial information, especially as it relates to their need for, receipt, and expenditure of money. And these are no small amounts – Americans gave US$410 billion to charitable organizations in 2017 alone. Almost one-third of this money went to religious organizations – this is more than all combined donations to education, health, and culture and humanities charities. Financial communicators responsible for generating these donations are *fundraising* professionals. Animal shelters, food pantries, college and universities, and even United Nations engage in fundraising activities to support their operations and

For use at 11:00 a.m. EST
February 19, 2021

MONETARY POLICY REPORT

February 19, 2021

Board of Governors of the Federal Reserve System

Figure 2.1 Monetary policy report. *Source*: Board of Governors of the Federal Reserve System. February 19, 2021.

advance their causes. For example, the United Nations Refugee Agency developed a campaign in partnership with Kickstarter to raise money for a refugee humanitarian crisis.

These fundraising jobs have similar requirements and expectations to investor relations jobs. It is vital for fundraising professionals to be exceptionally knowledgeable about the organizations they work for. Donors may have different preferences and different capabilities – it is essential for fundraisers to align what the donors can and want to support with the needs of their nonprofit. Donors often want to stay engaged with the organizations they support – so, building and maintaining these relationships also becomes an important job of the fundraising professional. And, of course, it is important to report to the donors on how their money is spent and what the progress is of the initiatives these donors supported – not that different from updating the investors of a corporation on the progress the corporation made in the annual reports.

A recent job advertisement from Yale University, looking for a fundraising officer, describes the responsibilities of a future hire:

1. Identifies, cultivates and solicits Yale alumni/alumnae and friends who are capable of making gifts to the University.
2. Devises and implements cultivation and solicitation strategies. Evaluates various gift opportunities and giving vehicles; recommends the most suitable for a particular donor. Develops, writes and presents proposals in keeping with university needs and in line with donor's interest and financial situation.
3. Initiates and maintains contact with current, past, and prospective donors, promoting positive donor relations. Engages volunteers proactively as needed. Determines and executes events and programs in support of development activities, assessing the success of such events/programs and recommending changes. Identifies disaffected or disinterested donors and devises strategies to encourage/redirect their interests as appropriate.
4. Interacts with internal contacts such as deans, directors, faculty, officers and other Development staff to consult on University needs, cultivation, solicitation and stewardship strategies, and potential donors. Keeps abreast of University events and disseminates University information to donors, prospective donors, volunteers and team members as appropriate.

The professional association for fundraising, the AFP has about 30,000 members. AFP is significantly larger than NIRI – this reflects the fact that there are more not-for-profit organizations that need fundraising than there are publicly traded corporations that need investor relations. The average salary of the fundraising professional is US$85,060. A typical title for the person leading the fundraising function at an organization is the *chief development officer* (CDO). CDO is the highest fundraising title. It is usually reserved for somebody who manages a large fundraising department or program. However, many fundraising professionals work for smaller organizations and typically are the only person in the department – in this case, they would have the title of *fundraising officer* or *fundraising manager*. Other titles in fundraising are vice president for development and advancement, director of philanthropy, or gifts officer.

Returning to the corporate sector of the economy, it is important to note that there are other financial communication jobs in corporations in addition to investor relations. In fact, there are many financial communication professionals in banking and insurance. Communicators working at banking institutions and credit unions communicate a large volume of financial information about credit cards, mortgages, savings accounts, and certificates of deposits. And, once again, often they have a responsibility to go beyond making the information available and instead focus on explaining and educating their audiences about all the nuances of their communications. Insurance is a subject with a very high complexity – life insurance alone can have many different categories with different payments, rules, premiums, and so on – term life insurance, whole life insurance, universal life insurance, variable life insurance, guaranteed issue life insurance, and more! All of this requires quality communications to help people understand the product and its purpose.

Investor Relations and Financial Communication Agencies

All the jobs described above – corporate investor relations jobs, communications jobs in banking and insurance, governmental financial communication jobs, or fundraising for not-for-profit organizations – represent *in-house* positions. These job functions are located within the organization they are trying to benefit. In addition to the in-house jobs, there are many financial communication jobs in the agency sector. There are many agencies that specialize in financial communication and investor relations and provide their expertise to a variety of organizations that need to supplement their in-house stuff.

One of the leading agencies with a strong reputation in investor relations is Prosek Partners. With offices in two leading financial centers of the world, New York City and London, Prosek has a sophisticated investor relations program that can support merger and acquisition transactions, help with shareholder activism, develop outreach to investors and financial analysts, plan events, and provide counsel to top management.

In addition to dedicated agencies in investor relations and financial communications, many big public relations and strategic communication agencies also offer specialized services in this area. Edelman, the largest public relation agency, has a strong financial communication practice. According to Edelman, its financial communication and capital markets practice employs more than 150 global advisors with backgrounds in finance, investor relations, communications, journalism, and government services.

A financial communication agency may be a great place for entry into the investor relations job. Agencies have no problems hiring recent college graduates with little or no experience. Working at an agency exposes you to many different clients in a variety of industries and builds experience very fast. Eventually, one of the agency clients may offer you an in-house job. It is a common way to transition from an agency job to a corporate job. Salaries in agencies are usually smaller than on the corporate side and, as a result, many agency employees eventually move to corporations, while agencies bring in more new entry-level employees with little or no prior experience.

The new hires at agencies usually have the titles of *intern* or *account assistant*. An agency client is called an *account*, thus an account assistant is the one who helps working on a client's account. Once an agency employee gains sufficient experience, they may be given an account to manage on their own – then, they become *account coordinator*. Later, they may be promoted to larger accounts where multiple agency employees are involved – then, their title would reflect that as they grow through jobs of *assistant account executive*, *account executive*, *senior account executive*, and, finally, *account director* or *account supervisor*. As agency employees continue to advance up the career ladder, they gradually become more involved in managing the agency as a whole rather than managing separate accounts. The senior-level positions at agencies are *vice president*, *senior vice president*, *executive vice president*, *partner*, and, finally, *senior partner*. In large multinational agencies with regional offices, it is possible to be a *regional director* or a *president/CEO* of an agency subsidiary or a branch. Of course, at the very top, the agency would have the *CEO* of the whole organization and, sometimes, a *chairperson*.

This variety of titles and levels may seem confusing and unnecessary, but it is actually important for agencies to have such a structure because work at each level of this hierarchy is billed to the client at different levels. For example, a typical financial communication agency would charge about US$100 for an hour of work of an account assistant, while it would charge US$200 for an hour of an account executive – double the hourly billing rate. If an account requires involvement at the level of a vice president, the billable rate may be US$400 or US$500 an hour.

Billable hours are the lifeblood of an agency – it is important to track and monitor all the work in order to bill the clients fairly for all the work. Many agencies celebrate and reward employees who produce the most billable hours in a week or in a month. Most often agency employees work on multiple accounts at the same time. It is not uncommon in the agency world to work on four or five accounts at the same time. As a result, it becomes important to monitor closely how employees spend their day so that appropriate clients can be billed the correct amount of hours at an accurate rate.

Education and Training

Most people working in investor relations do not have an educational background in investor relations. It is not surprising considering there are pretty much no majors in investor relations. At best, one can find a standalone course in investor relations, financial communication, or business journalism. Only a small number of educational institutions have minors or specializations. For example, Newhouse School at Syracuse University launched a financial and investor communications emphasis that prepares students for jobs in investor relations, financial services, and corporate communications. As a result, just taking a class or two in investor relations or financial communication already puts a student ahead of many other job seekers. Some students interested in investor relations build their own program of study combining courses from accounting, finance, law, and strategic communications. Such students may major in communications to hone their writing and public speaking skills, while minoring in accounting to develop a good understanding of financial statements.

A study of IROs who are members of NIRI found that most IROs today have a business background. More than two-thirds of IROs in the survey reported having their bachelor's degree from one of the business school majors – finance, accounting, or management. IROs with communication education were in a minority. Some IROs also reported having no business and no communication education – instead they grew into their investor relations job from an operational background and, as a result, they reported education in medicine, chemistry, aeronautics, engineering, and so on. Since the investor relations job requires an IRO to be an expert in what the company does, it is not much of a surprise that a specialist in the company's business could become an IRO. Who better to explain the complexities and potential of a new chemical compound for future production of medicine than a chemist or a medic?

At the same time, investor relations is its own profession that has unique and challenging demands. As a result, many professionals once they become IROs seek additional training to professionalize themselves in this occupation. In fact, the same survey of IROs, reported that almost 70% of all IROs had a second, graduate, degree. It is a good idea to supplement the skills and knowledge learned during undergraduate studies and acquired throughout professional experience with a graduate degree. It gives the chance for a person with degree in communication to learn about finance and accounting, and it gives the chance to a person with a business degree to learn about communication strategies and tactics.

The variety of educational backgrounds and professional experiences in investor relations also makes the role of professional organizations in the field exceptionally important. For many IROs, a professional organization is the only place where they can actually learn about the profession itself. NIRI, the leading professional organization in investor relations, takes this responsibility seriously. NIRI organizes a lot of training sessions, seminars, and webinars. One of the most popular among these educational opportunities is Fundamentals of Investor Relations, a must-attend event for people new to investor relations. No matter what previous education or occupation a person has had, this seminar brings everyone up to speed on the practice of investor relations, covering key components of investor relations – finance, communication, marketing, and law. NIRI also maintains an investor relations accreditation, the *Investor Relations Charter* (IRC). IRC is important recognition in the investor relations profession and has a requirement for continuing professional education to maintain the credential.

Ethics and Professionalism

NIRI and other professional organizations play an important role in developing and promoting an ethical and professional code of conduct for investor relations professionals. NIRI's investor relations *Code of Conduct* consists of 12 points:

1. Maintain my integrity and credibility by practicing investor relations in accordance with the highest legal and ethical standards.
2. Avoid even the appearance of professional impropriety and act as an advisor to colleagues to avoid unethical, questionable, or inappropriate behavior or situations.
3. Recognize that the integrity of the capital markets is based on transparency of relevant financial and non-financial corporate information, and will to the best of my ability and knowledge work to ensure that my company or client fully and fairly discloses this important information.
4. Provide analysts, institutional and individual investors, and the media fair and equal access to corporate information.
5. Honor my obligation to serve the interest of shareholders and other stakeholders.
6. Discharge my responsibilities completely and competently by keeping myself abreast of the affairs of my company or client as well as the laws and regulations affecting the practice of investor relations.
7. Maintain the confidentiality of information acquired in the course of my work for my company or client company.
8. Not use confidential information acquired in the course of my work for my personal advantage nor for the advantage of related parties.
9. Exercise independent judgment in the conduct of my duties and responsibilities on behalf of my company or client.

10. Avoid any professional/business relationships that might affect, or be perceived to potentially affect, my ethical practice of investor relations.
11. Report to appropriate company authorities if I suspect or recognize fraudulent or illegal acts within the company.
12. Represent myself in a reputable and dignified manner that reflects the professional stature of investor relations, and comply with the provisions of NIRI's Participation and Engagement Code of Conduct and NIRI's eGroups Code of Conduct.

Although NIRI does not have much power to enforce these ethical guidelines, the association can terminate the membership of anyone who is found in violation of these principles and who has been sanctioned by government agencies or judicial bodies. NIRI also maintains an *Ethics Council* that can provide guidance to IROs on issues involving ethical decision-making, offer educational opportunities, and develop recommendations to NIRI's Board of Directors.

Financial communicators engaged in other aspects of the communication industry outside of investor relations often belong to other professional organizations with their own training resources, accreditation processes, and codes of ethical and professional conduct. For example, many financial communication professionals in the banking sector are members of the *Financial Communications Section* of the PRSA. The PRSA *Code of Ethics* focuses on six professional values:

1. Advocacy. We serve the public interest by acting as responsible advocates for those we represent. We provide a voice in the marketplace of ideas, facts, and viewpoints to aid informed public debate.
2. Honesty. We adhere to the highest standards of accuracy and truth in advancing the interests of those we represent and in communicating with the public.
3. Expertise. We acquire and responsibly use specialized knowledge and experience. We advance the profession through continued professional development, research, and education. We build mutual understanding, credibility, and relationships among a wide array of institutions and audiences.
4. Independence. We provide objective counsel to those we represent. We are accountable for our actions.
5. Loyalty. We are faithful to those we represent, while honoring our obligation to serve the public interest.
6. Fairness. We deal fairly with clients, employers, competitors, peers, vendors, the media, and the general public. We respect all opinions and support the right of free expression.

NIRI's Code of Conduct and PRSA's Code of Ethics, as well as codes of related professional associations, have quite a few things in common. First of these is the purpose of investor relations and financial communication. This purpose is more than just serving the management who signs the IRO's paycheck. Investor relations professionals have a broader responsibility to the shareholders, and to society, in general. Shareholders in the company are the highest authority in publicly traded companies as they are the ones who appoint the Board of Directors, who, in turn, appoints the CEO. Thus, the responsibility of the IRO is to the company and its shareholders, not to the CEO. Tesla is more than just Elon Musk and Facebook is more than just Mark Zuckerberg.

In addition, as discussed earlier, investor relations is one of the key providers of timely and accurate information to the financial markets and this serves as the basis of modern capitalist society. Investors cannot invest without knowledge and understanding of what they are investing in, and companies won't have sufficient capital to grow and expand without these investments. This can bring the whole economy to a halt. Thus, IROs serve the economy in general.

Another important point that these ethical guidelines make is the necessity for independence and expertise. This means that investor relations and financial communication professionals have a unique set of knowledge and skills that others do not necessarily have. Thus, it is important for them to be able to make their own judgment on what the proper course of action is in various situations. IROs should not be delegated only technical tasks of writing news releases or updating websites – they need to be able to implement proactive strategic decisions about what needs to be done, when, and why. In the same way as the CEO of a hospital should not tell a surgeon how to operate, the CEO of a corporation should not tell the IROs how to perform their investor relations functions.

Finding a Job in Investor Relations and Financial Communication

As we discussed earlier, many investor relations professionals do not start their careers in investor relations. Instead, they transition to investor relations from accounting, finance, communications, law, or operations of the company. Thus, one way to land an IRO role is to start working at a large corporation in almost any capacity and show an interest in investor relations. A chance to transition to investor relations may eventually present itself.

At some companies, IRO is a *rotational* role. What this means is that the role of IRO is assigned for a year or two before a person transitions to another job, and another person steps into the role. General Electric is one of the examples of a company with rotational IRO responsibilities. The benefit of this approach is the ability to train future executives in the role of an IRO. As mentioned previously, IROs must become experts in everything the company does and develop a deep understanding of the company as a whole – its mission, its value, its unique business proposition – this is very useful for future leaders of the company. As a result, before advancing somebody to the executive role, it is beneficial to have that person serve in the role of an IRO for a couple of years.

In addition, a big part of an IRO's job is externally oriented, especially one-on-one and small-group meetings with institutional investors. These high-stakes meetings are great training opportunities for future corporate executives who would be involved in plenty of high-stakes meetings in their leadership roles. It is also beneficial to start building relationships between investors and future company leaders as it helps establish trust and credibility – a solid foundation for mutual understanding. Future executives learn to think from the investors' perspective and learn to appreciate their perspective.

Another access route into investor relations jobs is through an agency. Many financial communication agencies are willing to hire new graduates for entry-level positions. Whether these graduates come with a background in finance and accounting, or public relations and strategic communications, agencies are willing to provide additional training to beef up their skill sets and make them proficient in what is required for investor relations. For example, Corbin Advisors, an investor relations and financial communication agency with headquarters in Connecticut, hires recent graduates for entry-level jobs, and even provides internship opportunities for current students in graduate and undergraduate programs. Beginning a career at an agency can expose you to many different companies: from the largest Fortune 100 corporations to start-ups looking for their first investors. This helps future IROs build relationships and practice a variety of investor relations and financial communication tasks. It is not uncommon for an agency employee to transition to the in-house role at one of the clients that this employee used to work with. In fact, quite a typical route in investor relations is when a student after graduation joins a financial communication agency, and, then, several years later, leaves the agency to take a job at one of the corporations that is a client of that agency, as they would have developed a relationship with this company and would have proven their value.

Many of the professional associations have job boards where one can search for job vacancies. For example, if you are interested in investor relations jobs, the NIRI career center is a great resource. People interested in financial communication jobs in the banking sector may want to check out the PRSA job center. People interested in fundraising and donor relations can look for jobs on the AFP website.

For example, at the time of writing, one of the jobs listed on the NIRI career center website is for investor relations manager at Bruker Corporation. The position of manager of investor relations is described as a job that "will combine business acumen, financial modelling and analysis, investor and corporate communications expertise to develop and deliver clear, differentiated messages and effective strategies for communicating with internal and external stakeholders" (NIRI, 2020). These are the job responsibilities listed in the announcement for this position:

- Serve as a corporate spokesperson and day-to-day interface for existing shareholders, prospective investors, sell-side analysts and other external constituencies.
- Together with the Director of IR [investor relations] and Corporate Development, plan and execute a strategic, comprehensive and proactive investor relations program and annual plan. This includes maintaining existing investor relationships and proactively targeting new investors to help the Company achieve its optimal shareholder mix.
- Effectively organize Wall Street conferences, Non-Deal Roadshows, meetings, Investor Days and other events with the goal of maximizing the effectiveness of management time with IR activities.
- Manage the quarterly earnings release process including conference call logistics, conducting business and financial analyses, drafting earnings releases and earnings call slides and scripts, preparing talking points, and preparing Q&A for the management team that cover financial, business, market and competitive issues.
- Prepare presentations for industry and investor conferences, meetings, and events presented by the CEO, CFO and other management.
- Provide business, financial, and market intelligence to the senior management team and identify industry trends, shareholder concerns, and competitor actions that might impact the Company.
- Monitor analyst reports, including consensus and analyst expectations, and summarize key insights.

- Monitor trading activity in the Company's stock and trends and changes in share-holder ownership.
- Write and develop external communications including press releases, regulatory filings, annual reports and other investor collateral such as investor kits, fact sheets, and newsletters. Maintain the Investor Relations website.
- Maintain the Investor Relations database and processes that monitor and measure the effectiveness of the Company's investor relations and communications efforts.
- Contribute to the quarterly Board of Directors IR report and generation of Board materials.
- Ensure compliance with corporate policies and securities regulations.
- Maintain relationships with contacts at institutional investors.
- Manage and maintain vendor relationships within the IR function.
- Play a leadership role in making the function and the Company more efficient and effective.
- As needed, participate in important business/function initiatives or special projects and manage them to successful completion.
- Work and manage effectively across the Company's matrixed organization to improve efficiency and achieve desired results.
- Perform other duties as required.

As mentioned previously, investor relations is a rather small profession. There are not that many IROs. Once you enter this profession, you learn about your peers and about job opportunities quickly. As a result, word of mouth is also a very important avenue for finding a job in this field. It is important to take advantage of various networking opportunities – virtually or in person, locally or nationally. Annual professional conferences are among the best networking opportunities available. NIRI's annual conference is usually held in June alternating between the east and west coasts. PRSA's annual conference is usually held in October, and also moves from city to city. Other professional organizations organize conferences as well. In addition to being great networking opportunities, these events serve as excellent professional development events.

Key Terms

Account
Account assistant
Account coordinator
Account director
Account executive
Account supervisor
Agency
Assistant account executive
Association of Fundraising Professionals
CCO
Central bank
CDO
CEO
CFO

Chairperson
Code of Conduct
Code of Ethics
COO
Ethics Council
Executive vice president
The Federal Reserve System
Financial Communications Section
Form 8-K
Form 10-K
Form 10-Q
Fundraising
In-house
Intern
International Association of Business Communicators
Investor Relations Charter
IRC
National Investor Relations Institute
One-on-one meetings
Over-the-counter market
Partner
Public company
Public Relations Society of America
R&D
Regional director
Senior account executive
Senior partner
Senior vice president
Stock exchange
Vice president

Discussion Questions and Activities

1   How does the membership of NIRI compare with that of other professional associations? Do you expect NIRI's membership to grow or decline in the future?
2   What does it mean for the investor relations profession and IROs to work within such a small community? Identify and discuss pluses and minuses.
3   Does it matter which executive oversees the investor relations function? What are the benefits and drawbacks of different investor relations corporate structures?
4   Discuss different types of financial communication jobs – compare differences and similarities working in different sectors of the economy and different industries.
5   Find a recent posting for an investor relations or financial communication job. Analyze the key requirements for the candidate, as well as the job's responsibilities. Discuss what kind of training and education such a job requires.

3

Stockholders and Stakeholders

Investor relations, as suggested by its name, focuses on investors as its main audience. *Investors*, those who invest in the company, are also often called *stockholders* or *shareholders* because they own shares of stock in the company. However, investors are not the only people important to investor relations officers (IROs). These other audiences are called *stakeholders* because they have a particular stake in the company, a certain connection, or an interest in the company. For example, company employees are not stockholders, but they are definitely stakeholders. Stakeholders are sometimes also called *publics* – a group of people who focus on a particular issue related to the company. These stakeholders may play a very important role in investor relations. Thus, it becomes part of the investor relations program to identify, prioritize, and build relationships with all these stakeholders in addition to the company's stockholders. This chapter reviews the different types of stockholders and stakeholders that investor relations professionals work with.

Investors: Stockholders

Corporations do not appear out of thin air. They are not naturally born either. Somebody creates them. For example, let's imagine a person has an idea for a social media application. This social media application can be designed and put in the Apple Store for other people to download. The person who developed the app is the sole proprietor of this app. Now, let's imagine that the app is becoming really popular and millions of people install and use it. The sole owner of the app may realize that it is impossible to provide support for and continue development of the app alone and more people need to be hired – designers, coders, marketers, lawyers, and many more. This requires money. The owner of the app may decide to create a company to support this app and invite an outside investor or several investors to help with all these initial expenses for new hires. Although there are different ways to set up a company, a typical approach would identify what part of a corporation, or share of a corporation, belongs to whom. For example, the original owner of the app may approach some investors and offer them 10% of the new corporation ownership if they invest US$1 million in the company. If the investors agree, they provide this money to the corporation so that it can grow and develop, and, in exchange, they become part owners of the

Investor Relations and Financial Communication: Creating Value Through Trust and Understanding, First Edition. Alexander V. Laskin.

company. For example, Facebook started as an app run by Mark Zuckerberg and Eduardo Saverin, but as they needed extra cash to roll out the app nationally, and then internationally, they offered about 10% of Facebook for a US$500,000 investment from venture capitalist Peter Thiel. Later, many other investors and investments followed. These early investors are called *angel investors* or *venture investors* – they invest in young start-up companies. These investments carry lots of risks as many start-ups go bankrupt without making any money. In this case, venture capitalists lose their investment as the value of their share of stock becomes zero when the company goes out of business. Often, venture investors are the only opportunities for these start-ups to get going because they would not be able to get a loan at the bank with no track record or history of revenues – something that bank loan officers look at.

Even for professional investors it is quite risky to evaluate the future prospects and fair value of such start-up companies. Back in the nineteenth century many people were deceived by fake prospects of investing in the gold fields of California or other "blue sky" enterprises; therefore, the government has a variety of regulations in place to protect investors. Disclosure of information is a required part of trading stock in the United States. However, many small and start-up companies do not have the resources and expertise for proper disclosure; indeed, some of them may be just an idea with no history or activity to disclose. How would these companies get their funding? The process is different in different countries, but in the United States there is a category of investors who are allowed to invest in these unproven securities. These investors are called *accredited investors* or *sophisticated investors*. These investors are considered to be experts in what they are doing and, as a result, they do not need any additional protection from the US government. Thus, they are allowed to invest in new and unregistered securities that do not provide normal disclosure. In addition, these accredited investors have large net worth (above US$1 million for individuals or US$5 million for organizations). This ensures that they can survive a bad investment or two. A special category of these accredited investors is *qualified institutional buyers* (QIBs). QIBs are the largest and the most sophisticated group of investors – their assets under management exceed US$100 million (with certain exceptions for broker-dealers and savings and loan associations).

As a result, a new start-up company may start growing from just its founder or founders to include additional venture investors. It issues shares to those investors, but the shares are not available to the general public. The company is a *private shareholder company*. Going back to Facebook, after Peter Thiel's investment of US$500,000 in 2004, other investments followed: Accel Partners, Greylock Partners, Meritech Capital, Microsoft, and others.

Once a company establishes itself and can show a proven track record of revenues, the company may decide to *go public* – offer its shares for sale to the general public. This process is called an *initial public offering* (IPO), and it involves registering the securities and disclosing detailed information about the company in a document called a prospectus. Facebook, for example, filed its prospectus with the Securities and Exchange Commission (SEC) on February 1, 2012, and its stock began trading publicly on May 18, 2012. Facebook shares were offered at US$38 a share. At this time, Facebook already had 845 million active users, an estimated value above US$100 billion, and was a household name, thus attracting lots of attention to its stock. This helped the company set records on its opening day for the highest valuation for an IPO and the highest trading volume for an IPO. In 2021, Facebook shares are traded at about US$335 – an almost tenfold increase – making it a good investment for those who purchased the shares on the IPO day.

Retail Shareholders

Once the company is a *public shareholder company*, all restrictions for share ownership are removed and anyone can buy and sell its stock. Any private individual can buy shares of publicly traded companies like Microsoft, Netflix, Disney, or Facebook, and then hold them or sell them whenever they want – if the share price increases by the time the shareholders sell the stock, they make a profit; if the price decreases, they lose money. These private individual investors are called *retail shareholders*. They may buy shares because they see a good investment opportunity, they may invest because they like and use the products of the company, or they may invest because they support the company's mission. Tesla stock is a great example of the former. Many Tesla shareholders believe in the mission of the company and want to support the green company building electric cars and solar panels. It does not matter much to them if the company misses its earnings estimate or falls behind on its delivery schedule – they are very loyal investors. One such retail investor, Brandon Smith, invested about US$90,000 in Tesla stock and so far has never sold a single share. As of 2021, his investment is worth more than US$1 million. Another Tesla millionaire, Basel Termanini, has been driving Tesla cars since 2012 and is passionate about the brand – as a result, he also bought Tesla stock and his investment in 2021 is worth US$2.5 million (Hull, 2020). The CEO of Tesla, Elon Musk, consistently shows his appreciation for retail investors and values their direct experience with the company's product.

Another type of retail investor is company employees who want to buy shares of their employer. As these investors also work at the company they have significant knowledge about what the company does. Some of these investors are called *insiders* – these are usually senior-level employees who have access to information not available to other investors – *nonpublic information*. For example, the CEO of a company is likely to find out good or bad news about the company or its products before anybody else. As a result, the CEO would have a chance to buy or sell the stock before the price changes based on this new information. This practice of using nonpublic information to benefit from stock is called *insider trading*. Since this would be unfair to all other investors, insider trading is illegal, and insiders must report their trading activity to the SEC.

Some employees also receive shares of the company as part of the *stock compensation* or *stock bonus*. For example, an employee may receive a certain number of shares if the company meets a specific sales benchmark – this encourages all employees to put their best efforts toward reaching the corporate goal as they know they will be rewarded for that. In other cases, stock may be given to employees based on their longevity; for example, employees who have worked at the company for 5, 10, or 20 years may receive company stock as a reward.

It is quite common for corporations to encourage their employees to buy their stock – it essentially aligns the interests of employees with the interests of the company at large. As a result, many companies add stock to various retirement saving programs or develop special stock purchase programs for employees. For example, in 2020, Sanofi, one of the largest global pharmaceutical companies, introduced "Action 2020," a stock program where Sanofi employees can buy shares of the company at only 80% of the market price. In addition, for every five shares purchased, Sanofi will add one extra share for free. According to Sanofi, the goal of this program is "to better associate its employees who are key contributors in this value creation, to the future development and results of the company" (2020).

Institutional Investors

On the opposite side from retail investors, there are *institutional investors* or *professional investors*. There are many types of professional investors, with the main ones being pension funds, mutual funds, hedge funds, endowments, and sovereign funds.

Pension funds, also called *superannuation funds*, are designed to provide retirement income to their beneficiaries. The largest pension fund in the world is the *Federal Old-Age and Survivors Insurance Trust Fund*. To many people in the United States, this fund is known as *Social Security*. It manages assets exceeding US$2.7 trillion. Social Security, however, is different from most other pension funds because it is funded through taxes and the fund is not allowed to invest in shares of companies or any other marketable securities.

A typical pension fund however, is funded by contributions from the employees and employers. Then, these contributions are invested in various securities, including shares of corporations. *California Public Employees' Retirement System* (CalPERS) is one such fund, with US$300 billion in investments. The value of investments may increase or decrease with fluctuations in the market. For example, it is estimated that in 2009 during the financial crisis CalPERS lost about US$55 billion. The *Australian National Superannuation Scheme* manages more than US$1.7 trillion of assets funded by a 9.5% contribution from every employee in Australia. The Scheme has about 500 funds with different investment strategies and management structures, with people being able to choose how to allocate their investments between these funds.

Mutual funds, similarly, accumulate funds from many individuals and organizations and invest them on their behalf. For example, a retail investor may buy shares in Apple, Microsoft, Facebook, Tesla, and Walmart directly or such an investor may invest in the Vanguard 500 Index Fund, which automatically invests in the 500 largest US companies including Apple, Microsoft, and so on. This Vanguard 500 Index Fund has over US$620 billion in assets and, as a result, investing in such a fund creates more diversification and economies of scale. The funds typically charge a management fee for operating the investments on behalf of their clients. Mutual funds also have different investment strategies and an investor can align their investment philosophy with a particular fund. Vanguard in addition to the 500 Index Fund operates many other funds with different strategies; for example, the Vanguard FTSE Social Index Fund screens its investments based on environmental, social, and corporate governance criteria, and excludes stock in alcohol, tobacco, weapons, adult entertainment, fossil fuels, and gaming companies.

Hedge funds are similar to mutual funds but usually involve more risks and use more complex investment strategies and investment instruments, such as derivatives. As a result, hedge funds tend to be limited to sophisticated investors and not open to the general public. Similarly to the unregistered securities discussed earlier, the US government protects regular people from potential fraud, while professional investors do not need this protection as they should be able to evaluate the risks on their own. One of the complex investment strategies that hedge funds use is short selling. Short selling essentially means selling securities that the hedge fund does not own. For example, a hedge fund may sell 100 shares of Microsoft stock without having any Microsoft shares on its balance sheet. The logic behind the short sale is the hedge fund expects the share price to decline soon, and the fund would be able to buy the shares in the future at a cheaper price than the price they are selling the shares for at this very moment. It is easy to make money when all the stock prices are going up, but short selling is a way to make money when the prices are going down.

Short selling is important for investor relations professionals. In fact, IROs should monitor the trade in stock of their company for signs of short selling. Short selling is essentially a bet against the company's success; it is an expectation that the company is going to fail. For IROs, it is important to understand why a bet like this is made, what fuels those expectations, and how much it can affect the share price. Since short sellers do not have to own the stock to sell it, theoretically they can even sell more stock than the company has issued. All this puts pressure on the stock price. In fact, by going on a selling spree, short sellers can push the stock price down even without any under-lying reason – just because of a large sell-off.

On the other hand, short selling carries significantly more risk than traditional investing and that is why it is limited only to professional investors. In the case of investing US$1 million in shares of a company, the most an investor could lose is US$1 million. But shorting US$1 million worth of stock could lead to a loss of US$1, US$10, or even US$100 million if the price of the securities goes up instead of going down – there is no limit to how much the price could increase. For example, in January 2021 one of the hedge funds, Melvin Capital, needed a bailout of US$2.75 billion after its short position against the shares of GameStop backfired as the stock's price jumped through the roof reaching at one point US$450 from only US$4 a year earlier.

Another type of professional investor is *endowments*. Many colleges and other non-profit organizations have financial endowments that manage investments in order to support the mission of the organizations. For example, the endowment of Harvard University is made up of 14,000 different funds with a combined value of almost US$42 billion in investments. Most Harvard investments are in hedge funds, followed by private equity and public equity investments.

Finally, *sovereign funds, sovereign investment funds*, or *sovereign wealth funds* are state-owned funds. Some consider Social Security as a sovereign fund, but since its pri-mary purpose is retirement most people treat it as a pension fund. An example of a sovereign fund is the Abu Dhabi Investment Authority from the United Arab Emirates, which has an estimated US$800 billion in assets. The fund has a variety of investments including Nestlé Skin Health, ThyssenKrupp Elevator, and Citigroup among others.

All these types of institutional investors may have different approaches to investing. It is important for investor relations professionals to know how these investors decide what companies to invest in. In general, investors can be classified into two large groups according to their investment approach: *passive investing* versus *active invest-ing*. Active investing is what many people imagine when they think about investing – picking stocks that can outperform the market. Active investors analyze a company's business, its revenues and profits, stock performance, and many other indicators to make a decision when to buy and when to sell stock. Indeed, a timely investment in a stock on the rise can significantly reward the investor. For example, Amazon went public on May 15, 1997 with a share price of US$18. Today, one share of Amazon stock is traded at above US$3,200. In other words, just US$1,000 invested in 1997 could have been US$1,200,000 today. Unfortunately, it was difficult, if not impossible, to predict Amazon's success in 1997. Even the strongest believers in remote mail-order shopping would not have considered Amazon, a discount bookseller, as their primary investment target, opting perhaps for Sears instead with its leading catalog business that seemed destined to succeed in the Internet era. Yet, while Amazon was growing, Sears was declining, filing for bankruptcy on October 15, 2018. This is the challenge with continuously picking the winning stocks – it is easy to do in hindsight, but very difficult looking forward.

Thus, the other approach to investing is passive investing. Instead of picking winners to buy and losers to sell, an investor can buy the whole market; for example, one share in every company. This so-called *total market investment* protects from many risks because even if some stocks go bankrupt, some will surely wildly succeed. On average, the overall value of stocks tends to increase over time. As a result, a passive investor eliminates a lot of risks and almost guarantees future growth. In addition, many active professional investors demand high fees for their service, while passive funds charge just a fraction of active managers' costs. For example, US$10,000 invested in the Vanguard Total Stock Market Index Fund in 2010 would have become US$37,197 in 2020 – a significant growth considering the very low risk of the investment.

Another common passive investing strategy is to follow a particular stock index. Perhaps the most popular index is *Standard & Poor's 500*, or S&P 500, or simply S&P, an index combining the 500 largest stocks in the United States. One of the leading proponents of investing in S&P 500 funds is a famous investor, Warren Buffett, who believes this is the best investment strategy for most investors. Many other indexes and, as a result, funds that track those indexes exist. For example, while S&P 500 focuses on the largest companies, *Morningstar Small Core Index* combines stocks of small companies, and the *Russell Midcap Index* combines mid-size companies. There are indexes that focus on a specific industry; for example, people who believe that the transportation industry is set for strong growth may invest in Dow Jones Transports, also called the *Dow Jones Transportation Average* (DJTA), the oldest stock index, which combines stocks of 20 transportation corporations – airlines, railroads, marine transportation, trucking, delivery services, and rental and leasing services. Another example is the *Dow Jones Utility Average* (DJUA), or simply *Dow Jones Utilities*, an index that focuses on 15 leading utility companies in the United States.

The index funds are not limited to the United States. Many countries have indexes combining the largest stocks in those countries and there are passive investment funds that follow those indexes. For example, in the UK, the most popular index is the *Financial Times Stock Exchange 100* (FTSE 100), an index of the 100 largest stocks on the UK stock market. There are many investment funds that follow this index; for example, HSBC FTSE 100, iShares Core FTSE 100, or UBS ETF FTSE 100.

Some investment funds follow indexes that catalog the companies by other criteria. For example, the *FTSE4Good Index* is a collection of shares of socially and environmentally responsible companies. It is not the only index focused on socially responsible companies – others are the *Calvert Social Index* and the *MSCI KLD 400 Social*

Index. As a result, there are funds that track those indexes, allowing investors to focus on environmentally and socially responsible investments.

While passive investing focuses on a specific index or other criteria and passively follows it, active investors, as the name applies, actively participate in the decision-making process on what securities to invest in. Although there are many different classifications of active investors, we will focus on three types: traders, portfolio builders, and shareowners.

Traders

Traders are the type of investors who may own a stock in a company for just a fraction of a second before selling it and buying another stock and then another stock and then another stock. In many cases, traders use sophisticated algorithms to do the trading for them – the computer is fed a variety of data on trading patterns of different stocks with the goal of trying to outperform the market through fast and efficient trades. Traditionally, traders would rely on technical analysis – an analysis of past stock price movements. Looking at the past supply and demand, traders attempt to predict what will happen to the stock in the near future. Traders use a variety of complex trading algorithms and rely on industry-standard and proprietary indicators such as moving average, relative strength index, Bollinger bands, Fibonacci retracement levels, and others. Sometimes, traders who rely purely on technical data are called *noise traders* because they make their decisions based on what's happening in the market without even knowing what the companies they are buying and selling are actually doing! They do not read annual reports, do not visit the company's website, and do not talk to the investor relations professionals to learn more about the company. They react to a noise about the company not the actual company that is responsible for that noise.

The opposite approach to this technical analysis is *fundamental analysis*, which is when a trader focuses on fundamentals about the company – revenues, profits, technologies, competition, and so on. However, studying fundamentals is a time-consuming process and for traders who enter and exit stock positions many times in a matter of hours, minutes, or even seconds this may be simply impossible.

Of course, as it is often the case, in reality modern investors are *quantamental* and combine all kinds of information available to them – fundamental and technical – it is rare to find a purely technical trader or a purely fundamental trader. An investor may make a decision to enter the pharmaceutical market based on the fundamental data about the global pandemic and estimating that medical companies will profit in this scenario. Then, such an investor would use algorithms to decide what stock and when to buy and sell, using technical data. But this investor may also decide to intervene and update the algorithms, if they happened to learn about a company getting approval for a new vaccine for example, using fundamental data again.

Portfolio Builders

Another type of active investors is *portfolio builders*. The goal of a portfolio builder is to create a portfolio that provides less risk than a passive portfolio and/or generates more return than a passive portfolio. For example, a famous investor, Benjamin Graham, built his portfolio around fundamental analysis and focusing on a company's value. Instead of blindly investing in all S&P 500 stock as a passive investor would do, he selected only companies that have low debt and above-average profit margins. The idea was to focus only on companies that would provide a better return than the market on average.

Another active investor, John Templeton, created a series of Templeton funds with different investment strategies. He was called the greatest stock picker of the twentieth century for his ability to build a portfolio out of stocks that could outperform the market. One of the current actively managed Templeton funds, Templeton Emerging Markets Small Cap Fund, looks for small companies that nobody else in the world may know about, trying to identify success stories that could bring exceptional return on investments. Chetan Sehgal, the fund manager, explains the fund's strategy as looking "for emerging market small-cap stocks consistent with Templeton's philosophy of investing in overlooked and under-researched companies" (Franklin Templeton, 2020).

Although much research has shown that passive investing is generally the best strategy, there have been quite a few success stories among portfolio investors. One of the most famous investors, Warren Buffett, generated an enormous return through his investment company, Berkshire Hathaway. Investment of just US$10,000 in the fund in 1965, when Warren Buffett took control of the company, would produce about US$250 million today, significantly outperforming a passive investment in the S&P 500 index fund over the same period.

Since portfolio builders do not focus on just one stock but instead on many stocks that meet certain criteria, for example, stock from a particular country or region, or stocks that are environmentally responsible, or stocks that show great future potential, these investors decrease their risk. Even if one company fails to perform and goes bankrupt, only part of the portfolio will lose value, not the whole portfolio. It is also more likely that at least one of hundreds or thousands of stocks invested will be the next unicorn and bring large returns in the future versus investing in just one stock and hoping to make it big. To make good decisions on adding stocks, portfolio investors utilize fundamental analysis significantly more than frequent traders in order to learn about the companies they invest in. They also utilize special portfolio-building algorithms and use a variety of portfolio-building strategies in order to develop a balance between risk and reward, gain exposure to various types of securities, sectors, and companies desired, and develop a desired level of diversification. Overall, the main focus is on the quality of the portfolio as a whole rather than on the individual stocks in it. Although portfolio investors tend to buy and hold stock, it would not be a big problem for portfolio managers to sell any stock in their portfolio, if needed. No single stock has any special significance as the focus is on the portfolio performance overall and fund managers would do whatever it takes to improve this performance.

Shareowners

Shareowners are different from traders and portfolio builders because they tend to focus on a specific singular stock. The reasons for this focus may be different, but typically it is somebody who really believes in the company and is hoping to make a very big return over the years. Ford Motor Company, for example, along with many other legacy automakers was not doing very well in 2020 reporting billions of dollars in losses. Twenty years ago the company's shares were above US$90, but by the end of December 2020, the stock was hovering around US$9 per share. Yet the chief operating officer of Ford, Jim Farley, bought US$1 million worth of Ford stock during 2020 showing his confidence in the car manufacturer's future. It is doubtful he did it to profit on trade imbalances as traders might do, or to improve his portfolio diversification as portfolio investors would do – instead it seems like he believes in the future of the company and wants to send a positive message by owning this stock long term.

Thus, these types of investors are called shareowners versus traditional shareholders – it is done to emphasize that they do not just hold the stock temporarily, sometimes not even knowing anything about the company behind the stock. Instead, they are owners of the stock for long periods of time – usually years – and they know and care about the company. These are the investors IROs tend to build long-term relationships with and these are the ones who want to know as much as possible about the company. They are also sometimes called *strategic investors*.

A certain subtype of these shareowners is *activist investors*. A typical investor tends to sell the stock of the company if they do not like what the company is doing or how it is managed. They are said to *vote with their feet* or *vote with their wallets*. Activist investors, however, instead of selling the shares, try to influence the management of the company through a variety of means to change whatever they do not like about the company. Such activist behavior also tends to require significant effort from the investor relations personnel as they work in the middle between the company's shareholders and the company's management.

Warren Buffett is an example of such a strategic investor, who often uses activism to make the changes he deems necessary. One of the companies Warren Buffett invested in over the years was Salomon Brothers. In 1987, Buffett's Berkshire Hathaway became the largest shareholder of Salomon Brothers. As the years progressed and Buffett learned more about his new investment, he did not really like what he saw. The firm was found to violate the rules established for trading of securities, overstretched its resources to become one of the most leveraged companies, and took too much risk in junk bonds trading. But instead of cutting his losses and selling the stock, Warren Buffett used his shares to make himself a chairman of the board of Salomon Brothers, fired the existing leadership responsible for bad decisions, and made significant strategic changes at the company, including modifying its investment philosophy, making employees "owner-operators," and demanding compliance with all rules and regulations (Loomis, 1997).

This example is, of course, as active as it gets – even activist investors typically do not start running the company themselves, but they tend to be very vocal about what they think should be done. Activist investors often meet with the company's management to discuss what they think and give their suggestions to the company's management, go public with their concerns to the press and social media, and often utilize annual shareholder meetings to make their concerns known to other shareholders and to try to persuade them to join forces against the management. Carl Icahn, a famous activist investor, purchased about 1.4% of Motorola stock, and with that stock launched a campaign to get a seat on the Board of Directors accusing current Board members of rubber-stamping everything the management proposed and not acting in the best interests of shareholders. Since his share of stock was not sufficient to get on the board, he launched a campaign to reach other shareholders trying to persuade them to vote for him. Although Icahn initially failed, with time he increased his ownership in the company and achieved his goal by having Motorola sell its cell phone business to Google with a huge premium for Motorola shareholders (Tonello, 2014).

Common vs. Preferred Stock

Another way to classify shareholders is based on the type of stock they own. At the most basic level, shares can be divided into *common shares* and *preferred shares*. Preferred shares are the type of stock that does not come with voting rights. In other words, holders of preferred stock are *silent owners* of the corporations – the stock still represents ownership in the company, but these owners cannot vote on any issues during the company's annual shareholder meeting. However, in order to offset this lack of voice, preferred stock usually compensates its holders with a *dividend* payment.

A dividend is a payment a company makes to its shareholders as distribution of some of the company's earnings. While common shares may receive a dividend as well, preferred stock owners usually receive a higher dividend. For example, the Bank of America has common stock that recently paid US$0.18 dividend per share, while its preferred stockholders received US$0.38 dividend per share. In many cases, preferred stock has a guaranteed dividend payment, while common shares may receive a dividend one year and receive no dividend the following year.

Another important distinction of the preferred stock is its bankruptcy protection. In the case of a company going bankrupt, preferred stock owners are paid from whatever is left after the company's liquidation before the common stock owners are paid. In fact, usually there is nothing left for owners of common shares. This means that preferred shareholders carry less risk than holders of the common stock. For example, after Enron went bankrupt in December 2001, the court ordered the company to pay US$7.2 billion back to the shareholders. But preferred shareholders received preferred treatment – for each preferred share of Enron investors were given US$168.50, while for each share of common stock investors received only US$6.79.

There are many subtypes of preferred stock – many of these types have to do with how the dividend is calculated: is it paid annually or quarterly, is it a specific monetary amount or is it a percentage of company profit, or any other options. A unique type of preferred stock is *convertible shares*. Convertible shares are the preferred stock that may be converted into common stock – this may be especially beneficial for investors in new unproven start-ups. While the company is still at its early stages, an investor has preferred stock with higher protection against bankruptcy and guaranteed dividends, but if a company becomes a success, preferred stock can be converted into common stock, giving investors a chance to participate in having a say in the company's development and allowing a better chance for stock value appreciation.

Of course, many companies have even more complicated stock structures with several classes of common and preferred shares. For example, Facebook common stock is divided into Class A common stock and Class B common stock. Class A is a traditional common stock that everyone can purchase on a stock market. Class B shares, however, are common shares owned by Facebook founders and employees, including Mark Zuckerberg. The key difference is that each Class A share of Facebook gives you 1 vote, while each Class B share gives you 10 votes. This makes Facebook insiders more powerful when it comes to voting than regular Facebook shareholders.

Value vs. Growth Investors

Yet another way to classify investors is by their investment philosophy. Although almost every single investor is unique in how they approach and manage their investments, two broad groups of investors are usually recognized: *value investors* and *growth investors*.

Growth investors are investors who are trying to identify companies with high growth potential. The companies may have zero profits, they may not even have any sales yet, but an investor may believe that they have the potential to grow rapidly because of their unique product or service, and a large potential market for said product or service. Imagine an electric car company today. There are hardly any electric cars on the road today in comparison with gasoline and diesel cars and trucks. Some investors, however, believe that in the future all cars will be electric – this creates an enormous growth potential for electric car makers. Imagine if every single gas car in the world had to be replaced with an electric car – this would require electric car manufacturers to grow at an unprecedented pace – doubling and tripling their sales every year for many years. This creates an outstanding opportunity for growth investors.

What about other growth segments? Solar panels, for example. If investors believed that in the future every roof will have solar panels on it, they would want to invest in companies designing, producing, and installing solar panels. Of course, it is difficult to predict the future – early investors in Zune believed that it would be a growth leader, yet it never caught on in the market. However, if you get it right, you can make significant returns on your investments.

Value investors have a different approach. Instead of trying to predict the future they look at the company's record today. The goal of value investors is to identify the companies with value that they would understand better than other investors. For example, Walmart has received negative press about its treatment of its employees, and, as a result, many investors were compelled to sell shares of Walmart, pushing its stock price down. However, value investors would identify this as a perfect opportunity to buy the Walmart stock – Walmart's business did not really change much after the bad press, its sales did not decrease, its profit did not diminish, and its customers did not stop shopping there. Its underlying value is still the same as it was before the media posted negative stories about it; however, the price to purchase its stock suddenly decreased – this presented a great opportunity for value investors to buy Walmart at a cheaper price. The stock is said to be *on sale*. After all, people will still be shopping at Walmart no matter what – for many communities Walmart is the only retailer in the area, with no alternatives other than online orders that may take days to arrive.

In order to find undervalued stocks, value investors follow a simple rule: buy when everyone is selling, and sell when everyone is buying. The most famous investor in the world, Warren Buffett, follows value investing principles. As the stock market crashed at the onset of the COVID-19 pandemic, many investors rushed to sell their stocks, while Warren Buffett saw it as an opportunity to buy stocks – indeed, all stocks suddenly became 30% cheaper. His famous quote sums it up: "Whether we're talking about socks or stocks, I like buying quality merchandise when it is marked down" (as cited in Frankel, 2019).

Investors: Debt Holders

Although traditionally investor relations is associated with *equity investors*, owners of common or preferred stock, recently more and more investor relations professionals focus on *debt investors*. The key difference between shares and debt securities is the fact that debt is repaid. If an investor holds a bond with a principal amount of US$10,000 from a company, the full US$10,000 will have to be paid back to the investor at the predetermined date. For example, in 2018 Apple issued US$1 billion of green bonds – bonds to fund Apple projects focused on environment and sustainability – with a *maturity date* in 2031. The maturity date for a bond is the date when the investor will have the bond principal amount repaid. In other words, bond investors have guaranteed expectation of payment on the maturity date. Shareholders may see the price of shares they own go up, go down, or stay the same, while bond holders know exactly what is going to happen with their investment. If a bond's principal amount is US$10,000, and an investor can buy this bond today for US$9,000, the profit is secured at US$1,000.

In addition to the discount on the purchase price from the principal amount, bonds tend to pay monthly, quarterly, or annual interest. This is somewhat similar to dividends paid on shares; however, dividends are often not guaranteed as they tend to depend on a company making a profit, while bond interest is guaranteed. For example, the green bonds from Apple mentioned earlier pay 0.5% on November 15 every year until the maturity date on November 15, 2031.

This guaranteed stream of income over many years with a full repayment at the end makes bonds an attractive and low-risk investment choice. Another benefit of bonds is that, in the case of bankruptcy, bond holders are first in line during a company's liquidation, before stockholders, even before holders of the preferred shares. This makes bond investment even less risky.

While debt securities carry less risk, they also carry less potential for reward. There is no limit to how much a share price can increase. For example, in just one year, 2020, the share price of Tesla increased eightfold, from about US$90 in January to over US$700 in December. Shareholders can realize such enormous increases in the share price, but with bonds there is no potential for explosive growth like this, the bond holders are simply paid the principal amount of the bond. As a result, bond investments are considered conservative choices and are less popular than share investments. There are also fewer regulations around bond securities. Since there are fewer retail investors on the bond market, there is an assumption that bonds are designed more for professional investors and, as a result, fewer regulations and protections are needed. Nevertheless, a company issuing debt is still expected to prepare and release details about its business, securities to be released, and all other relevant information.

Sell-side

Investors are the most important audience for investor relations professionals, whether they invest in equity or debt. However, IROs also work extensively with various intermediaries who facilitate the smooth operation of the financial market. The key intermediary is the *sell-side*. The name sell-side is coined as the opposite to investors, who are labeled *buy-side*. Indeed, buy-side are those who actually buy the securities available on the equity and debt markets. Sell-side, then, are the companies responsible for facilitating the sales of securities. Sell-side can be compared with the department stores that sell products from different manufacturers. For example, when Uber publicly sold its shares in 2019, it used a network of 29 banks. These banks, the sell-side, were selling shares of Uber to investors, the buy-side. Among them were the largest sell-side banks, such as Morgan Stanley, Goldman Sachs, and Bank of America Merrill Lynch.

Sell-side companies facilitate selling of the securities during the IPOs and on the secondary market. On the secondary market sell-side companies are usually referred to as security brokers, or simply brokers. They buy and sell shares for the clients. The clients, the buy-side, can be retail shareholders, mutual funds, pension funds, or any other type of organization. For example, if you were to decide to buy a share in Amazon, you would most likely use one of the Internet brokers, like E-trade or Robinhood – they make buying and selling securities fast and easy. Sell-side organizations are also actively involved on the bond market, including corporate bonds and government bonds. E-trade, for example, on its website states that it can help its clients trade stocks, bonds, and other securities, can provide guidance and recommendations, and can even manage your capital for you.

To do all this, many sell-side organizations employ *financial analysts*, who analyze stocks and bonds and issue investment recommendations to their clients on which securities to buy, which to sell, and which to hold. For example, Tesla stock is analyzed by 33 financial analysts. At the beginning of 2021, 8 of these financial analysts were recommending selling the stock, 11 recommending buying it, and 14 taking a neutral position of holding the Tesla stock. This sell-side function is called *research*. Research work is very important for IROs – investor relations professionals become responsible for sharing information with the financial analysts and educating them on all the important details about the company. If financial analysts do not understand the company's vision or its business model, they cannot provide an accurate recommendation for their clients.

One of the key measures for investor relations professionals is the consistency in the analysts' estimates, and their variance from the *consensus estimate*. Financial analysts tend to predict future earnings for a company they analyze based on their understanding of the company's business. Many investors tend to rely on these estimates in making their stock buy and sell decisions. The average of all analysts' estimates is called a consensus estimate. If all analysts' estimates are pretty similar, there would not be much variance from one analyst to another, and all estimates would be close to the consensus estimate. This indicates similar levels of understanding and appreciation of the company's business and, as a result, it is usually considered an indication of good work by the company's IROs. If, however, the IROs have not properly educated the analysts on the company's strengths and weaknesses or have not communicated all relevant information to all analysts, it is possible to see large variations from one estimate to another. As a result, with large variations between estimates, the analysts may make contradictory recommendations, like in the earlier example of Tesla stock, where some analysts recommend buying the stock, while others are recommending selling the stock. This may indicate very different levels of understanding of the future of this company.

For many small companies getting access to the sell-side and to sell-side research is the only way to get noticed and get exposure to the buy-side. Investors may never find out about some small company in Alachua, Florida, unless sell-side financial analysts write a research report on them and share it with their clients. As a result, one of the key tasks for IROs at new or smaller companies is establishing or increasing the coverage of the stock by the financial analysts. This requires identifying the analysts who would be appropriate for a particular stock and developing relationships with them.

Sell-side analysts tend to focus on a specific industry or industries – this makes them experts not just in finance but also in that particular industry – as a result, they tend to develop a good understanding of technology and business. To be industry-level experts, financial analysts are interested in much more than just financial numbers. In fact, to proper evaluate the company it is not enough to look at the balance sheet alone. It is important to understand the company as a whole: What are its competitive advantages? What is unique about its products? How does it compare with others in the industry? For example, one of the largest investment banks, UBS, recently tasked its analysts with studying battery technologies for the electric car market. The battery is one of the main components in an electric car and, thus, whoever has the lead in the battery technology is well positioned for the future as sales of electric cars are expected to grow. Financial results are based on what happened in the past; for financial analysts, however, it is of primary importance what is going to happen in the future. In order to answer this question, analysts must understand what is going to happen with the company and the whole industry. Tesla sells more electric vehicles than its competitors, but whether it will be able to maintain its leadership depends to a large extent on the developments in the battery technology by Tesla and by its competitors – Volkswagen, General Motors, and others. UBS financial analysts concluded that, although Tesla has an advantage in the battery technologies, its reliance on battery suppliers like LG and Panasonic presents a weakness for the company versus having its own battery production. Financial analysts would then communicate that information to fund managers and other investors who make a decision on buying and selling stocks.

Meetings with financial analysts may be helpful not just for enhancing analysts' understanding of the company, but also to help the company's management enhance their understanding of the industry as a whole. Sometimes company may see their own business in a new light or from a different perspective and get an insight into the potential future directions of company development. For IROs it may be a challenge to maintain relationships with the financial analysts – analysts may be covering many companies, and this workload tends to increase with time. At many sell-side companies, financial analysts are an expense account – brokers do not charge their clients for research, it is offered for free. The only payments are trade commissions when clients buy or sell securities – as a result, while traders bring income, financial analysis is seen as an expense. Some companies, however, do charge for research and sell the analysts' research reports, but even in this case research income pales in comparison with trading income.

Internal Stakeholders

Not all the work of investor relations professionals is targeted outside the company: internal work occupies a very significant portion of an IRO's day. A lot of work is focused on the company's top management. It is common for investor relations professionals to prepare reports for the company's executives about share price fluctuations, trading volume, changes in ownership, and even relaying feedback from investors and analysts about the company's business. IROs also work with the company's executives on preparing them for various public appearances – from *one-on-one meetings* with investors to interviews on CNBC. Investors and financial analysts love hearing directly from the company's management and cherish opportunities to ask them questions directly; however, there are a lot of rules and regulations on what can and cannot be said. As a result, it becomes the responsibility of the IRO to train executives on proper communications with the investment community.

IROs also work closely with the company's top management as well as other departments such as public relations, accounting, and marketing on producing annual and quarterly reports that often become more than just legally required disclosure vehicles, serving also as an opportunity for a company to promote its vision and enhance its reputation among not just investors, but also customers, suppliers, employees, and others. In addition to periodic reporting, IROs spend time with company executives anticipating and reacting to unexpected developments with emergency current filings, as needed.

Investor relations work is dependent on extensive understanding of the company's business. As a result, investor relations professionals develop working relationships in every department of the company – research, production, sales, human resources, customer support, and so on. The company's competitive advantage can reside in any of these areas and it is important to communicate and educate buy-side and sell-side on the strengths and weaknesses of the company to establish a fair evaluation for the company's securities.

Another reason internal stakeholders are vitally important for investor relations is the fact that employees tend to be vigilant consumers of all information related to the company. It is not a secret that company's employees read annual reports, listen to earnings calls, and attend annual meetings. This is a fast and reliable way to learn more about the company as a whole, and for employees this knowledge is important. As a result, when IROs prepare messages for investors, they should always take into account how these messages will affect the internal stakeholders. It is an imminent disaster if there is a dissonance between what is communicated externally to investors and internally to employees about sales, revenues, competition, or future prospects. It will hurt the employee morale immediately, and with time this disagreement will become public knowledge, further hurting relationships internally and externally. Finally, it is quite common for employees to own shares in their companies – they may receive shares as part of the compensation package or simply buy them on the secondary market. Thus, they often need to be treated as both employees and shareholders.

Other Stakeholders

Many other stakeholders occupy an IRO's attention. Journalists are an important audience for investor relations, especially financial and business journalists. A negative story in the business media can hurt the company and its fair valuation, thus it is important to work with journalists and develop relationships with them. Helping journalists find facts and educating them on the company's business is not that different from educating investors and financial analysts. Although relationships with journalists are usually a prerogative of public relations, investor relations professionals must participate in this effort as well. If a journalist misunderstands information related to a company's business performance, it may lead to negative outcomes for the corporation. It is important that the media knows who to contact and to be available to the media in the same way as IROs are available to investors and analysts. It is also important to know key reporters covering the company and the industry. These relationships may be vital in a crisis when fast and accurate communications are important. These relationships are also important when something positive is happening – like the launch of a new product or a scientific discovery that can bring profits to the company – working with journalists on covering these stories may have a positive effect on the stock and the company as a whole.

Investor relations is one of the most regulated communication professions; as a result, IROs work closely with a variety of regulatory agencies. In the United States, the key regulator is the SEC. The SEC focuses on "protecting investors, maintaining fair, orderly, and efficient markets, and facilitating capital formation" (2020). To achieve these goals, the SEC oversees the federal securities laws, maintains the disclosure of financial information by publicly traded companies, and can bring enforcement actions against violators of the securities law. The SEC is headed by five commissioners. The commissioners are appointed by the President of the United States for a five-year term. The SEC must be a bipartisan body. In order to achieve this, no more than three commissioners can belong to the same political party. One of the commissioners is designated by the US President to be the Chair of the Commission. As of 2021, the Chair of the Commission is Allison Herren Lee.

Today the SEC employs almost 3,500 people. The Commission's organization chart consists of 4 divisions and 19 offices. The Division of Corporate Finance is directly charged with overseeing corporate disclosure practices and making sure that all investors, from Wall Street financial analysts to retired teachers in rural Iowa, have equal access to the corporate financial information. The Division reviews required disclosure documents filed by companies planning to sell their securities to the general public, as well as periodic disclosures by publicly traded corporations. The Division encourages corporations to provide extensive and timely information, both positive and negative, about a company's business to ensure that investors can make an educated decision whether to buy, hold, or sell securities of the company.

The Division of Trading and Markets provides oversight over securities trading. It controls the work of stock exchanges, brokers, dealers, transfer agents, clearing agencies, credit rating agencies, and others. The goal of this Division is to ensure reliable and efficient operations of the securities trading markets.

The Division of Investment Management is in charge of mutual and pension funds operating in the United States. A large portion of the money in these funds is collected from many private investors who are saving for retirement, college, a new house, or for any other purpose. Professional fund managers pool together money from millions of such individuals and manage it on their behalf. The Division ensures that fund managers act in the best interests of all individual investors and provide full disclosure of fund activities to them.

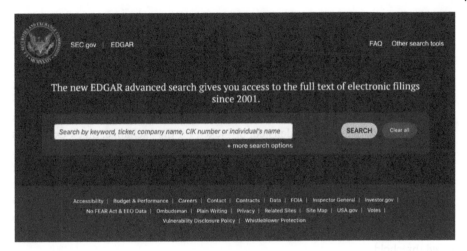

Figure 3.1 EDGAR home page managed by the United States Securities and Exchange Commission.

The Division of Enforcement investigates securities law violations, obtains evidence of unlawful activities, and can bring civil actions in courts. This Division also collects complaints from private and professional investors and monitors market activities daily to ensure legality of all operations. The Division recovered US$1.2 billion for harmed investors during the most recent fiscal year as a result of enforcement actions against wrongdoers (SEC, 2020). One of the largest examples was Wells Fargo. The SEC charged the Wells Fargo CEO and Chairman of the Board as well as the head of Wells Fargo banking with misleading investors and exaggerating the success of the banking operations at Wells Fargo between 2014 and 2016. Specifically, the SEC noted the usage of metrics that relied on unused, unneeded, or even unauthorized accounts. Stephanie Avakian, Director of the SEC's Division of Enforcement explained: "If executives speak about a key performance metric to promote their business, they must do so fully and accurately, The Commission will continue to hold responsible not only the senior executives who make false and misleading statements but also those who certify to the accuracy of misleading statements despite warnings to the contrary" (SEC, 2020, para. 4).

The SEC is arguably best known for its data service. The SEC is responsible for *EDGAR (Electronic Data Gathering, Analysis, and Retrieval system)* (Figure 3.1). All publicly traded companies are required to submit their financial information to EDGAR and that information becomes available to anybody who has a computer with an Internet connection. You do not have to own shares in a company to see its reports. Anyone with an Internet connection can access annual and quarterly reports of any public company as well as other filings submitted to EDGAR.

In addition to the SEC, other regulators important for investor relations and financial communication professionals are: the Federal Reserve Board, the Commodity Futures Trading Commission, and the US Department of Treasury, especially its Office of Domestic Finance, among others. The US Treasury's Office of Domestic Finance is responsible for regulations of banking and financial institutions, as well as capital markets.

Another important stakeholder for a company's IROs is the *stock exchange* where securities are traded. Stock exchanges have their own rules and requirements that companies must follow in order to become and to remain listed on a stock exchange. Only companies that are listed can be traded on a stock exchange. The most common listing requirement is the size of the company; for example, the New York Stock Exchange only lists companies valued at no less than US$100 million. If a share price goes down and the company's overall value, or its *capitalization*, goes below this threshold the company can be delisted, or kicked off the exchange. Stock exchanges may have also rules related to a single share price, total number of shares, and similar. However, exchanges can introduce any other rules as well. For example, at the end of 2020 Nasdaq introduced a proposal for all its listed companies to have at least one woman and at least one "diverse" member (underrepresented minority or LGBTQ) on the Board of Directors. Each company would be responsible for reporting the makeup of its Board of Directors and explaining how it meets or why it does not meet the proposed threshold.

Traditionally, three stock exchanges are considered the top exchanges where companies want to get listed: the New York Stock Exchange, Nasdaq, and the London Stock Exchange. However, there are many other regional stock exchanges with less stringent listing requirements that may be a better option for a particular company. New exchanges also appear. For example, September 2020 saw the launch of three new stock exchanges – the Long-Term Stock Exchange (LTSE), the Members Exchange (MEMX), and the Miami International Securities Exchange – bringing the total number of US exchanges to 19.

In addition, the SEC continues to approve *alternative trading systems* (ATSs) – also known as *dark pools* – with 54 currently in operation in the United States. The term dark pool indicates that the prices and trading volumes are not public, unlike regular, or *lit*, exchanges where bids and offers are posted publicly. Almost one-third of all trading in the United States occurs on dark pools, with the rest split across the lit exchanges. As more trading venues and exchanges launch, especially dark pools, it makes it significantly more difficult for the investor relations professionals to know where a stock is traded, by whom, what it means for the price, and who the buyers and sellers are (Ashwell, 2020).

Key Terms

Accredited investor
Active investing
Activist investors
Alternative trading system
Angel investor
ATS
Australian National Superannuation Scheme
Berkshire Hathaway
Buffet, Warren
Buy-side
California Public Employees' Retirement System
CalPERS

Calvert Social Index
Capitalization
Common share
Consensus estimate
Convertible share
Dark pool Debt investor
Diversification
Dividend
DJTA
DJUA
Dark pool
Dow Jones Transport
Dow Jones Transportation Average
Dow Jones Utilities
Dow Jones Utility Average
EDGAR
Electronic Data Gathering, Analysis, and Retrieval system
Endowment
Equity investor
Federal Old-Age and Survivors Insurance Trust Fund
Financial analyst
Financial Times Stock Exchange 100
FTSE 100
FTSE4Good Index
Fundamental analysis
Go public
Graham, Benjamin
Growth investor
Hedge fund
Icahn, Carl
Initial public offering
Insider
Insider trading
Institutional investor
Investor
IPO
Lit exchange
Maturity date
Morningstar Small Core Index
MSCI KLD 400 Social Index
Mutual fund
Noise trader
Nonpublic information
One-on-one meetings
Passive investing
Pension fund
Portfolio builders

Preferred shares
Private shareholder company
Professional investors
Publics
Public company
Publicly traded company
Public shareholder company
QIB
Qualified institutional buyer
Quantamental
Research
Retail shareholder
Russell Midcap Index
S&P
S&P 500
SEC
Securities and Exchange Commission
Sell-side
Shareholder
Shareowners
Short selling
Silent owner
Social Security
Sophisticated investor
Sovereign fund
Sovereign investment fund
Sovereign wealth fund
Standard & Poor's 500
Stock bonus
Stock compensation
Stock exchange
Stakeholder
Stockholder
Strategic investor
Superannuation fund
Technical analysis
Templeton, John
Tesla millionaire
Total market investment
Trader
Value investor
Venture investor
Vote with your feet
Vote with your wallet

Discussion Questions and Activities

1 Some companies have specific plans to increase the amount of retail shareholders. Who are retail shareholders and why do companies want to attract them?

2 Discuss how IROs should develop relationships with three types of investors: traders, portfolio builders, and shareowners. Recommend key strategies for each type.

3 What are the key differences between common and preferred stock? Discuss what should be the differences in IROs communications, if any, depending on what types of stock they own. What about debt holders?

4 Describe various stakeholders other than stockholders that are important for IROs. What roles do they play in investor relations?

5 Identify any actively managed equity fund and analyze its investment approach. Compare its performance with various market indexes and other funds. If you were an IRO of a corporation, how would you pitch this fund to invest in your company?

Part II

Disclosure

4

Communicating Financial Information

A good working knowledge of accounting and finance is essential for investor relations professionals and financial communicators because a very large part of disclosure focuses on financial information. Whether it is a new company drafting a prospectus, an existing company submitting a quarterly report, or a company sending proxy documents to shareholders in preparation for an annual general meeting, financial information is a key component of all these communications. So, what is included in the financial disclosure?

Regulation S-X provides specific details on what information, including financial information, must be included in corporate disclosure. It identifies three main financial statements that form the foundation of the financial disclosure: *balance sheet*, *income statement*, and *cash flow statement*.

Income Statement

An income statement is a document that describes the earnings and spending of a company over a period of time – for an annual report, the time period is a year. An income statement can be compared with a person's tax return – both of these documents show all the income received during the year, and all the expenses for the same time period. The document, then, shows how much tax must be paid by the corporation or by the individual.

Table 4.1 is Microsoft 2020 annual income statement retrieved from Microsoft's annual report, *Form 10-K*, filing with the US Securities and Exchange Commission (SEC). The top lines of the income statement describe the sales or *revenues* of the company. In the case of Microsoft, revenues are divided into two groups: sales of products and sales of services. The year 2020 was important for Microsoft: if you look carefully at the revenues, you will notice that 2020 is the year when revenues from services surpassed revenues from products (in 2019 and 2018, sales of products brought more revenues than sales of services). So, in 2020 Microsoft became a service company. This is an important discovery for financial analysts and, no doubt, led to many discussions with Microsoft's investor relations professionals and executives. Analysts would want

Investor Relations and Financial Communication: Creating Value Through Trust and Understanding, First Edition. Alexander V. Laskin.
© 2022 John Wiley & Sons, Inc. Published 2022 by John Wiley & Sons, Inc.

Table 4.1 Microsoft 2020 income statement.

(In millions, except per share amounts)			
Year ended June 30	2020	2019	2018
Revenue:			
Product	$ 68,041	$ 66,069	$ 64,497
Service and other	74,974	59,774	45,863
Total revenue	143,015	125,843	110,360
Cost of revenue:			
Product	16,017	16,273	15,420
Service and other	30,061	26,637	22,933
Total cost of revenue	46,078	42,910	38,353
Gross margin	96,937	82,933	72,007
Research and development	19,269	16,876	14,726
Sales and marketing	19,598	18,213	17,469
General and administrative	5,111	4,885	4,754
Operating income	52,959	42,959	35,058
Other income, net	77	729	1,416
Income before income taxes	53,036	43,688	36,474
Provision for income taxes	8,755	4,448	19,903
Net income	$ 44,281	$ 39,240	$ 16,571
Earnings per share:			
Basic	$ 5.82	$ 5.11	$ 2.15
Diluted	$ 5.76	$ 5.06	$ 2.13
Weighted average shares outstanding:			
Basic	7,610	7,673	7,700
Diluted	7,683	7,753	7,794

Source: Microsoft Corporation financial statements. Retrieved from: https://www.sec.gov/Archives/edgar/data/0000789019/000156459020034944/msft-10k_20200630.htm#ITEM_8_FINANCIAL_STATEMENTS_AND_SUPPLEM. Public Domain.

to know what services are growing, what their future prospects are, and what is the opinion of Microsoft leadership on these trends in sales. Perhaps they would want to discuss the shift from selling Microsoft Office products to the Microsoft Office subscription model as a change from product revenues to service revenue. Whatever discussions were held, however, they would go beyond what can be found in the financial statements and would focus on the developments in operations, marketing, technology, and so on. The financial statement is the starting point of this conversation, but additional information is needed to understand properly what is going on with Microsoft, or any other company for that matter. The revenue section then sums up all the revenues of the company: for 2020 revenues totaled US$143 billion.

The next section of the income statement describes *costs of goods sold* (COGS), or cost of sales, or cost of revenues. Every time Microsoft sells an Xbox or Surface or Office, Microsoft has to spend money buying raw materials, components, technology, patents, and so on. To build a Surface tablet, Microsoft has to buy a processor, display, memory, battery, and many other components. Microsoft also has to pay employees to produce those tablets; thus, there is also a salary component involved. Generally, costs of sales are proportionally related to sales – in other words, to sell more Surface tablets, Microsoft has to buy more components and hire more employees. If sales go down costs can proportionally go down as well. In the case of 2020 Microsoft, total cost of revenues was US$46 billion.

Subtracting costs from revenues gives us *gross margin*: US$143 billion minus US$46 billion leaves us with a gross margin of US$97 billion. This is the number that financial analysts look at closely. There is no clear-cut rule of what a good gross margin is. It depends on the industry, on the products and services, on the general state of the economy, on the competition, and on the life cycle of the industry, products, and services. Financial analysts would compare Microsoft's gross margin with previous years and with the company's competitors. However, even without doing that, we can observe that Microsoft's gross margin being more than twice the size of its costs of sales, is a very good indicator of Microsoft's financial health. This basically suggests that for every dollar Microsoft invests in building its products and services it gets US$3 in sales.

Next, the income statement lists additional expenses of the company for the year. These expenses are often called *selling, general, and administrative expenses* (SG&A). The key difference of these expenses from cost of sales is the fact that SG&A are not proportionally related to sales. If sales of Surface tablets, for example, decline, Microsoft can cut its costs of sales by buying less of the raw materials and components it needs to build the tablets. It can also lay off some of the employees putting the tablets together to save on salary expenses, but Microsoft won't be able to make its Super Bowl ad cheaper because the price of the Super Bowl ad is not related to the number of units Microsoft sells. If Microsoft borrowed money from the bank, the interest payment on that loan won't change either based on Microsoft's declining sales.

One of the important expenses for Microsoft is *research and development (R&D) expense*. R&D is the foundation for future sales – the company must work on developing new Office, new Xbox, new Surface, new video games – all this requires significant investment. The income statement shows that in 2020 Microsoft invested almost US$20 billion in R&D. There is little doubt that financial analysts would want to know more about these investments: what products and services are being developed, what seems to be an early success, what are the challenges, and so on. Again, analysts and investors would need to go beyond the basic financial statements to evaluate this information. Once again, there is no universally accepted rule on what the right amount is to spend on R&D. On one hand, these expenses are taken out of a company's earnings and lower the company's profitability; on the other hand, without developing new products there will be no earnings in the future. Financial analysts and investors expend significant effort talking with investor relations officers (IROs) and company management to understand R&D expenses, comparing them with competitors and with the industry as a whole, taking into account the development stages of various products and services. Other expenses described in this part of the income statement are sales, marketing, advertising, public relations, and general administrative expenses. These are all expenses needed to run the business – the company needs to pay for electricity, water, rent, printing costs, Internet connection, repay the loans with interest, buy new equipment, and so on. These expenses typically would not proportionally correlate to the sales of the company's products.

Once all these expenses are paid what is left is *operating income*. In the case of Microsoft, it is almost US$53 billion. Operating income (or operating loss) is a very important indicator because it shows how much money the company is making from its main business. Many income statements also show a measure called *earnings before interest, depreciation, taxes, and amortization* (EBIDTA). EBIDTA shows the income before subtracting interest paid on loans, depreciation and amortization expenses on equipment and real estate, and taxes. Many financial analysts like using EBIDTA for analyzing a company's stock because it is a more direct indicator of the company's operations over a period of time. Companies may have very different tax structures (their headquarters may be in different countries) or different loans with different repayment formulas, so removing all these variables from the equation makes for an easier comparison on actual day-to-day operations between companies.

In addition to EBIDTA, financial analysts also use *earnings before interest and taxes* (EBIT), and then, finally, *earnings before taxes* (EBT). Each step is useful in financial analysis as it allows the evaluation of how much a company is paying in interest, and then, how much it is paying in taxes, and also allows the creation of a fairer criterion for comparing companies with each other. It is possible for a company to make lots of money from operations and have a good gross margin but lose money elsewhere by having too much real estate, or paying too much in employee perks, or borrowing too much at a very high rate. It is important to analyze the company as a whole in order to make a good investment decision, not just its products or its sales.

In the end, after all expenses are subtracted and taxes are paid, what is left is *net income* or *net profit* – the final results after all earnings and all expenses have been taken into account. Since this is the last line in the income statement calculations, this is known as the proverbial *bottom line*. In the case of Microsoft, 2020 net income was US$44 billion.

Income statements for publicly traded companies also tend to divide the net income by total number of shares to arrive at *earnings per share* (EPS). In the case of Microsoft, EPS for 2020 was US$5.82 and it showed a very strong growth in comparison with a 2019 EPS of US$2.13. This can be compared with the share price of Microsoft on the stock market, which at the start of 2021 was about US$240. Dividing the share price by the EPS gives investors and analysts the most popular metric for evaluating stocks: *price/earnings (P/E) ratio*. In the case of Microsoft the ratio is about 40. In other words, Microsoft shares are valued at 40 times the company's earnings. Once again, there is no right or wrong number for P/E. It is important to compare this number historically with previous years as well as with the company's competitors, or *peers*. For example, Adobe P/E is above 55 and Salesforce P/E is above 85 – this means their shares are more "expensive" from the P/E standpoint than shares of Microsoft. On the other hand, Google P/E is about 36, and Facebook P/E is about 32 – meaning their shares are less "expensive" from the P/E standpoint than shares of Microsoft.

Balance Sheet

If an income statement can be compared to a person's tax return, a balance sheet is more like a credit card application. On a credit card application, applicants are asked to describe all their assets, such as houses, cars, boats, money in checking and savings accounts, and whatever else the person owns. The individuals also describe all their liabilities such as credit card debts, mortgages, car loans, and whatever else the person owes. All of this is based on a particular point in time – usually, as of the time of the application. This is an important difference from the income statement – the income statement describes what happened over a certain period of time, a year for an annual income statement, while a balance sheet is a snapshot of a particular moment in time – it may already be outdated the next day.

So, what is on a company's balance sheet? Table 4.2 shows Microsoft's 2020 balance sheet, also taken from the Microsoft annual report, Form 10-K, submitted to the SEC. All balance sheets, including Microsoft's, have two main sections: *assets*, the section that describes what the company has; and the section labeled *liabilities and stockholders' equity*, where the company describes how it financed all its assets. The reason a balance sheet is called that is because both parts must always be in balance – everything a company has must correspond to a liability or equity. In this Microsoft balance sheet both sections are equal to $301.311 billion.

On a typical balance sheet, assets are divided into two large categories – *current assets* and *noncurrent assets*. The distinction between the two is their lifespan. As a general rule, if an asset's lifespan is less than a year, then it is a current asset. Current assets are also assets that are easy to convert into cash. A checking account is a good example of current assets because one can quickly withdraw cash from a checking account. Another example is inventory – all the Xbox consoles that Microsoft has already built are likely to be sold within a year. Another example is accounts receivable – Microsoft provided a service and sent a bill to the client and is now waiting for the payment. Since bills are typically due within 30 days, accounts receivables are also current assets. In the current example, Microsoft's total current assets are equal to almost $182 billion.

Noncurrent assets are long-term assets, sometimes also called *capital assets* or *fixed assets*. Factories and plants are examples of capital assets – the company is going to use them for many years, including the equipment inside, to produce the products and services, and won't sell them within a year. In fact, noncurrent assets are usually not easy to sell and convert into cash because it is unlikely somebody would want to buy a Microsoft's factory built to make Xboxes.

The most complex part of noncurrent assets is usually *intangibles* and *goodwill*. We will talk in more detail about intangible assets in the next section, but this category includes such assets as brand value, copyrights, patents, trademarks, and so on. Sometimes intangible assets are also called *nonfinancial assets* because it is very

Table 4.2 Microsoft 2020 balance sheets.

(In millions)		
June 30	2020	2019
Assets		
Current assets:		
Cash and cash equivalents	$ **13,576**	$ 11,356
Short-term investments	**122,951**	122,463
Total cash, cash equivalents, and short-term investments	**136,527**	133,819
Accounts receivable, net of allowance for doubtful accounts of **$788** and $411	**32,011**	29,524
Inventories	**1,895**	2,063
Other current assets	**11,482**	10,146
Total current assets	**181,915**	175,552
Property and equipment, net of accumulated depreciation of **$43,197** and $35,330	**44,151**	36,477
Operating lease right-of-use assets	**8,753**	7,379
Equity investments	**2,965**	2,649
Goodwill	**43,351**	42,026
Intangible assets, net	**7,038**	7,750
Other long-term assets	**13,138**	14,723
Total assets	$ **301,311**	$ 286,556
Liabilities and stockholders' equity		
Current liabilities:		
Accounts payable	$ **12,530**	$ 9,382
Current portion of long-term debt	**3,749**	5,516
Accrued compensation	**7,874**	6,830
Short-term income taxes	**2,130**	5,665
Short-term unearned revenue	**36,000**	32,676
Other current liabilities	**10,027**	9,351
Total current liabilities	**72,310**	69,420
Long-term debt	**59,578**	66,662
Long-term income taxes	**29,432**	29,612
Long-term unearned revenue	**3,180**	4,530
Deferred income taxes	**204**	233
Operating lease liabilities	**7,671**	6,188
Other long-term liabilities	**10,632**	7,581
Total liabilities	**183,007**	184,226
Commitments and contingencies		

(Continued)

Table 4.2 (Continued)

(In millions)		
June 30	2020	2019
Stockholders' equity:		
Common stock and paid-in capital – shares authorized 24,000; outstanding **7,571** and 7,643	**80,552**	78,520
Retained earnings	**34,566**	24,150
Accumulated other comprehensive income (loss)	**3,186**	(340)
Total stockholders' equity	**118,304**	102,330
Total liabilities and stockholders' equity	$ **301,311**	$ 286,556

Source: Microsoft Corporation financial statements. Retrieved from: https://www.sec.gov/Archives/edgar/data/0000789019/000156459020034944/msft-10k_20200630.htm#ITEM_8_FINANCIAL_STATEMENTS_AND_SUPPLEM. Public Domain.

difficult to measure them and to estimate their value in US dollars. For example, what value would you assign to the Google's search ranking algorithm? Google wouldn't exist without it, but Google today is much more than just its search. Or what is the brand value of Rolex? The price difference between a watch with the Rolex name on it and a similar watch without the name may be thousands of dollars. It becomes very difficult, yet very important, for financial analysts and investors to properly understand what is hiding behind the numbers in this part of the balance sheet; this segment requires a lot of work from IROs and company management to educate investors on the value of the company's intangibles.

The second section of the balance sheet describes liabilities and stockholders' equity. Similar to assets, liabilities tend to be divided into *short-term liabilities*, or *current liabilities*, and *long-term*, or *noncurrent liabilities*. As with the assets, the difference between the two is usually a one-year term – current liabilities are due within a year, and long-term liabilities are due in more than a year. Corporations, in the same way as people, get bills for electricity, water, rent, and credit card spending – all these must be paid well within a year, usually every month.

Among current liabilities, there is usually a line that reads "*current portion of long-term debt*." Although it may seem counterintuitive to have long-term debt in the short-term liabilities section, what this actually means is that long-term debt is usually repaid over a long period of time but within this long period of time there are recurring payments with some of them having to be paid in the near term. For example, if you have a mortgage, it is a long-term debt, but every month you have to pay a part of the overall amount of the mortgage, its monthly payment. So, although the overall mortgage is a long-term liability, the portion of the mortgage that has to be repaid within a year becomes a short-term, or current liability. In the case of the Microsoft 2020 balance sheet, the current portion of long-term liabilities equals US$3.749 billion. Short-term and long-term liabilities together for Microsoft are slightly over US$183 billion.

Shareholders' equity, or stockholders' equity, is the other way companies can finance their assets. Instead of borrowing money from a bank, a company can issue shares and sell them. These shares would be reflected in stockholders' equity. The Microsoft balance sheet shows 7.571 billion outstanding shares representing US$80.552 billion. Outstanding shares means shares that are issued and sold to investors out of the total amount of shares authorized that a company can potentially sell to investors.

Finally, the balance sheet shows *retained earnings*. This is the profit from the income statement that the company has accumulated over the years. The company can pay out the income to shareholders as dividends as discussed in the previous section or the company can keep the profits to reinvest them into growing its business. In 2020, Microsoft's retained earnings reached US$34.566 billion – quite a significant amount and considerably more than Microsoft reported just a year earlier at US$24.150 billion. Retained earnings are recorded in shareholders' equity because these earnings belong to a corporation, and the shareholders are the corporation's owners. It does not mean, however, that shareholders can use this money any way they please. It is quite common though for shareholders to debate whether the company should pay out the earnings as dividends or save them as retained earnings. Steve Jobs, for example, was famous for refusing to pay dividends to Apple shareholders. Not all shareholders were happy about it, especially when Apple was making billions of dollars in profits. Jobs' logic, however, was that by reinvesting the profits in Apple's growth he could grow the company even faster. Some say that companies that pay dividends are out of ideas since they do not know what to invest the money in to bring even more growth. Of course, other investors disagree and say that paying dividends is the right thing to do to reward investors for holding the stock as investors realize return from the securities without having to sell them. While this debate is likely to continue forever, large amounts of retained earnings can be very beneficial to a company as this makes it possible to acquire a competitor or another company if an opportunity presents itself. For example, in 2020 a relatively young social media platform, TikTok, was a target for acquisition and, because Microsoft has large amounts of retained earnings, it was considered to be one of the front-runners for buying TikTok. Although, in the end, Microsoft did not buy this social media app, without retained earnings it would not even have had such an opportunity.

Cash Flow Statement

The final financial statement to discuss is the cash flow statement. If an income statement can be compared with a tax return and a balance sheet can be compared with a credit card application, a cash flow statement could be compared with a checking account statement. The cash flow statement focuses on movements of cash over a period of time – similarly to an income statement, cash flow describes what happened over a period of time – a month, a quarter, or a year. Table 4.3 shows a Microsoft 2020 cash flow statement. For most corporations, the cash flow statement is divided into three large sections: *cash from operations*, *cash from financing*, and *cash from investments*.

Table 4.3 Microsoft 2020 cash flows statements.

(In millions)			
Year ended June 30	2020	2019	2018
Operations			
Net income	$ **44,281**	$ 39,240	$ 16,571
Adjustments to reconcile net income to net cash from operations:			
Depreciation, amortization, and other	**12,796**	11,682	10,261
Stock-based compensation expense	**5,289**	4,652	3,940
Net recognized gains on investments and derivatives	**(219)**	(792)	(2,212)
Deferred income taxes	**11**	(6,463)	(5,143)
Changes in operating assets and liabilities:			
Accounts receivable	**(2,577)**	(2,812)	(3,862)
Inventories	**168**	597	(465)
Other current assets	**(2,330)**	(1,718)	(952)
Other long-term assets	**(1,037)**	(1,834)	(285)
Accounts payable	**3,018**	232	1,148
Unearned revenue	**2,212**	4,462	5,922
Income taxes	**(3,631)**	2,929	18,183
Other current liabilities	**1,346**	1,419	798
Other long-term liabilities	**1,348**	591	(20)
Net cash from operations	**60,675**	52,185	43,884
Financing			
Repayments of short-term debt, maturities of 90 days or less, net	**0**	0	(7,324)

(Continued)

Table 4.3 (Continued)

(In millions)			
Year ended June 30	2020	2019	2018
Proceeds from issuance of debt	0	0	7,183
Cash premium on debt exchange	(3,417)	0	0
Repayments of debt	(5,518)	(4,000)	(10,060)
Common stock issued	1,343	1,142	1,002
Common stock repurchased	(22,968)	(19,543)	(10,721)
Common stock cash dividends paid	(15,137)	(13,811)	(12,699)
Other, net	(334)	(675)	(971)
Net cash used in financing	(46,031)	(36,887)	(33,590)
Investing			
Additions to property and equipment	(15,441)	(13,925)	(11,632)
Acquisition of companies, net of cash acquired, and purchases of intangible and other assets	(2,521)	(2,388)	(888)
Purchases of investments	(77,190)	(57,697)	(137,380)
Maturities of investments	66,449	20,043	26,360
Sales of investments	17,721	38,194	117,577
Other, net	(1,241)	0	(98)
Net cash used in investing	(12,223)	(15,773)	(6,061)
Effect of foreign exchange rates on cash and cash equivalents	(201)	(115)	50
Net change in cash and cash equivalents	2,220	(590)	4,283
Cash and cash equivalents, beginning of period	11,356	11,946	7,663
Cash and cash equivalents, end of period	$ 13,576	$ 11,356	$ 11,946

Source: Microsoft Corporation financial statements. Retrieved from: https://www.sec.gov/Archives/edgar/data/0000789019/000156459020034944/msft-10k_20200630.htm#ITEM_8_FINANCIAL_STATEMENTS_AND_SUPPLEM. Public Domain.

Not surprisingly a cash flow statement starts with net income, since this is the number representing how much cash a corporation has earned over this particular period of time. This number is taken directly from the income statement in Table 4.1. Microsoft's next income on the income statement for 2020 was US$44.281 billion, so this is what goes on the first line of the 2020 cash flow statement as well.

Then, all expenses that were paid in something other than cash are added back to the net income since they do not affect the company's cash flow. For example, if a company paid for something with stock rather than with cash this expense is properly recorded as an expense on the income statement, but it would not count as an expense on the cash flow statement since cash was not used in this case. Thus, this expense should be added back to the next income. In the case of the Microsoft 2020 cash flow statement we see that stock-based compensation was more than US$5 billion and this amount is added back to the net income. Some other noncash items have to be subtracted. For example, accounts receivable. Imagine that Microsoft provided a service to a certain company and sent them a bill for that service. While this amount may be reported as income, until the cash has been transferred, this money cannot be used on the cash flow statement. Thus, the Microsoft 2020 cash flow statement deducts US$2.577 billion as account receivables that have not been paid yet.

As a result, the cash flow statement removes all noncash transactions and records only movements of money from operations, financing, like issuing and repaying debt, and investing, like buying and selling equipment. This is similar to an individual's checking account statement: an individual may have completed a job, let's say an Uber ride, but until the money is transferred, the payment does not show up in the individual's checking account. In the end, the statement shows how the company's cash position changed, increased or decreased, over that particular period. Similar to the checking account statement showing how much cash arrived in the account and how much left the account, the end result is the *cash balance*. In the case of Microsoft, the company added US$2.22 billion to its cash at the end of the 2020 fiscal year, resulting in a total cash position of almost US$13.6 billion. This compares very positively with the final cash result for 2019 when the Microsoft cash amount decreased by US$0.59 billion. Financial analysts and investors would want to know what the reason for such a significant change in cash operations from year to year is, and what management thinks about it.

Statement of Stockholders' Equity

The statement of stockholders' or shareholders' equity (Table 4.4) is not always considered an essential standalone document, but it is a very important statement for publicly traded corporations. Much of that information can be found on the other statements described previously. For example, the common stock balance of US$80.552 billion, retained earnings of US$34.566 billion, and other income of US$3.186 billion are already reflected on the balance sheet in the stockholders' equity section. However, this statement provides additional details on each of these categories. The section on common stock, for example, explains why the amount of

Table 4.4 Microsoft 2020 stockholders' equity statements.

(In millions) Year ended June 30		2020	2019	2018
Common stock and paid-in capital				
Balance, beginning of period	$	78,520	$ 71,223	$ 69,315
Common stock issued		1,343	6,829	1,002
Common stock repurchased		(4,599)	(4,195)	(3,033)
Stock-based compensation expense		5,289	4,652	3,940
Other, net		(1)	11	(1)
Balance, end of period		80,552	78,520	71,223
Retained earnings				
Balance, beginning of period		24,150	13,682	17,769
Net income		44,281	39,240	16,571
Common stock cash dividends		(15,483)	(14,103)	(12,917)
Common stock repurchased		(18,382)	(15,346)	(7,699)
Cumulative effect of accounting changes		0	677	(42)
Balance, end of period		34,566	24,150	13,682
Accumulated other comprehensive income (loss)				
Balance, beginning of period		(340)	(2,187)	627
Other comprehensive income (loss)		3,526	1,914	(2,856)
Cumulative effect of accounting changes		0	(67)	42
Balance, end of period		3,186	(340)	(2,187)
Total stockholders' equity	$	118,304	$ 102,330	$ 82,718
Cash dividends declared per common share	$	2.04	$ 1.84	$ 1.68

Source: Microsoft Corporation financial statements. Retrieved from: https://www.sec.gov/Archives/edgar/data/0000789019/000156459020034944/msft-10k_20200630.htm#ITEM_8_FINANCIAL_STATEMENTS_AND_SUPPLEM. Public Domain.

common stock decreased from 2019 to 2020. It shows that some of the stock was bought back by Microsoft. It also shows that Microsoft paid dividends in 2020 to the amount of almost US$15.5 billion dollars, which represented US$2.04 per share of company's stock.

Financial Analysis

Receiving financial disclosure is only the first step in analyzing corporate financial information. Financial analysts and investors employ complex algorithms and a variety of analytical tools to evaluate what stock to buy, to sell, or to hold. One of the key components of financial analysis is ratio analysis. We have already talked about one ratio, P/E, but there are many other ratios used in analyzing financial information. Many of the financial ratios used today originate from the DuPont analysis, focused on calculating *return on equity* (Figure 4.1). The name refers to the DuPont Powder Company where this analysis was first developed as a calculation of return on internal investments in a standardized fashion as part of its management accounting practices. However, today these ratios are widely used to compare corporations and even whole industries between each other.

The first ratio in the DuPont formula is the *tax burden ratio*, which divides net income by EBT. This shows how much a company pays in taxes. On one hand, investors want the company to optimize its tax burden and pay as little in taxes as possible. On the other hand, if a company pays significantly less in taxes than its competitors it may be a cause for concern as it may lead to investigations by tax authorities or may generate a lot of negative publicity. In fact, when in 2019 it was disclosed that Amazon paid no federal taxes while recording record profits of more than US$11 billion, it led

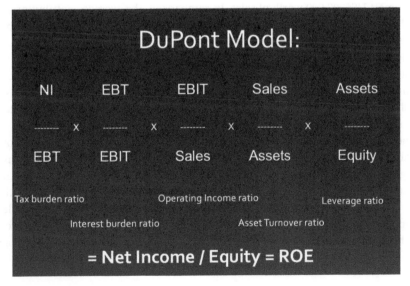

Figure 4.1 DuPont formula.

to a strong backlash against the company, including comments from President Trump and Senator Sanders.

The next ratio in the DuPont formula is the *interest burden ratio*, which shows what part of its earnings the company has to spend on interest payments to service its debt. Once again, on one hand, investors do not want to see a company burdened with too much debt. In fact, if a company borrows so much that it has to spend all its cash on interest payments, it may lead to bankruptcy. On the other hand, if a company can borrow money at a low interest rate and invest the money in business that will bring more profit than the required interest payments, investors would want the company to borrow. It is an indicator of a management team who knows how to make profits and grow business, and investors like to see that.

The next ratio is the *operating income ratio*, which compares EBIT with revenues. This is essentially the operating profit margin that shows how much profit a company makes from its main operations. This number is heavily dependent on the industry and is very commonly used to compare companies within the same business. Since taxes and interest payments are taken out of the calculations, it allows investors to focus on the actual effectiveness of the business operations of competitors.

The asset turnover ratio is a measure of how efficiently a company uses its assets, or, financially speaking, how many sales company assets generated. This allows the comparison of results from companies of different sizes – a large company is expected to have larger sales because it has more assets – so, the asset turnover ratio levels the comparison by dividing all sales by all the company's assets eliminating the influence of the company's size. In addition, in recent years, the employees' contribution to the corporate value has become more important than the assets that the company may own, so more and more companies are reporting *sales per employee*. Although this ratio is not part of the traditional DuPont formula, it really highlights the importance of employees, especially a highly educated and trained employee force, in the twenty-first century. In the case of Microsoft, for example, each employee on average generates almost US$900,000 worth of sales. In comparison, the average contribution of an employee at Netflix is above US$2.3 million, and an employee at Amazon contributes about US$350,000 of sales (Statista, 2021).

The last ratio in the DuPont model is the *leverage ratio*, which divides all assets by equity. Since a corporation's assets can be financed by either debt or by equity, this ratio compares the proportions of these two ways of financing. If the company has too much debt, it becomes too leveraged, potentially endangering the company's existence if the debt continues to grow out of control.

The result of the DuPont formula calculations is *return on equity* (ROE) or, in other words, net income divided by the total equity. This shows how much profit a company can generate using resources provided by the shareholders. This is a bottom line ratio in the DuPont model and is often simply called the *return to shareholders*. As with all the other ratios, this varies greatly between industries, but an average ROE for a large company is 14%. Microsoft's ROE, however, is closer to 40%, significantly outperforming the average number. On the other hand, Apple's ROE is above 70%, while Google's is below 20%.

There are significantly more ratios in use today for analyzing the value of corporations. It would be impossible to describe all of them. In addition, many investors and financial analysts use their own proprietary ratios and calculations that guide their decision-making and recommendations that others do not even know about. Yet, for investor relations professionals, it is extremely important to know about and monitor as many of these ratios as possible – the standard ones as well as those unique to their industries.

In addition, IROs and investors focus on stock level ratios. One of them is EPS, a quick and easy way to compare the profitability of different companies; another is P/E, which compares the price of the stock with earnings per stock. We have discussed these two measures in the "Income Statement" section. Another commonly used ratio is *price to earnings to growth (PEG) ratio*, which adds projected growth in earnings to the P/E ratio. This allows the estimation of the future potential of the company and attempts to predict its share price fluctuations. P/B is *price to book value ratio*. This ratio is important for value investors as it helps to identify undervalued companies by comparing the current share price on the stock market with the original value of the share of stock. Finally, investors interested in dividends often calculate *dividend yield* and *dividend payout ratio*. Dividend yield is dividend per share divided by the share price. It basically tells investors how much profit from dividends their investments in each share would bring. The dividend payout ratio (DPR) shows what percentage of profits a company tends to pay out as dividends versus retaining the profit as retained earnings. Microsoft's DPR is 33%, which indicates that Microsoft shares a third of its profits with its stockholders.

GAAP and Non-GAAP Financial Disclosure

An important consideration in financial disclosure is the consistency of calculations of all the numbers. Indeed, what if one company has one way of valuating its assets, while the other company calculates its assets value differently? This would make comparison between the two impossible, or at least inaccurate. Without consistency in how financial results are measured, valued, and even presented and discussed, financial analysis cannot be trusted. As a result, general standards have been developed with specific guidelines. These standards vary from country to country. In the United States, the dominant standard is *Generally Accepted Accounting Principles* (US GAAP). In many European countries, the standard in use is *International Financial Reporting Standards* (IFRS). Other countries may have their own standards. It is also not uncommon for a company that has shareholders from all over the world, or the companies that are traded on stock exchanges in several countries, to prepare financial results according to multiple standards. For example, Gazprom, a Russian company, but with shares being traded at the London Stock Exchange, prepares two types of financial statements – one following *Russian Accounting Principles* (RAP), and one following IFRS. The difference can be substantial. For 2019, the net profit for Gazprom according to IFRS was about 930 million Russian rubles, while, according to RAP, net profit was only 650 million Russian rubles.

The problem with standardized accounting processes is that they do not readily capture the unique nature of each corporation. Take Google for example – the main asset of Google is its search algorithm, but how do you properly recognize its value on the accounting form? For Apple, on the other hand, it is possible to value its software and hardware businesses, but how do you assign a value to the iPhone and Mac users, who are among the most devoted users of any phone and computer products? As a result, many companies in addition to reporting GAAP or IFRS or any other standardized numbers, release nonstandardized numbers. In the United States, it is common to see GAAP and *non-GAAP* numbers. Practically any time a company releases non-GAAP numbers, investor relations professionals must be prepared to discuss and educate on why this deviation from general principles is needed and why it is important in order to properly understand the company's business.

Publicly traded companies are also expected to have their financial results verified independently. This process is called an *audit* and is conducted by a specialized outside organization. Large corporations usually rely on the *Big Four*, the four largest audit companies in the world. The Big Four auditors are: Deloitte, Ernst & Young, KPMG, and PricewaterhouseCoopers. Together these four are responsible for auditing the financial reports of the majority of large corporations in the world, including 99% of Standard & Poor's 500 corporations. In the case of the Microsoft financial reports discussed in this section, they were all audited by Deloitte. The role of the *auditor* is very important – they essentially tell investors that they verified the numbers and investors can trust these reports. As a result, the reputation of an auditor is of paramount importance. A large and well-established auditing firm is unlikely to help even a very big corporation to manipulate financial results. On the other hand, a new and small auditor would cause suspicion. This is the reason why auditing services are concentrated within just a few large firms. Of course, even this is not a guarantee of an accurate and trustworthy audit as the case of Enron showed. Arthur Andersen, one of the top auditing firms, former member of the *Big Five*, had to surrender its accounting license and went out of business after it was involved in the Enron scandal as Enron's auditor. Although the Supreme Court later reversed the guilty conviction for Arthur Andersen, the firm's reputation was already destroyed and the Big Five became the Big Four with the demise of Arthur Andersen.

Key Terms

Annual report
Asset
Asset turnover ratio
Audit
Auditor
Balance sheet
Big Five
Big Four
Bottom line
Capital assets

Cash balance
Cash from financing
Cash from investments
Cash from operations
Cash flow statement
COGS
Cost of goods sold
Cost of revenues
Cost of sales
Current asset
Current liabilities
Current portion of long-term debt
Dividend payout ratio
Dividend yield
Earnings before interest, depreciation, taxes, and amortization
Earnings before interest and taxes
Earnings before taxes
Earnings per share
EBIT
EBIDTA
EBT
EPS
Equity
Fixed assets
Form 10-K
GAAP
Generally Accepted Accounting Principles
Goodwill
Gross margin
IFRS
Income statement
Intangibles
Interest burden ratio
International Financial Reporting Standards
Leverage ratio
Liability
Long-term liabilities
Net income
Net profit
Noncurrent asset
Noncurrent liabilities
Nonfinancial assets
Non-GAAP
Operating income
Operating income ratio
Peer

PEG
P/B
Price to book value ratio
Price to earnings to growth ratio
R&D
RAP
Regulation S-X
Research and development expense
Retained earnings
Return on equity
Return to shareholders
Revenues
ROE
Russian Accounting Principles
Sales
Sales per employee
Selling, general, and administrative expenses
SG&A
Shareholders' equity
Short-term liabilities
Stockholders' equity
Tax burden ratio

Discussion Questions and Activities

1 What is known as the bottom line in financial statements? What calculations are needed to arrive at this bottom line?

2 If you were a shareholder in a corporation, what would be your arguments for and against dividend payments? How important do you think dividends are when making a decision to buy stock in a company? Calculate dividend yield and DPR for a few companies you may consider investing in.

3 Discuss what the importance of a cash flow statement is. What advantages or problems can the cash flow statement reveal that cannot be found in other statements?

4 Choose any publicly traded corporation and download its most recent financial statements from EDGAR (Electronic Data Gathering, Analysis, and Retrieval). Calculate key financial ratios for this company: tax burden ratio, interest burden ratio, operating income ratio, asset turnover ratio, leverage ratio, sales per employee, ROE, EPS, and P/E.

5 Find two competing publicly traded companies in the same industry and of similar sizes. Compare their financial performance based on the latest available statements. Identify key differences and try to explain them based on the publicly available information you can find online.

5

Communicating Nonfinancial Information

Financial information is an important part of mandated corporate disclosure. However, companies are required to disclose more than just their finances. In fact, the annual report, Form 10-K, has 15 sections, or items as they are referred to on the form, organized into four parts (Table 5.1). Financial statements, discussed in the previous chapter, make up Item 8 of the 10-K, but most other sections provide other, *nonfinancial data*. For many analysts and investors the most newsworthy section of the annual report is Item 7, *Management Discussion and Analysis of Financial Condition and Results of Operations*, or *MD&A*. This section allows a company's executives to explain, clarify, and refine the financial and operational data, and to educate investors on what the results actually mean for the company's business. Most importantly, MD&A gives company a chance to talk about the future, its business goals and plans, and link the previous years' results with the future trajectory of the company. The US Securities and Exchange Commission (SEC, 2021) provides examples of how companies address future risks and opportunities in their MD&A statements:

- A consumer company might discuss ways in which it seeks to meet changing tastes.
- A manufacturing company that relies on natural resources may discuss how it assesses commodity risks and conducts resource management programs.
- A financial institution may discuss ways that management monitors liquidity and assures adequate capital under various scenarios, such as a rise in interest rates or a ratings downgrade.
- A global company may discuss how it handles exchange rate risks.
- Companies may discuss how they handle competition, build their brands, or manage in an economic downturn.
- Companies also may discuss how they ensure compliance with laws and regulations, or how they are addressing the impact of new or anticipated laws and regulations.

In fact, over recent years the scope of the required disclosure is constantly expanding and includes more and more financial as well as nonfinancial information. The series of corporate scandals has led to stiffer regulations from the SEC and Congress. In recent years, two major pieces of legislation have had a significant effect on corporate disclosure: the Sarbanes–Oxley Act in 2002 and the Dodd–Frank Act in 2010. But even with constantly expanding required disclosure, investor relations professionals have to

Investor Relations and Financial Communication: Creating Value Through Trust and Understanding, First Edition. Alexander V. Laskin.
© 2022 John Wiley & Sons, Inc. Published 2022 by John Wiley & Sons, Inc.

Table 5.1 The structure of Form 10-K, annual report.

Part	Item	Content
Part 1	Item 1 Business	Description of the company's business, including its main products and services, what subsidiaries it owns, and what markets it operates in
	Item 1A Risk factors	Information about the most significant risks that apply to the company or to its securities
	Item 1B Unresolved staff comments	Company's response to comments it has received from the SEC staff on previously filed reports that have not been resolved after an extended period of time
	Item 2 Properties	Information about the company's significant physical properties, such as principal plants, mines, and other materially important physical properties
	Item 3 Legal proceedings	Information about significant pending lawsuits or other legal proceedings, other than ordinary litigation
	Item 4 Mine safety disclosure	Information concerning mine safety violations, if applicable
Part 2	Item 5 Market	Information about the company's securities and everything related to stock
	Item 6 Consolidated financial data	Key financial information for the company and its subsidiaries
	Item 7 MD&A	Management's discussion of the results and projections for the future
	Item 8 Financial statements	Main financial statements
	Item 9 Changes in and Disagreements	Changes in and disagreements with accountants on accounting and financial disclosure
	Item 9A Controls and procedures	Management's report on the effectiveness of the procedures of financial reporting
	Item 9B Other information	Any additional material information not previously reported
Part 3	Item 10 Directors, executive officers, and corporate governance	A list of key people in the company with their biographical details and other important information
	Item 11 Executive compensation	Information on their compensation

(Continued)

Table 5.1 (Continued)

Part	Item	Content
	Item 12 Security ownership	Information on the key people of the company ownership of securities, including stock compensation
	Item 13 Relationships, related transactions and director independence	Discussion of relationship between directors, executives, and the company; as well as disclosure of any conflicts of interests
	Item 14 Accounting fees	Information about processes and payments for audit and tax services
Part 4	Item 15 Exhibits	All the exhibits required, including the signatures
	Item 16 Summary	Summary of Form 10-K

go beyond publication of the obligatory disclosure documents. Investor relations is not about the amount of information provided; rather, it is about understanding. The job of investor relations is to help investors understand the company and its business model. As a result, investor relations officers (IROs) must focus on what is important to disclose to educate about the company, even if this information is not part of the legal requirements.

Investors themselves are changing. They are not satisfied with the information in the obligatory disclosure filings despite the increased amount of such information. They want to understand the company, its strategy, its vision, and its role in society. Favaro (2001) explains that today communications targeted at investors "have to be able to explain not only the numbers, but also the nature of the business, its long-term strategy, and non-financial information, as investors have learned to incorporate these higher-level questions into their buy and sell decisions" (p. 7). The financial equation from the DuPont model, return on equity (ROE), is being transformed into a new ROE: return on expectations, and managing these expectations becomes an important part of investor relations programs.

The nature of business itself is transforming as well. For many corporations, value creation does not depend on how much land they own or how many employees they have or even how big their factories are. Yet, financial statements were developed when such tangible assets were of utmost importance. Today, these tangible indicators do not predict success very well for companies with value being generated through unique brand or advanced technology. Instead, success today mostly depends on *intangible assets.*

Wallman, a former SEC Commissioner, once said: "When historians look back at the turn of the century, they will note one of the most profound economic shifts of the era: The rise of Intangible Economy" (2003, p. v). Things that companies valued in the past like access to water, electricity, land, and raw materials, play less important roles in the digital economy – these tangible assets are now commodities, available to everybody, and not capable of creating a competitive advantage for a company. What becomes important is intangibles that may not have a physical or financial form. Patents, bioengineered drugs, brands, strategic alliances, customer lists, a proprietary cost-reducing Internet-based supply chain are all examples of intangibles assets. Economists estimate that intangible assets account for more than half of the market capitalization of publicly traded companies.

In fact, the market value of many corporations today significantly exceeds their tangible assets even taking into account the difference between the current market price of assets and historical cost-based accounting. Baruch Lev calculates that the market value of all US publicly traded companies is several times larger than the balance sheet value of all their physical and financial assets. For Internet-related companies the market price can exceed their tangible assets by 100 times or more.

Yet, intangible assets are more difficult to quantify and more difficult to present on a balance sheet. US Generally Accepted Accounting Principles (GAAP) are notorious for failing to provide fair representation of intangibles, treating internally generated intangibles as costs not as investments, and often putting them all under general expenses. Thus, even more nonfinancial disclosure is needed to properly educate investors and analysts about these intangible assets.

If the investor relations function aims at building an improved understanding of the company and its business model, it becomes the job of the IROs to present, explain, and educate investors on the value of the company's intangibles, as well as their contribution to the overall business model and value of the corporation. There is no doubt that traditional financial disclosure is still important; however, investors also want to understand what stands behind the numbers. Koller of McKinsey & Company described the role of nonfinancial information at the National Investor Relations Institute's (NIRI) Conference by quoting Michael Starbird: "A 1,200 page calculus book consists of two ideas and 1,198 pages of examples and applications." These ideas are what nonfinancial information can communicate – they are the foundation of the company's business model, the underlying reason for its success or failure. Financial statements, then, become the applications – how well the business ideas are being managed and implemented.

Overall, the importance of nonfinancial information is readily recognized by everyone on the buy-side and on the sell-side. Most importantly, while financial indicators focus on the past performance of the company, nonfinancial information is usually about the future. The nonfinancial indicators that carry information on the company's corporate strategy, management, organizational capital, employees, research and development (R&D), market position, quality of products and services, and corporate social responsibility can satisfy this informational void and help investors value the company fairly. This makes them very important for investors. IROs' efforts, as a result, are often concentrated on educating investors and analysts about nonfinancial information and providing details on the value of the company's intangible assets. Thus, it is essential for IROs to be knowledgeable about the intangibles and nonfinancials of the company.

Defining Nonfinancial Information

There are many approaches to defining nonfinancial information. Leading accounting and auditing firms have developed their own classifications. Many scholars have created their own definitions as well (see Table 5.2). For example, PriceWaterhouseCoopers (PWC), one of the Big Four auditing companies, has studied nonfinancial information for many years. In their research, they refer to this information as *extra-financial information* – meaning that it adds an extra layer of knowledge and understanding on top of the financial data. In addition to defining and classifying extra-financial information, PWC interviewed buy-side and sell-side investors and financial analysts to get their perspectives on nonfinancials. The study concluded that this information is extremely important to properly analyze the company. PWC classified extra-financial information into nine categories:

- Quality of management
- Strength of market position
- Strength of corporate culture
- Quality of products and services
- Level of customer satisfaction
- Governance
- Ethical information
- Social information
- Environmental information.

Similarly, Ernst and Young, another Big Four firm, developed *Measures that Matter* project, which identifies critical nonfinancial data grouped into eight categories:

- Quality of management
- Effectiveness of executive compensation policies
- Strength of corporate culture
- Level of customer satisfaction
- Strength of market position
- Quality of products and services
- Effectiveness of new product development
- Quality of investor communications.

Many other classifications exist in academic and professional communities, but there are several key categories that unite all of them. First of all, the company's *strategy* is often considered one of the (or even the most) important categories of nonfinancial information. Many surveys and interviews of investors and financial analysts have shown that a company's strategy is the most important piece of nonfinancial information for evaluating the stock. This is one of the reasons MD&A is such an important part of Form 10-K – this is exactly where top managers have a chance to explain their vision of the company's strategy and connect it with the past performance and future plans.

Another important component of nonfinancial information is the *top managers* themselves. Think about Tesla without Elon Musk. His personality, his expertise, and his credibility are important factors behind the growth of the company. Would the share price be valued as high if somebody else was running the company? Jeff Bezos, for example, announced that he was stepping down from the role of CEO of Amazon after the market

Table 5.2 Classifications of intangibles and nonfinancials.

Laskin	Lev	Kaplan & Norton	Ernst & Young	PWC	Organisation for Economic Co-operation and Development (OECD)
Strategy					
Management			Quality of management; executive compensation	Quality of management	Organization and administration
Employees	Human resources	Internal business perspective	Corporate culture	Corporate culture	Human resources
Organizational capital	Organizational capital	Internal business perspective	Corporate culture	Corporate culture	Information system
R&D	Products/services	Innovation and learning perspective	New product development		Production and technology
Products and services	Products/services	Customer perspective	Products and services	Products and services	
Competitive market position	Customer relations	Customer perspective	Market position; customer satisfaction	Market position; customer satisfaction	Procurement, distribution, customer linkage
Corporate responsibility			Corporate culture	Social, ethical, and environmental	
Communications			Investor communications	Governance	

Laskin's classification is adopted from Laskin (2008). Lev's classification is adopted from Lev (2005).
Kaplan & Norton's classification is adopted from Kaplan and Norton (1992).
Ernst & Young's classification is adopted from Ernst & Young (1997).
PriceWaterhouseCooper's classification is adopted from PriceWaterhouseCoopers (2005).
The financial category comprises four indicators: balance sheet information; profit and loss information; cash flow information; and stock information and ratios (not shown in the table). The social, ethical, and environmental category comprises three indicators: social information; ethical information; and environmental information (not shown in the table). OECD's classification is adopted from Young (1998).

closed on February 2 with the price of Amazon at US$3,380 per share. The next day the price of shares saw a decline to US$3,312 per share. It is impossible to connect the share price decline directly to the Bezos' announcement; however, the stock market overall did not experience the decline on February 3, closing at 3,826 on February 2 and reaching 3,829 at the end of February 3. With no other significant news coming from Amazon that day, it is possible that the news about Bezos had a negative effect on the share price.

If markets run on trust, the credibility and track record of the management team become of paramount importance. Hill and Knowlton conducted a study of investors and analysts and concluded that "for the investment community, responsibility lies in the hands of those at the top. Other than financial performance the perceived quality of management is the single most crucial factor for an analyst's rating, prioritized even above market position, strategy, past performance and corporate governance" (2006, p. 1). It is not a surprise, then, that some companies deliberately work on developing their CEOs as standalone brands and turning their top executives into celebrities. The term *celebrity CEO* has recently appeared. It is not much different from a sports team making some of their athletes into celebrities to increase the attendance and viewership of the games as well as to attract more fans. And, of course, this has been a popular strategy for years for many music and movie franchises stacking their success on developing musicians and actors into celebrities.

CEOs and other top managers are very important for a company's success, but business is a team game. As a result, another important nonfinancial measure focuses on *employees* in general. Almost all of the classifications of nonfinancial information and intangibles discuss employee quality in one way or another. These measures usually look at employee productivity, the company's ability to attract and keep high-quality employees, policies on promotion, unique approaches to compensation and incentivizing employees, opportunities for professional development, education, and training, employee health and safety, working conditions, measures of diversity and inclusion, corporate culture, and various social policies. Depending on the industry and the company, these indicators can have different levels of influence on the total success of the organization; thus, investors and analysts may focus on some of these measures while ignoring the others.

A large category of nonfinancial information focuses on *organizational processes*. This category's indicators are unique business designs, business procedures, information technology, supply chain management, distribution systems, and customer connections. For example, Walmart is known for its unique ability to have the lowest possible price on many categories of products. To a large extent, this ability depends on its unique supply chain management and distribution systems that allow the expense of storing goods to be minimized as they are delivered just when they are expected to be in demand in a particular store so that goods do not spend much time just sitting on the shelf. This intangible advantage is very difficult to replicate. The same is true for Walmart's ability to get the best price from its suppliers due to its sheer volume of sales and established relationships. Again, this intangible advantage cannot be easily replicated by its competitors, but it is one of the key reasons behind Walmart's success.

The *R&D* category is dedicated to the ability of a corporation to perform product and process innovations. Ability to innovate is of great importance to shareholders and financial analysts, often ranked quite high in various surveys of financial professionals. Without research a company cannot produce new products and enter new markets – it is a foundation for growth. For many technology companies, R&D is a key category to communicate to investors and analysts.

At the same time, it is also a difficult category to explain. For example, Apple created a whole new market when it released its first iPod. This later led to iTunes, iPads, and iPhones – products that now generate significant profits for the company. Yet, when the first iPod hit the stores, the share price pretty much did not change. It is widely believed that many investors and analysts did not realize the potential behind the iPod. Not many could have envisioned how iPod could lead to large changes in many aspects of human lives and how important this product would become for Apple's profitability.

Arguably, the stocks most dependent on good R&D communications are stocks of pharmaceutical companies. These corporations invest billions in researching and producing a variety of chemical compounds, with only a handful of them becoming successful, profitable drugs. Many investors and analysts are actively searching for information on pharmaceutical companies' pipelines – showing medicines at different stages of development with expected dates to hit the market. This information can have stronger effect on the share price than financial information in the income statement as the pipeline talks about the future of the company and its future profits, while the income statement focuses on the past.

Nonfinancial information also includes details about the company's current *products and services*: product life cycle, product features, quality of products, and similar. *Competitive market position* is an extension of the products and services category. It is, however, often separated into its own category because instead of looking at the product itself, it looks at the industry and the company's customers. As such, it includes variables like market share, competition, threat of product substitution, customer satisfaction with the product, repeat sales, and so on. Another area is quality of communications. This includes advertising, marketing, and public relations campaigns. It also may include the quality of investor relations.

Finally, a category of growing importance focuses on *environmental, social, and governance* (ESG) issues: corporate social responsibility, environmental sustainability, social and ethical responsibility, and issues of governance. The information in this category is constantly expanding with more and more measures being added.

In fact, a variety of measures may even create a lack of clarity instead of improving understanding. For example, the apparel industry has hundreds of different indicators, including:

Fair Labor Association (FLA)
Worker Rights Consortium (WRC)
Worldwide Responsible Accredited Production (WRAP)
SA8000®
Ethical Trading Initiative (ETI)
Fair Wear Foundation.

Financial analysts who focus on a specific industry would often be familiar with the main indicators for that industry and would demand the information they specifically need. IROs may use the expertise of financial analysts to identify key metrics that should be communicated to the buy-side as well.

All these nonfinancial indicators vary in importance depending on the industry and the company. However, Ernst & Young conducted a study in which it analyzed how important different types of nonfinancial information are for buy-side and sell-side. They found that the most important types of nonfinancial information for investors and analysts are: strategy execution, management credibility, quality of strategy, innovativeness, and ability to attract talented people. All of these are long-term focused indicators, dealing with a company's ability to meet its long-term goals as specified in the corporate strategy. The least important indicators in the Ernst & Young study are: compensation ratios, use of employee teams, and awards – in other words, the indicators that are less strategic and more current or even focused on the past.

A study by Laskin (2008) found that IROs generally value nonfinancial information highly as well and communicate it to the investment community. Overall, IROs see nonfinancial information as comprising three main groups: product information – information about company's products, R&D, and market position; process dimension – information about the company's strategy, internal structure, and management; and support dimensions – information about corporate social responsibility and corporate communications. The products and process indicators are generally regarded as important, while support information is believed to be less relevant for understanding the company's business and is communicated less frequently. However, the study found that one specific type of information is significantly undercommunicated by IROs: information about the company's management. Investors often rate this information as among the most important; but IROs do not see it as important. This dissonance can harm the stock valuation and the way investors perceive the future of the company. Thus, IROs should consider providing more information about the quality of management to the investment community and allow for face-to-face time between investors and management.

Lack of Nonfinancial Disclosure

Surprisingly, despite the recognized importance, neither managers nor investors can manage, communicate, or evaluate intangibles as well as they can manage, communicate, and evaluate tangible assets. Many research projects in the academe and the industry have indicated that investors consistently fail to estimate properly the value of nonfinancials and intangibles. The answer might lie in the inability of investors, essentially outsiders of the company, to fully grasp the value of complex, intangible profit-making capabilities. Or in the time constraints of financial analysts who have to cover many corporations and digest large amounts of information to present their recommendations to the investors, and thus often resort to simplified financial models that do not take into account much intangible value. The answer may also lie in the lack of disclosure about intangible assets and their value-creating contribution in the information that IROs provide to the financial markets. Such a shortage of information can no doubt harm investors' understanding and, subsequently, evaluation. Baruch Lev argues, "But look carefully beneath the shiny veneer of intangibles and you will find a knotty and unattractive reality, one in which information deficiencies both at companies and in the capital markets feed negatively on one another" (2004, p. 110).

The lack of nonfinancial disclosure is an important contributor to the problem. Standard corporate financial reports are poor providers of nonfinancial information. Modern accounting standards do not include nonfinancial indicators of corporate performance and do not require the companies to disclose much information on intangibles. Recently, professionals and academics have started calling for a complete revision of accounting standards because they perpetuate the information deficiencies.

As a result, investors and analysts are often required to estimate the value of intangibles without having much information about them – an impossible task. Some studies even question the usefulness of accounting reports altogether: "Internally developed intangible assets ... are generally not permitted by generally accepted accounting standards (GAAP) to be recognized in the financial statements, but instead are immediately expensed. These assets, such as patents, technology and brand names, are often of significant value to a company" (Gelb & Siegel, 2000, p. 307). Others suggest that current accounting standards are simply outdated and are not appropriate for modern businesses: "The traditional financial performance measures worked well for the industrial era, but they are out of step with the skills and competencies companies are trying to master today" (Kaplan & Norton, 1996, p. 71).

Nevertheless, it is unlikely to be the only reason. Another issue is the complexity and difficulty of evaluating these assets. One might argue that the burst of the dot-com bubble was partially caused by the inability of financial analysts and investor to correctly evaluate business models built on intangible assets. In fact, intangibles suffer from the inability to be evaluated by comparison. With tangible assets investors can often rely on the market prices of such assets because there is a market for land, office space, cars, oil, tools, and other means of production. This helps to evaluate and compare the companies. When intangibles are involved, however, it is rare, or outright impossible, to find comparable intangibles traded on an open market. Often such intangibles are unique to a specific firm and cannot be transferred to another corporation – like a unique organizational structure or historical ties with a supplier.

Lack of timely, extensive, and accurate disclosure of nonfinancial information, inability to reliably measure its value, and the nonexistence of market prices and comparables can lead to a systematic undervaluation of intangibles, causing companies to suffer by harming their cost of capital and limiting their growth potential. R&D is often one of the most undervalued intangible assets. R&D can potentially generate a substantial value for a company and, subsequently, its investors. Unfortunately, investors often fail to recognize that. This makes the role of IROs even more important for companies with a large contribution to the bottom line from R&D as well as from other intangibles. Investors and analysts, in those cases, have to rely on accurate and extensive nonfinancial information to help them properly understand the corporate return from these intangible assets, and an IRO's job is to provide them exactly the information they need.

Future of Nonfinancial Information

This importance of intangibles, and, subsequently, the need for disclosing nonfinancial information, is only going to increase with time as *commodization* of physical assets will diminish their contribution to corporations' value-generation potential and bring the competition into the intangibles sphere. Furthermore, it is incorrect to think that intangibles are only limited to so-called new technology, or Internet, companies. Instead, they have become a foundation for value creation in every industry, from retail to mining. Intangible assets and nonfinancial information have become a vital component of investor communications for publicly traded companies in every industry. Intangibles are creating competitive advantages for companies and, as a result, intangibles are the foundation of companies' business models. Intangibles underline the financial results and thus understanding a company requires understanding of its intangibles. Intangibles allow IROs to better explain a company's financial results and prospects for future growth. Intangibles also focus attention on long-term performance and are better aligned with long-term organizational strategies and objectives instead of short-term financial results. Finally, nonfinancial disclosure can help cultivate long-term relationships with investors and shareholders as it enhances understanding and appreciation of the company's business.

Investors and analysts are actively searching for nonfinancial information. So, even if a company's IROs fail to share these data, the investment community will still need to find the answers in another place. It may be more beneficial for the company to be upfront. The Ernst & Young report on the importance of nonfinancial information, *Measures That Matter*, concludes : "Sell-side and buy-side investors alike make their own inferences about non-financial performance and then act upon these inferences, whether companies strategically manage and disclose non-financial factors or not" (1997, p. 13).

It is also important to note that the terms intangibles and nonfinancials are often used interchangeably. Indeed, one of the leading definitions of intangibles specifies that these assets are nonfinancial: intangibles are claims to future benefits that do not have a physical or financial embodiment (Lev, 2001). However, this does not always mean that these assets never have a tangible component or that they cannot be represented financially. For example, a *brand* is often considered an intangible and nonfinancial asset, yet there are many organizations that estimate values of brands and assign them financial values. Interbrand, one of the leaders in evaluation of brands, estimates that the brand Coca-Cola is worth almost US$57 billion, while the Pepsi brand is estimated at less than US$19 billion. There are approaches to estimating financial values of R&D programs, employee resources, and even location.

The same applies to tangibility of resources; for example, a piece of software, an intangible asset, is often recorded on a disk, a tangible asset. The intangible concept of operational efficiency may depend on owning a large fleet of trucks, a tangible asset. In other words, there is always a connection between tangible and intangible, financial and nonfinancial. Once again, it is often a job of the IRO to educate investors and financial analysts on how all this interplay manifests itself at a particular company, and how this company constructs its competitive advantage on its tangible and intangible assets. To do this, IROs conduct extensive disclosure of financial and nonfinancial information. The relationships between all the components of corporate business are likely to increase in complexity making an IRO's job more and more complicated in return. For example, Tesla, a maker of tangible automobiles, has a significant component of its value in intangible assets. In fact, many Tesla drivers buy the car for its intangible components such as self-driving rather than for anything else. Or take an example of an airline like Delta that flies tangible planes but is most appreciated for such intangible indicators as on-time departures and arrivals.

Key Terms

Annual report
Brand
Celebrity CEOs
Commodization

Competitive market position
Employee
Environmental, social, and governance
ESG
Extra-financial information
Financial information
Form 10-K
Intangible assets
Intangible economy
MD&A
Management discussion & Analysis of Financial Condition and Results of Operations
New ROE
Nonfinancial information
Organizational process
Products and services
R&D
Research and development
Return on equity
Return on expectations
ROE
Strategy
Tangible assets
Top management

Discussion Questions and Activities

1 Discuss various items of Form 10-K, and their importance for investors. Are there any additional items you would like to see added to the form?
2 Thinking about some large corporations you are familiar with, describe the intangibles that generate value for them. Compare the intangible and tangible resources these corporations have and discuss which ones could lead to a stronger competitive advantage. Which ones are harder to build and replicate?
3 Why do you think investors repeatedly call a company's strategy and its top management team the two most important components of nonfinancial information? What are the best ways to evaluate this information? Why do you think IROs do not communicate the information about top managers often?
4 Explain why it is often believed that the focus on intangibles is better aligned with long-term corporate success versus the focus on quarterly financial results?
5 The chapter discusses key executives who are connected with the success of the companies they run: Elon Musk and Jeff Bezos. Identify other companies with strong, influential leaders. What do you think their roles in and contributions to the overall corporate value are?

Part III

Context

6

Legal and Regulatory Environment of Investor Relations and Financial Communication

Investor relations is a highly regulated activity in many countries. In the United States, the primary agency responsible for oversight of the stock market is the US *Securities and Exchange Commission* (SEC). On the agency's website, the SEC states its main mission is "to protect investors, maintain fair, orderly, and efficient markets, and facilitate capital formation." To achieve these goals, the SEC oversees the federal securities laws, maintains the disclosure of financial information by publicly traded companies, and can bring enforcement actions against violators of the securities law. The SEC works in close cooperation with several other US government agencies, such as the Federal Reserve Board of Governors and the Department of the Treasury.

Even before the establishment of the SEC and before enactment of the federal regulations of investor relations, individual states passed their own laws to protect their citizens from investment fraud. These state laws, referred to as *blue sky laws*, were enacted in response to a growing number of fraudulent speculative schemes targeted at the general population. The schemes were not backed up by any assets or reasonable plans – all the fraudulent claims were "out of the blue sky." Thus, these con artists were referred to as "blue sky merchants" and the state laws protecting against these blue sky schemes were labeled blue sky laws.

Nevertheless, in the early 1930s it became apparent that state laws alone could not combat securities fraud. The stock market crash of 1929, including the Black Tuesday market collapse on Tuesday, October 29, 1929, and the Great Depression clearly demonstrated the importance of the stock market and called for increased regulation to prevent another market collapse. In addition, the development of communication and transportation networks made inter-state trade of securities easily accessible. State laws, however, were inadequate in dealing with inter-state fraud. The Federal Government needed to step in and create federal regulations. As a result, two pieces of federal regulations were developed: the Securities Act of 1933 and the Securities Exchange Act of 1934. Although modified throughout the years, both of these legislations continue to govern securities markets today.

Investor Relations and Financial Communication: Creating Value Through Trust and Understanding, First Edition. Alexander V. Laskin.
© 2022 John Wiley & Sons, Inc. Published 2022 by John Wiley & Sons, Inc.

Securities Act of 1933

The Securities Act of 1933, the *Truth in Securities Act*, requires any original inter-state sale or offer of securities to be registered. The goal of the registration is twofold: first, it allows the government to make sure that there is no deceit or fraud behind such an offer of securities. Second, it allows the authorities to ensure that the company fully discloses any relevant information pertaining to such an offer and thus enables investors to evaluate this offer properly. The Act describes in detail the registration process and information that must be filed by a company. In general, the company must file a document called a *Registration Statement*, or *Form S-1* for US companies or *Form F-1* for foreign companies. The key part of the form is the *prospectus*, which describes the specific types of securities offered, and supplies information about the company and its business, information about the management, and the financial statements certified by independent accountants. All this information becomes publicly available and any interested parties, including potential investors and financial analysts, have access to it. The information enables market participants to make an informed decision whether to invest or not to invest in the stock, thus protecting investors from fraud.

The Act also provides some exceptions for companies to avoid the process of registration. The two most common exceptions, often used by foreign companies, are *Rule 144A* and *Regulation S*. Rule 144A stipulates that foreign companies can be exempt from the registration process if they do not offer their securities to private individuals in the United States but only to large institutional investors or qualified institutional buyers (QIBs). QIBs have over US$100 million in assets and typically employ financial analysts who can request the information from the issuer, analyze the offer of securities, and make qualified decisions on the valuation of such securities themselves. As a result, the SEC believes that QIBs do not require the same protection as private investors or small institutional investors have under the Securities Act of 1933.

Regulation S, or simply Reg. S, also allows an issuer to be exempt from the registration if the securities do not have a connection to the United States – in other words, the company is located outside of the United States and issues securities outside of the United States. In addition, the company does not engage in direct selling efforts to US investors. Many foreign companies also rely on Regulation S to avoid the registration requirement.

Securities Exchange Act of 1934

While the previously described Securities Act of 1933 regulates the initial offer of securities, the *Securities Exchange Act of 1934* aims at regulating the secondary trade of securities. The Act provides regulation of brokerage firms, transfer agents, clearing companies, stock exchanges, and so on. The Act establishes the guidelines for periodic reporting of major corporations with more than US$10 million in assets and with more than 500 shareholders. The periodic reporting is primarily based on *Form 10-K*, the *annual report*, and *Form 10-Q*, the *quarterly report*. The 1934 Act established the SEC responsible for securities regulation. The SEC maintains *EDGAR* (*Electronic Data Gathering, Analysis, and Retrieval*), a database where corporate disclosure is maintained, including forms like 10-K and 10-Q. Anyone can access EDGAR and all the filings for free.

Another important component of the 1934 Act disclosure regulations are *current disclosures*, sometimes called extraordinary disclosures. If something happens with the company that could affect its share price and that a reasonable investor would like to know about, a company cannot wait for the next periodic report, like 10-K or 10-Q, and must instead file Form 8-K. The events that lead to filing Form 8-K are called *material events*, and Form 8-K is called a *current report*. There is a long list of what is considered a material event that can trigger a filing requirement, for example, bankruptcy, acquisition of another company, or revisions of the financial statements, but, in general, companies are expected to err on the side of publicity and disclose any information that may have an effect on the share price.

In addition to corporate reporting requirements, the Securities Exchange Act regulates *annual shareholder meetings*, also called *annual general meetings* (AGMs), and the meetings' *proxy solicitation* process. At least once a year, publicly traded companies must organize a shareholder meeting where they report on their results and allow shareholders to select the *Board of Directors*, a group of shareholder representatives to provide an oversight of the management, including the appointment and dismissal of the company's CEO. Many of the key corporate decisions must also be approved by the Board of Directors in order to ensure that these decisions are in the best interests of shareholders. The Act of 1934 requires publicly traded companies to send all shareholders prior to the shareholder meetings a *proxy statement* that provides detailed information on all the issues that would be up for a vote at the meeting, such as information on the Board of Directors candidates, financial and operational results, the compensation of top executives, and the proposed auditor for the company.

The Securities Exchange Act also requires disclosure from anyone who tries to acquire significant control over a public company. Specifically, if anyone purchases more than 5% of the company's total voting shares, they must disclose it by filing a form, *Schedule 13D*, with the SEC, making this information public. Similarly, when people with a connection to the company, like managers or representatives from the Board of Directors, trade the company's stock they must also disclose this information. These people are often called *insiders* and this type of trading is called *insider trading*. The disclosure is done by filing one of the insider trading forms: *Form F-3, Form F-4,* or *Form F-5*. Some types of insider trading are illegal in the United States, especially if the trade is based on nonpublic privileged information that insiders have access to owing to their position in the company. Thus, the SEC provides an oversight over transactions done by the insiders.

The Act of 1934 also provides strict guidelines for security exchanges, trading platforms, brokers and dealers of securities, transfer, clearing, and depositary agencies, and other market participants to ensure they act in the best interest of shareholders.

True Indenture Act of 1939

The True Indenture Act of 1939 focuses specifically on debt securities versus equity securities. The Act covers notes, bonds, debentures, and certificates of interest that are available to the general public, and provides similar protections for debt investors as the Acts of 1933 and 1934 did for equity investors. The Act defines eligibility of trustees, preferential collection methods, and established reporting requirements, including periodic reports by the obligor in order to protect investors and the public interest.

Investment Company Act of 1940

The Investment Company Act of 1940 focuses on regulations for investment organization, including mutual funds. Once again, the Act creates significant disclosure requirements in order to bring transparency to the markets, requires investment funds to be registered prior to engaging in operations, classifies various types of investment organizations, and provides guidelines for record-keeping and accounting. The Act created a filing requirement for investment organizations, *Form N-8A*, the *notification of registration*, which is required to be filed with the SEC by the investment organization. One of the main goals of the Act is to eliminate or minimize the conflict of interest that arises for mutual funds that have their own securities trading publicly.

Investment Adviser Act of 1940

The Investment Adviser Act of 1940 is a very important document for sell-side organizations that provide investment advice and manage assets for others. These organizations must register with the SEC before offering their services. One of the key contributions of the Act was the attention brought to the issue of investment advice and the actual definition of the adviser. The Act of 1940 stated that an *investment adviser* is someone "who, for compensation, engages in the business of advising others, either directly or through publications or writings, as to the value of securities or as to the advisability of investing in, purchasing, or selling securities, or who, for compensation and as part of a regular business, issues or promulgates analyses or reports concerning securities" (SEC, 2019). The SEC takes the protection of investors seriously and takes actions against investment advisers who violate the Act of 1940. For example, in February 2021, the SEC filed a complaint against an investment adviser, GPB Capital, for violating the Investment Adviser Act as well as other securities regulations by lying to investors, misrepresenting their fees and compensation, and even failing to register with the SEC. As a result, the SEC has suggested that more than 17,000 retail investors were defrauded of US$1.7 billion (SEC, 2021).

Regulation FD

Although the Securities Act of 1933, the Securities Exchange Act of 1934, the Investment Company Act of 1940, and the Investment Adviser Act of 1940 are the foundation of the US stock market and generally function well at developing trust in the market, it turned out that they do not protect all shareholders equally well. If we look back at the efficient market hypothesis discussed in Chapter 1, one of the key assumptions of this hypothesis is equal access to information for all participants. However, quite often, companies actually reported important information first to the key financial analysts during a conference call or to institutional investors at a private meeting. Then, the information would trickle down the chain to smaller institutional investors, brokers, and private shareholders. Thus, large institutional investors and financial analysts with close connections to the corporations would get access to material information first before other investors and would have a chance to receive higher returns on their investments by outperforming, or *beating*, the market. This situation was unfair to private shareholders but there was no way to make information available to everybody from New York to California instantaneously.

The end of 1990s, however, brought the widespread adoption of the Internet. People became capable of accessing information themselves including directly from the SEC filings or companies' websites. In addition, more and more people were engaging in self-trading of securities using online brokerage firms. They needed to have access to information at the same time as large institutional investors did. The inequalities in the stock market became painfully obvious and the government had to step in.

As a result, the SEC adopted a new rule, *Regulation FD*, or *Regulation Fair Disclosure*, or simply *Reg. FD*, in October 2000. The key stipulation of Regulation FD was to eliminate the practice of *selective disclosure* – in other words, disclosure of information to some select parties (largely, institutional investors and financial analysts). Instead, Regulation FD requires that when a company, or a person acting on its behalf, discloses material nonpublic information to certain enumerated persons (in general, securities market professionals and holders of the issuer's securities who may well trade on the basis of the information), it must make public disclosure of that information. Such disclosure must also be done simultaneously to securities market professionals and everybody else, thus eliminating the opportunity for professional investors to *beat the market* by receiving information earlier. Regulation FD also makes provision for unintentional disclosure of information, in which case the company must follow up with public disclosure in a very limited timeframe.

Regulation FD was a significant change for investor relations officers (IROs). It was quite common for investor relations professionals to organize private one-on-one meetings between the CEO of the company and a large investor, or an important financial analyst. At this meeting, it was also quite common to discuss things that were not public information – in fact, it was often a key purpose of these meetings. Some IROs had a practice of sharing *exclusive content* with some investors and analysts before the information became public. This helped improve relationships between the company and these investors and analysts, similarly to how media relations professionals my share exclusive details with just one or two journalists or media companies. Yet, all these practices became illegal after Regulation FD. Many IROs were strongly against this regulation; many large investors were against it, too. There was a fear that investor meetings would become irrelevant since no new information can be disclosed there anyway.

However, many of these fears have turned out to be unsubstantiated. Investors and financial analysts are still interested in getting in the same room with the company's top management, and they still ask clarifying questions to better understand already available information. IROs now train CEOs and other executives before one-on-one meetings about what information can be shared and what cannot, what is publicly available and what is not. There are also provisions in the regulations to safeguard the company in case nonpublic information gets disclosed by accident during those meetings – the company would just need to make it publicly available right after the meeting in order to satisfy Regulation FD.

Regulation FD led to a significant improvement in the equality of the disclosure practices, and promoted full, fair, and timely disclosure to all market participants, but it did not eliminate all problems completely. There is little doubt that small and retail investors benefited greatly from the law, but still the competition among financial analysts pushes them to seek privileged information, testing IROs and executives almost daily through emails, phone calls, and one-on-one meetings. Regulators do not always enforce the provisions of Regulation FD strictly and consistently, creating a situation where it becomes an obligation of the IROs to balance the demands of financial analysts and investors with the stipulations of the Regulation FD.

For example, TherapeuticsMD, a publicly traded company, had a meeting with the US Food and Drug Administration (FDA) about its drug approval. The company issued a press release about the meeting, making the information publicly available to satisfy Regulation FD. However, financial analysts were looking for more information and, since they had access to the company's IROs and other top management, they sent emails asking for more details. One of the emails from the company to the analysts provided a description of the FDA meeting as "very positive." The next day the share price of TherapeuticsMD went up almost 20%. The SEC found that these emails constituted selective disclosure because for a pharmaceutical firm any details on its interactions with the FDA are of the utmost importance and, thus, comprise material information that must be disseminated fairly and appropriately to all, not just to a few financial analysts. So, simply using the phrase "very positive" in an email response to financial analysts led to a violation of Reg. FD.

In March 2021, the SEC charged AT&T and its three investor relations professionals individually for contacting financial analysts from almost 20 different firms with information about smartphone sales. Since this information is important, or material, for the cell company and the information was not disclosed publicly but rather in private phone conversations, the SEC claimed the actions of those IROs violated Regulation FD. Thus, it is important for the corporations to remain vigilant in following corporate governance protocols to ensure full compliance with Reg. FD to avoid being a subject of investigation by the SEC.

Sarbanes–Oxley Act of 2002

The Public Company Accounting Reform and Investor Protection Act was enacted on July 30, 2002. It is often referred to by the name of its sponsors: Senator Paul Sarbanes (D-MD) and Representative Michael G. Oxley (R-OH), as the *Sarbanes–Oxley Act*, or simply *SOX*. President George W. Bush, when signing the law, stated that the Sarbanes–Oxley Act comprises "the most far-reaching reforms of American business practices since the time of Franklin D. Roosevelt." Others also call SOX "a most welcome gift to shareholders."

SOX primarily focuses on further improving the quality and quantity of financial disclosure. To some extent, SOX was a governmental response to a wave of corporate scandals that shook corporate America at the beginning of the twenty-first century. Many of these scandals were directly related to senior management's manipulation of information disclosed to investors, and, as a result, the inability of investors, both private and corporate, to properly understand the company's business and its value. In the chain of corporate scandals even companies once believed to be among the leaders in their respective fields, such as Adelphia, Global Crossings, WorldComm, Tyco International, Kmart, and

Waste Management, experienced significant drops in their share prices and some even bankruptcies. Of course, the largest scandal of all was Enron: "The collapse of energy giant Enron is the largest bankruptcy and one of the most shocking failures in US corporate history" (Allen, 2002, p. 206). Enron is referred to as the *Business Watergate* because of the enormous effect it had on the relationships between large businesses and the general public – the same way as the Watergate Scandal violated the trust of people in the political system, Enron shattered their trust in business. The government had to restore the confidence of domestic and international investors in the very model of American capitalism.

SOX became the key step in restoring the investors' confidence. First, SOX created a *Public Company Accounting Oversight Board* (PCAOB), an independent board charged with improving the audit process. As described earlier, in accordance with the Securities Act of 1933 and the Securities Exchange Act of 1934, public companies must have their financial statements verified by an independent accountant. The PCAOB's goal is then to regulate the process of such audits and the companies that provide them. SOX creates specific requirements for auditing companies and explains what auditor's independence from the company means.

SOX also expands the scope of disclosure by public companies. The enhanced disclosure includes off-balance sheet transactions, liabilities, and obligations. Companies must also report on the transactions carried out by company executives.

SOX emphasize the importance of accuracy and completeness of disclosures by public companies and introduces personal responsibility of senior corporate executives for such disclosures. Specifically, *Section 302* requires senior executives to certify:

- The signing officers have reviewed the report.
- The report does not contain any untrue statements of a material fact or omit a material fact required to avoid a statement being misleading.
- The financial statements and related information fairly present the financial condition and the results in all material respects.
- The signing officers are responsible for internal controls and have evaluated these internal controls within the previous 90 days and have reported on their findings.
- A list is supplied of all deficiencies in the internal controls and information on any fraud that involves employees who are involved with internal activities.
- Any significant changes in internal controls or related factors that could have a negative impact on the internal controls are indicated in the report.

A variety of other SOX provisions detail specific requirements for establishing internal structures to facilitate these new disclosure procedures, introduce corporate and criminal fraud accountability, and enhance white collar crime penalties.

Not everyone was welcoming of the Act. Some of SOX's critics pointed to the significant expense of compliance with the new requirements introduced by SOX. Creating the necessary internal control structures and hiring an expensive audit company might become a cost burden for smaller publicly traded companies. However, others claim that this is money well spent and that it is worth paying for enhanced understanding of the company's business by shareholders and improved transparency of the markets in general.

Dodd–Frank Act of 2010

The Dodd–Frank Wall Street Reform and Consumer Protection Act (Table 6.1), enacted on July 21, 2010, was a response to the Great Recession and focused on improving financial regulations in the United States. The law consists of 15 titles focused on various aspects and components of the financial markets. Section 9 specifically targets securities regulations and investor protection. This part of the law restructured the SEC, creating the *Office of the Investor Advocate* charged with four tasks: to provide a voice for investors, to assist retail investors, to study investor behavior, and to support the SEC's Investor Advisory Committee.

One of key pieces of legislature introduced in the Dodd–Frank Act is the enhanced *whistleblower protection* and creation of a *whistleblower reward program*. A person who steps forward to report corporate misdoings, a *whistleblower*, is guaranteed confidentiality and also a reward in proportion to the money that the whistleblower helps recover. The concept of the whistleblower was already introduced in Section 21F of the Securities Exchange Act of 1934; however, the SEC *Office of the Whistleblower* was only established in 2010. The first monetary award to a whistleblower was issued in 2012. Since then, the SEC has awarded about US$687 million to 109 individuals, which represents between 10 and 30% of money collected in the enforcement actions based on the information received from these whistleblowers. In October 2020, the SEC announced the largest award given to a whistleblower of US$144 million. The SEC Office of the Whistleblower reported: "After repeatedly reporting concerns internally, and despite personal and professional hardships, the whistleblower alerted the SEC and the other agency of the wrongdoing and provided substantial, ongoing assistance that proved critical to the success of the actions" (Norberg, 2020). The Dodd–Frank

Table 6.1 Dodd–Frank Wall Street Reform and Consumer Protection Act.

Title 1	Financial Stability
Title 2	Orderly Liquidation Authority
Title 3	Transfer of Powers to the Comptroller, the FDIC, and the Fed
Title 4	Regulation of Advisers to Hedge Funds and Others
Title 5	Insurance
Title 6	Improvements to Regulation
Title 7	Wall Street Transparency and Accountability
Title 8	Payment, Clearing, and Settlement Supervision
Title 9	Investor Protections and Improvements to the Regulation of Securities
Title 10	Bureau of Consumer Financial Protection
Title 11	Federal Reserve System Provisions
Title 12	Improving Access to Mainstream Financial Institutions
Title 13	Pay It Back Act
Title 14	Mortgage Reform and Anti-Predatory Lending Act
Title 15	Miscellaneous Provisions

Act also added additional protection from retaliation against whistleblowers and streamlined the process of reporting.

A rather controversial provision of the Dodd–Frank Act focused on executive compensation. Public companies are now required to provide detailed information on the compensation of top managers of the company. This information must also be compared with the company's performance and with the median salary of all the company's employees, allowing the calculation of the ratio between CEO pay and the pay of other employees. Furthermore, in addition to disclosure, companies were required to put the executive compensation up for a vote to the shareholders at the annual shareholder meeting – a provision that became known as *say on pay*. Although the shareholders' vote on the executive compensation is nonbinding, meaning that the companies do not have to follow the outcome of the vote, when shareholders do not approve the pay for top executives it sends a very powerful message. As discussed earlier, the quality of the management team is one of the main nonfinancial contributors to the value of the corporation and a negative vote on executive pay puts on display a lack of investors' confidence in the management team. In fact, a study of failed say-on-pay votes concluded that the number one reason for the negative vote on pay is shareholders' unhappiness with the performance of the corporation (Equilar, 2013).

Jumpstart Our Business Startups Act

The *Jumpstart Our Business Startups Act*, also known as the *JOBS Act*, and sometimes called the Crowdfund Act, was enacted on September 23, 2013. This legislation focused on helping companies get access to the capital markets. In fact, the average size of a company going public in the United States was steadily increasing year after year. This made access to the stock market difficult, if not outright impossible, for small and medium-sized companies. As a result, according to statistics of the National Bureau of Economic Research, over the past 20 years the number of publicly traded companies in the United States has decreased by almost half – from 8,025 to 4,101. Among many reasons cited for this decline is the complexity of regulations governing publicly traded corporations. The JOBS Act aimed to ease the burden.

Specifically, the law waived many securities regulations for smaller companies. The law defined those companies based on their revenues – specifically, companies were exempt if their annual revenues were below US$1 billion. Then, the company would be considered an *emerging growth company* and could be exempt from such regulations as securities registration and periodic disclosures. The Act is composed of seven sections: section 1 focused on emerging growth companies, section 2 on access to capital for job creators, section 3 – crowdfunding, section 4 – small company capital formation, section 5 – private companies, section 6 – capital expansion, and section 7 talked about the outreach efforts to inform small and medium-sized business about the provisions of the Act.

Section 3 of the Act, focused on *crowdfunding*, addressed a significant gap in the legislation since crowdfunding was not addressed directly prior to the JOBS Act. Any person or organization looking to crowdfund is required to disclose key information to potential investors including name, address, legal status, website information, name of company's officers and owners of more than a 20% stake in the company, description of business and future plans, and detailed information on the current financial condition, including audited financial statements for offerings of over US$500,000.

The reception of the legislation was uneven. Many financial actors praised the relaxation of regulations for smaller companies. On the other hand, many shareholder protection organizations noted that the rollback of regulations may lead to more fraud and hurt retail investors, whom the government should protect the most. The American Association of Retired Persons (AARP) was one of the most outspoken opponents of the law, noting the lessening of investor protections can endanger the market integrity. AARP noted that "older investors, who with a lifetime of savings and investments, are disproportionately represented among the victims of securities fraud" (Rogers, 2012, p. 1). AARP warned of the return of the penny stocks fraud of the past that specifically targeted unsophisticated and vulnerable investors and that crowdfunding sites may become turbo-charged pump-and-dump operations of the Internet age, sucking money away from investors into speculative ventures without much due diligence or disclosures about their operations.

There is little doubt that laws and regulations governing investor relations work have advanced significantly over the years from the state level laws to complex federal regulations. There is also little doubt that compliance with these regulations is now an important component of IROs' day-to-day operations. At the same time, the laws are still far from perfect and will continue to be modified. Many professionals and professional associations have divergent viewpoints on how the regulations must change as there are many competing interests among the investment market participants. Thus, IROs must stay up to date on all the changes in the regulatory landscape and work in close cooperation with the company's legal team.

Key Terms

AGM
Annual general meeting
Annual report
Annual shareholder meeting
Beat the market
Blue sky laws
Board of Directors
Business Watergate
Crowdfunding
Current disclosure
Current report
Dodd–Frank Wall Street Reform and Consumer Protection Act
EDGAR Exclusive content
Electronic Data Gathering, Analysis, and Retrieval
Emerging growth company
Enron
Extraordinary disclosure
Form 8-K
Form 10-K

Form 10-Q
Form F-1
Form F-3
Form F-4
Form F-5
Form N-8A
Form S-1
Insider
Insider trading
Investment adviser
Investment Adviser Act of 1940
Investment Company Act of 1940
JOBS Act
Jumpstart Our Business Startups Act
Material events
Notification of registration
The Office of the Investor Advocate
The Office of the Whistleblower
PCAOB
Prospectus
Proxy solicitation
Proxy statement
Public Company Accounting Oversight Board
The Public Company Accounting Reform and Investor Protection Act
QIB
Qualified institutional buyer
Quarterly report
Registration statement
Reg. FD
Reg. S
Regulation Fair Disclosure
Regulation FD
Regulation S
Rule 144A
Sarbanes–Oxley Act
Say on pay
Schedule 13D
SEC
Section 302
Securities Act of 1933
Securities and Exchange Commission
Securities Exchange Act of 1934
Selective disclosure
SOX
True Indenture Act of 1939
Truth in Securities Act
Whistleblower

Whistleblower protection
Whistleblower reward program

Discussion Questions and Activities

1 Define blue sky laws. Explain why blue sky laws became less and less sufficient as the twentieth century progressed. What laws were needed to replace blue sky laws?

2 Compare the two main securities acts of 1933 and 1934. What are the main differences and the main similarities between the two?

3 What is Regulation FD and why was it needed? Discuss how Regulation FD changed the practice of investor relations.

4 After reading about all the current regulations, brainstorm how regulations will continue developing in the twenty-first century. What new problems do you expect to come up? What areas will future laws need to focus on?

5 Choose any publicly traded company. Try to find its most recent 10-K, 10-Q, and 8-K. Where did you find these documents – the company's website, EDGAR, somewhere else? Study 8-K closely. Why do you think it was filed? Could the information contained in the 8-K wait for the next periodic report instead?

7

Corporate Governance, Environmental Sustainability, and Social Responsibility

A large part of investor relations and financial communication professionals' responsibilities involves managing strategic and tactical issues for the organization. Research indicates that most issues stem from *incongruence* between organizational expectations and the expectations of various stakeholders of the organization. For example, shareholders may want a corporation to pay them dividends after a successful year, while the corporate management may want to keep the profits in order to reinvest them in future operations. The complexities of modern-day operations also prevent the traditional approach of finding a middle ground. Among the varieties of stakeholders tied into complex relationships, the middle ground rarely exists. If we continue with our previous example, in addition to shareholders and management, a corporation would also have customers – and they may want the company to lower the prices of their products and sacrifice some of the profits instead of collecting and reinvesting profits into business development or instead of paying profits out as dividends. A corporation also has employees, who may want to have higher salaries and better benefits instead of dividends, profit reinvestment, or lowering of the product prices. There are also suppliers, maybe dealers or stores or other members of the supply chain, local communities, governments, competitors, and many more stakeholders, with very diverse interests. It is impossible for a corporation to satisfy all of these demands – pleasing one of the publics could inadvertently hurt another, and finding a middle ground, or a compromise, that all stakeholders agree on may prove impossible.

Although this example relates to a corporation, it is not much easier for nonprofit or governmental organizations – they also face a complexity of managing interests of diverse publics, or stakeholders. As a result, the process of issue management is essential for all types of organizations.

Issue management is commonly defined as the anticipatory strategic management process of identifying and responding to issues facing an organization. The *issues* are not static – they grow or shrink, the number of stakeholders involved changes, and the issues increase or decrease in importance to those stakeholders. Heath (2018) identified the life cycle of issues: early stage, emerging stage, current stage, crisis stage, and dormant stage; and types of issues: issues of fact, issues of value, issues of policy, and issues of identification. For example, an issue of policy for Walmart was its treatment of its hourly employees. For years, it was a dormant issue not attracting much attention from anybody except from those involved: Walmart hourly employees. However, the issue grew beyond the organization and spilled into the mass media. The issue turned into a full-blown crisis when *Human Rights Watch* began an investigation of Walmart's treatment of its employees. With customers boycotting the stores, employees leaving, class action lawsuits piling up, constant media coverage keeping the issue at the top of the agenda, and government pressure mounting, Walmart had to respond and modify its policies, but at this point the price of the response was significantly higher than it would have been if Walmart had been able to identify and manage the issue before it became a crisis.

Issue management is built on the idea that the best crisis is the one that never happens. Predicting and managing issues to avoid future crises can save an organization from monetary and reputational losses. Issue management, however, is not only about avoiding losses; it is also about identifying opportunities. A new emerging technology or a change in customer preferences may allow a company to capitalize on the opportunity before its competitors seize this chance. This makes issue management an important part of the organizational process that involves all divisions and all employees. For investor relations and financial communication professionals, important issues of today are often represented by the abbreviation *ESG* (*environmental* issues, *social* issues, and *governance* issues).

Environmental Sustainability

Since United Nations raised the profile of sustainability and sustainable development in political, economic, and social agendas in the 1980s, corporations have been expected to publicly disclose their impact on the environment. The term sustainable development is generally traced back to the United Nations report, *Our Common Future*. The Secretary General of the United Nations, Javier Perez de Cuellar, established the World Commission on Environment and Development chaired by Gro Harlem Brundtland in 1983. The result of the work of this Commission was the *Our Common Future* report, unofficially also known as a *Brundtland Report*. The report provides a well-recognized definition of the concept: "*Sustainable development* is development that meets the needs of the present without compromising the ability of future generations to meet their own needs" (World Commission on Environment and Development, 1987, chapter 2). The foundational principle of this definition is preserving our habitat while improving our standard of living – a noble desire, yet often called impossible, as improving standards of living for the ever increasing number of people demands ever increasing amounts of resources and thus invariably leads to the depletion of natural capital.

Several attempts have been made over the years to make the concept of sustainability more meaningful by developing a precise framework for measuring and operationalizing the concept. These frameworks were developed from a variety of standpoints and approaches. Among those frameworks are the Triple Bottom Line, the Natural Step, the Ecological Footprint, the Sustainability Hierarchy, and many more. Yet, the challenge endured as the concept remained elusive. For example, Norman and MacDonald (2004), having reviewed one of these conceptualizations, the Triple Bottom Line, concluded that it may be just a "good old-fashioned single bottom line" (p. 258) with the addition of some vague environmental promises.

Yet, despite this vagueness, investors and analysts demand environment disclosure from organizations. Sustainability reporting as part of broader corporate reporting is a function of investor relations. Since one of the key purposes of investor relations is to provide full and timely disclosure in order to enable investor and shareholders as well as other relevant stakeholders to better understand the business model and the fair value of the company. Sustainability activities have an effect on a company's valuation and, as a result, are part of such disclosure.

The beginning of sustainability reporting is generally associated with a rapid increase in the external pressure from various stakeholders. These stakeholders were eager to better understand the true impact of organizations, whether positive or negative, toward sustainable development. In fact, *Global Reporting Initiative (GRI)* one of the leaders in standardizing sustainability reporting, defines impacts, as one of the central concepts of its reporting, as the "effect an organization has on the economy, the environment, and/or society, which in turn can indicate its contribution (positive or negative) to sustainable development" (2020, p. 27).

Sustainability reporting is then defined as "an organization's practice of reporting publicly on its economic, environmental, and/or social impacts, and hence its contributions – positive or negative – towards the goal of sustainable development" (GRI, 2020, p. 3). The language of sustainability reporting calls for objectivity as its stated goal is to provide "a balanced and reasonable representation of an organization's positive and negative contributions" (p. 3). This once again places sustainability reporting squarely in the domain of broader corporate reporting with its function of fair and timely disclosure of all relevant information to help outside stakeholders make informed decisions about the organization.

More and more companies produce sustainability reports. For example, a recent study by Governance & Accountability Institute showed that 65% of all companies in the Russell 1000 Index produce sustainability reports; if the sample is limited to the 500 largest companies the number of companies producing those reports increases to 90%. The growth in sustainability reporting is commonly celebrated as it is suggested that such an increase has a correlation with the increased importance of the role sustainability plays in the corporate world.

Unlike other corporate reporting, especially financial reporting, sustainability reporting lacks standardization. There are several competing formats that corporations can freely choose to align with. Among the most recognized are: GRI, the *International Integrated Reporting Council (IIRC)*, and the *Sustainability Accounting Standards Board (SASB)*. Another important distinction is that sustainability reporting is mainly voluntary – thus, a company may choose to completely avoid this disclosure.

As a result, countless corporations, their investors, and financial analysts are struggling with producing and consuming reporting on ESG performance because of the many required, semi-required, and voluntary standards and procedures in ESG reporting. The Investment Company Institute, a professional association of investment funds, commented that when it comes to ESG disclosure asset managers are put in "an untenable position as they navigate an increasingly crowded field of duplicative, overlapping or conflicting" requirements. Many investors operate in a global environment, yet they have to deal with state-based regulations that can vary greatly between American, Asian, and European countries.

Adding to this complexity is the increased need for information that goes beyond what is commonly available. Recently, a group of the world's largest investment and pension funds, including the California Public Employees' Retirement System (CalPERS), the California State Teachers' Retirement System (CalSTRS), the New York State Common Retirement Fund (NYSCRF), BNP Paribas Asset Management, and Boston Trust Walden, signed a letter asking companies to disclose if they engaged in any lobbying activities related to climate and specifically how their climate lobbying efforts align with the Paris Climate Agreement. This disclosure will definitely help expose the *greenwashers* – the companies that may be *talking green*, but behind closed doors are *lobbying brown* to scale back environmental regulations and protections.

Despite the challenges, investors value and act on the ESG information. NYSCRF, a pension fund managing over US$200 billion in assets, announced that it will divest all fossil fuel investments in the near future. This means that the fund will sell all its stock in oil and gas companies, as well as oil services, pipelines, and companies in related businesses. Such an enormous volume of shares for sale is likely to put pressure on the price of the stock. This decision, on one hand, is based on the desire to achieve a net-zero carbon emission goal by 2040 as stipulated in the *Paris Agreement*. On the other hand, this is also an investment decision – with an expected decline in demand for oil and gas, these companies are simply not the best investments. Similarly, the Retail Employees Superannuation Trust, an Australian pension fund with 1.7 million members and assets of over US$40 billion, pledged to readjust its portfolio to achieve net-zero emissions by 2050.

There are special investment organizations that use environmental issues as the main guiding principle for their investments. In fact, the number of such funds is growing year after year. These environmentally friendly investment vehicles can be divided into two categories: positive screeners and negative screeners. *Negative screening* refers to the process of avoiding investments in companies that are bad for the environment – such as in the earlier example when NYSCRF decided to eliminate investment in fossil fuel companies. This approach is now gaining mainstream momentum, with many investors being concerned with climate change and arranging their investments to mitigate this risk.

Positive screening, on the other hand, is not as common among mutual and pension funds; however, specific investment vehicles are appearing with positive screening as their main investment strategy. Positive screening companies are deliberately seeking out organizations that do good for the environment and investing only in them. These may be solar panel manufacturers, wind farms, electric cars, or food waste processors. These funds can make investors feel good about the companies they support. Some argue that it is not just a moral decision, but also a smart business move. For example, Vanguard FTSE Social Index Fund, one such *socially responsible fund*, with almost US$11 billion under management, outperformed the Standard and Poor's 500 (S&P 500) investment over the past year. Thus, ESG investments may not just be good for the world, but also good for the wallet.

Social Responsibility

In addition to the issues of environment impact, investors also consider how the company addresses large societal issues. The company's impact on society has long been a topic of debate in the academic and professional community. In fact, since the introduction of the term *corporate social responsibility* (*CSR*) arguments around its meaning have not subsided. Among the most accepted definitions is the one by Davis (1973): "The firm's considerations of, and response to, issues beyond the narrow economic, technical, and legal requirements of the firm to accomplish social benefits along with the traditional economic gains which the firm seeks" (p. 312). More recently, Kotler and Lee (2005) added that CSR is "a commitment to improve community well being through discretionary business practices and contribution of corporate resources" (p. 3).

The funds that want to avoid doing harm to the environment, or the funds that want to focus on doing good, often consider societal issues in addition to the issues of sustainability. For example, these funds may avoid investments in companies involved with the tobacco industry, weapons, or gambling. These stocks are known as *sinful stocks*. Even at the end of the nineteenth and the beginning of the twentieth centuries, certain investors, for example, Quakers avoided any investment in sinful stocks.

On the other hand, positive screening funds may invest in companies focused on education, medicine, or elimination of poverty and hunger. Some investors have introduced the concept of *impact investing* – looking to bring about positive change through the companies they invest in. One of the earliest socially responsible investment funds, *PaxWorld*, dates back to 1971, when two United Methodist Church ministers, Luther Tyson and Jack Corbett, looked to use investments not just to make profits but also to affect peace, housing, and employment opportunities, and to allow investors in their fund to align their investments with their religious values.

The financial industry in general is investing heavily in the *DEI* causes: diversity, equity, and inclusion. In fall 2020, for example, JPMorgan Chase committed to invest US$30 billion to eliminate the wealth gap between White and Black Americans. Specifically, the bank plans to allocate US$14 billion for housing loans for Black and Latino borrowers, US$8 billion for affordable housing projects, US$4 billion for refinancing, US$2 billion for small business lending, and the final US$2 billion for related philanthropic causes. The CEO of JPMorgan Chase, Jamie Dimon, stated, "We can do more and do better to break down systems that that have propagated racism and widespread economic inequality, especially for Black and Latinx people. It's long past time that society addresses racial inequalities in a more tangible, meaningful way" (Rabouin & Witherspoon, 2020, p. 1).

A certain subset of social issues involves doing business in or with certain countries. For example, in the past investors sold their investments in corporations located in South Africa or involved with the apartheid regime. This became known as the *protest divestment campaigns*. The South African protest divestment campaign started on college campuses. As students protested apartheid, they discovered that their own colleges invested in companies doing business with the apartheid regime. Although initially colleges ignored the students' demands, by 1988 over 100 colleges had pledged to stop investing in companies working with South Africa. Eventually, the movement spilled from college endowments to pension funds and mutual funds, and then to the US Congress, which enacted sanctions against South Africa. In more recent years, similar protest divestment campaigns have focused on Sudan, Syria, and Russia.

Corporate Governance

Investor relations is necessary because management is separated from ownership in modern corporations. In other words, the people who own the company are not the same as people who run it on a daily basis. In a small family business, for example, the managers and the owners are often the same people. Thus, there is no need for corporate governance and disclosure – owners know everything there is to know about the company because they are part of its day-to-day operations. However, if ownership is separated from management, it is important for owners to make sure that managers act in the best interests of the company's owners; this requires knowledge about what's happening with the corporations and what decisions managers are making.

Adam Smith was famously pessimistic about the separation of managers and owners. He worried that corporate executives

> being the managers rather of other people's money than of their own, it cannot well be expected that they should watch over it with the same anxious vigilance with which the partners in a private copartnery frequently watch over their own. Like the stewards of a rich man, they are apt to consider attention to small matters as not for their master's honour, and very easily give themselves a dispensation from having it. Negligence and profusion, therefore, must always prevail, more or less, in the management of the affairs of such a company. It is upon this account, that joint-stock companies for foreign trade have seldom been able to maintain the competition against private adventurers.
>
> *(Smith, 1776/2007, pp. 574–575)*

Thus, the system of modern corporations requires a system of control over the managers. There should be some kind of an oversight process that allows the shareholders to ensure that managers act in the best interests of owners rather than in their own self-interest. This oversight is called *corporate governance*.

The key theory that focuses on this interaction between managers and shareholders is the *agency theory*. In the agency theory, shareholders are *principals*, and managers are *agents*. The principal provides money or other resources, and the agent uses these resources to advance the interests of the principal. Principals employ agents to act on their behalf and to represent principals in day-to-day operations. In order to achieve this, agents are authorized to make decisions in place of principals. However, the theory posits that people may have disagreements and different perspectives on the same events, and, as a result, may prefer different courses of action, especially if the self-interests are different for different groups of people.

Thus, the agency theory proposes to *align the incentives* of agents with the interests of principals to ensure the agents always act in the best interest of the principals. For example, managers of corporations may receive bonuses if the share price of the corporation increases during a particular time period. Elon Musk, CEO of Tesla, famously does not take a salary from the company, but Tesla created an incentive plan for him to align his interests with the interests of Tesla shareholders. In a 2018 proxy statement, Tesla confirmed: "The basic premise is simple – Elon's compensation will be 100% aligned with the interests of our stockholders." Under the plan, Musk must increase the share price of Tesla stock by more than 10 times, raising the total value of Tesla to above US$650 billion. When he reached the target, he was scheduled to be awarded US$56 billion, making him the highest-paid CEO of any company on the planet. Of course, since his incentive package was based on Tesla stock as well, the total value of the award was even higher, when Tesla stock was trading above US$850 per share.

Part of the agency theory also focuses on *risk* – specifically, it studies the interesting paradox that principals carry all the risk since they can lose all the resources they provided, but make no decisions; at the same time, agents carry virtually no risk, but make all the decisions. This situation may encourage risky behavior as managers seem to be more open to taking chances than owners would be. Thus, it becomes important to develop corporate governance mechanisms that can mitigate the risky behaviors of agents and introduce the incentives that could also control the risk.

A key component of governance in the corporate environment is the *Board of Directors*. The directors on the Board are representatives of shareholders and are tasked with protecting and advancing shareholders' interests. Coca-Cola's 2020 proxy statement describes the important role of its Board of Directors:

> The Board is elected by the shareowners to oversee their interests in the long-term health and overall success of the Company's business and financial strength. The Board serves as the ultimate decision-making body of the Company, except for those matters reserved to or shared with the shareowners. The Board over-sees the proper safeguarding of the assets of the Company, the maintenance of appropriate financial and other internal controls and the Company's compliance with applicable laws and regulations and proper governance. The Board selects the Chief Executive Officer and oversees the members of senior management, who are charged by the Board with conducting the business of the Company.

Coca-Cola specifically points out that one of the key missions of the Board is the overall strategic direction of the company. In fact, the Board has a dedicated meeting each year to focus exclusively on strategy.

Each company develops a list of qualifications for those interested in serving on the Board. In the same proxy statement, Coca-Cola lists the following requirements for serving on the Board:

> each Director be a recognized person of high integrity with a proven record of suc-cess in his or her field and be able to devote the time and effort necessary to fulfill his or her responsibilities to the Company. Each Director must demonstrate inno-vative thinking, familiarity with and respect for corporate governance requirements and practices, an appreciation of multiple cultures and a commitment to sustain-ability and to dealing responsibly with social issues. In addition, potential Director candidates are interviewed to assess intangible qualities, including the individual's ability to ask difficult questions and, simultaneously, to work collegially.

The Board typically consists of *independent directors*, those who do not participate in managing the company and have no material relationship with the company, and *internal directors*. For example, Coca-Cola CEO James Quincey also serves on Coke's Board of Directors. In fact, he is a Chairman of the Board.

The process for Board membership starts with nominations. Many companies accept self-nominations from people interested in serving on the Board, and some companies hire professional search firms to find candidates for the Board. A company's share-holders can nominate representatives for the Board, and the same can be done by the company's management. Eventually, all nominations end up with the current Board of

Directors. The Board would typically have a nomination committee that is responsible for reviewing all the nominations. In the case of Coca-Cola, for example, the Board has a *Committee on Directors and Corporate Governance* that screens nominees' qualifications, reviews the independence of directors and their potential conflicts of interests, and examines the overall balance of the Board. The Committee then presents their finalists to the full Board for review and approval.

After approval, the final list of candidates for the Board is published in the proxy statement for the annual shareholder meeting. At the meeting, all shareholders vote for the directors. In the case of the Coca-Cola 2020 annual general meeting, for example, the Board presented 12 candidates for 12 seats on the Board of Directors, with 10 being independent members of the Board. All 12 had served on the Board in the previous year – no new candidates were presented.

Members of the Board of Directors are usually compensated for their services. Coca-Cola, for example, awards its Board members cash and stock. See Figure 7.1 for the compensation details for 2019. Directors received between US$25,000 and US$70,000 as cash compensation. They also received shares in the Coca-Cola company in amounts between US$40,000 and US$200,000.

An important issue of corporate governance is representation. For example, the State of California introduced a racial/ethnic diversity mandate and gender diversity mandate for corporate Board compositions. These proposals follow years of research showing that companies with a diverse Board of Directors and executives outperform their competitors – in fact, diversity has been known to increase return on investment.

2019 Director Compensation Table

Name[1] (a)	Fees Earned or Paid in Cash ($) (b)	Stock Awards ($) (c)	Option Awards ($) (d)	Non-Equity Incentive Plan Compensation ($) (e)	Change in Pension Value and Nonqualified Deferred Compensation Earnings ($) (f)	All Other Compensation ($) (g)	Total ($) (h)
Herbert A. Allen	$70,000	$200,000	$0	$0	$0	$105	$ 270,105
Ronald W. Allen[2]	70,000	200,000	0	0	0	3,209	273,209
Marc Bolland	50,000	200,000	0	0	0	5	250,005
Ana Botín	50,000	200,000	0	0	0	105	250,105
Richard M. Daley[3]	25,000	40,000	0	0	0	23,746	88,746
Christopher C. Davis	50,000	200,000	0	0	0	1,312	251,312
Barry Diller	70,000	200,000	0	0	0	944	270,944
Helene D. Gayle	66,000	200,000	0	0	0	5	266,005
Alexis M. Herman	70,000	200,000	0	0	0	36,344	306,344
Robert A. Kotick	50,000	200,000	0	0	0	105	250,105
Maria Elena Lagomasino	94,000	200,000	0	0	0	13,786	307,786
Sam Nunn[3]	35,000	40,000	0	0	0	55,404	130,404
Caroline J. Tsay	50,000	200,000	0	0	0	2,396	252,396
David B. Weinberg	50,000	200,000	0	0	0	1,644	251,644

[1] Mr. Quincey is a Company employee and therefore receives no compensation under the Directors' Plan. Muhtar Kent was an employee of the Company who also served as Chairman of the Board from January 2019 through the 2019 Annual Meeting of Shareowners when he stepped down as Chairman and therefore received no compensation under the Directors' Plan.

[2] Mr. R. Allen is not standing for reelection at the 2020 Annual Meeting.

[3] Messrs. Daley and Nunn did not stand for reelection at the 2019 Annual Meeting of Shareowners.

Figure 7.1 Compensation to the Coca-Cola Board of Directors members, 2019. *Source*: The Coca-Cola Company financial statements. Retrieved from: https://sec.report/Document/0001206774-20-000704/. Public Domain.

However, electing members of the Board of Directors is in the hands of shareholders, and, as a result, there may be not much a company or regulators can do one way or another, other than provide comprehensive and timely disclosure on the current Board makeup and the background of candidates for the Board of Directors. As of now, however, information on the racial and ethnic composition of the Boards and Board candidates is rarely included in the proxy documents for shareholders.

The Board is led by a *Chair of the Board*. In the case of Coca-Cola, the Chairman of the Board is also the CEO of the company. As a result, the Board has an additional position of the *Lead Independent Director*. This position is occupied by Maria Elena Legomasino, CEO of WE Family Offices, who states that in her role as "Lead Independent Director, I look forward to being the key point of contact at the Board level for our shareowners". In general, having the positions of CEO and Chair occupied by the same person is one of the most significant issues in corporate governance. Some even see this merger of two positions as the root of all evil:

> Beneath all the reporting on fatally flawed airplane design, serial ten-figure operating losses from big name startups, and Russian-linked presidential election information hackings, there lies an organizational leadership truth from the debacles at Boeing, WeWork, and Facebook: Be wary of giving the CEO job and the board chair job to one person.
>
> *(Mandato & Devine, 2020, p. 1)*

From the agency theory perspective, separation of these two positions is essential. Agency theory tasks the Board with oversight of management, and it weakens the shareholders' position if the person overseeing the management is the top manager. However, a *stewardship theory* of management stipulates that merging the two positions creates unity between the C-suite and the Board, making the company nimbler and more efficient. It also may be beneficial for shareholders because it creates a clear chain of command and responsibility.

In addition to the independence of the Chair, the overall *independence* of the Board is an important corporate governance issue and a topic of much debate. Many shareholders are fighting to increase the number of independent directors to 100%, arguing against any management being represented on the Board. But even seemingly independent Boards often have members who are friends, colleagues, or are otherwise connected to the company or its management. Such lack of independence may prevent the Board from acting in the best interests of shareholders and holding the management accountable. Recently, for example, shareholders of Boeing filed a lawsuit against the company's Board of Directors claiming the Board failed to provide proper oversight of management during the Boeing 737 Max crisis, ignored the red flags, and even engaged in a campaign to protect the management and mislead shareholders and the public at large. In the end, amid the 737 Max crisis, the Board allowed the CEO of Boeing to retire and to keep his US$38 million compensation instead of firing him.

The Board of Directors is typically organized into several committees focused on specific tasks. The Coca-Cola Board, for example, has six committees:

- Audit Committee
- Talent and Compensation

- Directors and Corporate Governance
- Public Policy and Sustainability
- Finance
- Management Development.

For each committee, Coca-Cola reports the number of meetings held in the previous year, the composition of the committee, the number of independent directors on the committee, and the main tasks of the committee.

The *Audit Committee* is responsible for the oversight of corporate disclosure, specifically focusing on the accuracy of financial statements and the integrity of the reporting process. The Committee oversees the audit process as well as compliance with all regulatory requirements and ethical standards. The *Talent and Compensation Committee* oversees overall policies and strategies for leadership, employee retention, corporate culture, and diversity and inclusion. This Committee is also responsible for approving the compensation packages for senior executives. As discussed earlier, the *Committee on Directors and Corporate Governance* oversees the nomination process for the Board of Directors as well as annual evaluation of the Board members. This Committee is also responsible for setting up corporate governance processes in the best interests of shareholders and the company. The *Finance Committee* provides oversight of Coca-Cola's financials and votes on major capital expenditures, mergers and acquisitions, and strategic investments. The Finance Committee also proposes the dividend payments to the shareholders. The *Management Development Committee* is charged with development of senior leaders at the company as well as succession planning. The *Public Policy and Sustainability Committee* focuses on issues of CSR and sustainability as well as other significant issue that can affect the company's business.

In addition to these committees, it is common for a company to have an *Executive Committee* of the Board of Directors. The Executive Committee performs the decision-making functions of the Board between the Board of Directors meetings or when the full Board is not available. The Executive Committee also act in a crisis situation to mitigate the damage to the company and its shareholders. A typical Executive Committee would include the Chair of the Board, Vice-Chair, and a Board Secretary.

Overall, the Board of Directors is the key instrument of corporate governance. It is responsible for creating corporate governance mechanisms that would align the interests of the company's management with the interests of shareholders, the company's owners. The Board is also responsible for providing constant oversight to ensure that these mechanisms are functioning properly, and the management is following all procedures developed. Of course, shareholders in addition to being represented through the Board of Directors, also have their own voice and a direct input into corporate governance. As part of the governance process, corporations are required to conduct an annual shareholder meeting. At the meeting, each common share of stock gives its holder one vote. In other words, a shareholder with 1,000 shares will have 1,000 votes, while a shareholder with one share will have just one vote.

As mentioned earlier, the key issue shareholders are voting on is the membership of the Board of Directors. Shareholders have the power to decide who will be their representatives. If shareholders do not vote for the CEO of the company to be on the Board of Directors, then the CEO is not going to make it onto the Board. Some companies' nominating committees manipulate the process, however, by presenting for the vote only the same number of candidates as there are seats on the Board. As shown earlier, Coca-Cola presented 12 nominations for 12 seats. Nevertheless, Coca-Cola's own bylaws stipulate that to serve as a director the candidate must receive a simple majority of all votes, otherwise the candidate must file a resignation letter to the Board. On the other hand, Coca-Cola bylaws also have a provision that the Board can decline the resignation letter and retain the director, even without the support of the majority of shareholders.

Another issue shareholders vote on during the annual general meeting is the appointment of the auditor who will verify the financial reporting of the company. Finally, the third item common for annual shareholder meetings is the *executive compensation* vote. Although the Board of Directors sets the executive compensation, shareholders have a chance to conduct an advisory vote and show their agreement or disagreement with what the Board has proposed. In the case of Coca-Cola, for its 2020 annual general meeting the Board recommended a compensation of over US$18 million for the CEO of the company, James Quincey, and over US$9 million for the CFO. The proxy statement submitted to the shareholders details what the compensation is composed of and why the Board considers it an appropriate compensation. At the end the of the discussion, the proxy statement tells the shareholders:

> Because your vote is advisory, it will not be binding upon the Board. However, the Board values shareowners' opinions, and the Talent and Compensation Committee will consider the outcome of the advisory vote when considering future executive compensation decisions. The Board has adopted a policy of providing for annual advisory votes from shareowners on executive compensation. The next such vote will occur at the 2021 Annual Meeting of Shareowners.

All the voting items described, such as Board membership, executive compensation, and selection of an auditor, are presented to the shareholders from the company and its Board of Directors. However, at the annual shareholder meeting, shareholders also have a chance to submit their own items for a vote. Such proposals can outline actions that a company, or its Board, should take in the case that the proposal is approved. *Shareholder proposals* are clearly labeled as shareholder proposals in the proxy statement. The company that received the proposal provides a recommendation on how to vote in response to the proposal, and its own response to the proposal. For example, for the 2020 Coca-Cola annual shareholder meeting, one shareholder proposal was included on the proxy statement. See Figure 7.2 for the meeting agenda. The proposal was submitted by John C. Harrington, owner of 100 shares in Coca-Cola. The proposal asked the company to evaluate how its products are related to public health issues that are increasingly important in society. Specifically, the proposal stated:

> Be It, Therefore, Resolved, that shareholders request the board of directors issue a report on Sugar and Public Health, with support from a group of independent and nationally recognized scientists and scholars providing critical feedback on our Company's sugar products marketed to consumers, especially those Coke products targeted to children and young consumers. Such report to shareholders should be produced at reasonable expense, exclude

Items of Business

Items of Business	Our Board's Recommendation	📄
COMPANY PROPOSALS		
1 Elect as Directors the 12 Director nominees named in the attached Proxy Statement to serve until the 2021 Annual Meeting of Shareowners.	✓ FOR each Director Nominee	11
2 Conduct an advisory vote to approve executive compensation.	✓ FOR	45
3 Ratify the appointment of Ernst & Young LLP as Independent Auditors of the Company to serve for the 2020 fiscal year.	✓ FOR	90
SHAREOWNER PROPOSAL		
4 Vote on a shareowner proposal on sugar and public health, if properly presented at the meeting.	⊗ AGAINST	93

Figure 7.2 Coca-Cola 2020 Annual general meeting agenda. *Source*: The Coca-Cola Company financial statements. Retrieved from: https://sec.report/Document/0001206774-20-000704/. Public Domain.

proprietary or legally privileged information and be published no later than November 1st, 2020, and include an assessment of risks to the company's finances and reputation associated with changing scientific understanding of the role of sugar in disease causation.

The Board of Directors of Coca-Cola recommended voting against this proposal and submitted a statement in opposition to the proposal.

The annual shareholder meeting and the Board of Directors are key components of the corporate governance mechanisms. The management of the company is hired by the shareholders to work for the shareholders. Sometimes, however, a conflict may arise between shareholders and the management. The corporation may try to limit the participation of the shareholders in the meeting to ensure that the vote is beneficial for the management. Companies may try to make a meeting announcement obscure in order to avoid shareholders showing up at the meeting or participating in the meeting in any way. In one example, a Russian publicly traded company announced its annual shareholder meeting was scheduled at the address where the penitentiary was located – needless to say, the shareholders who wished to attend were not allowed inside. The conflict between shareholders and managers can lead to proxy battles, shareholder activism, and full-blown crises.

Key Terms

Agency theory
Agent
Align the incentives

Audit Committee
Board independence
Board of Directors
Brundtland Report
Chair of the Board
Committee on Directors and Corporate Governance
Corporate governance
Corporate social responsibility
CSR
DEI
Environmental issue
ESG
Executive Committee
Executive compensation
Finance committee
Global Reporting Initiative
Governance issue
Greenwashing
GRI
IIRC
Impact investing
Incentive
Incongruency of expectations
Independent director
Internal director
International Integrated Reporting Council
Issue management
Lead Independent Director
Management Development Committee
Negative screening
Our Common Future
Paris Agreement
PaxWorld
Positive screening
Principal
Protest divestment campaign
Public Policy and Sustainability Committee
Risk
SASB
Sinful stocks
Shareholder proposals
Social issue
Socially responsible fund
Stakeholders
Stewardship theory
Sustainability Accounting Standards Board
Sustainable development

Talent and Compensation Committee
Talking green, lobbying brown
World Commission on Environment and Development

Discussion Questions and Activities

1 Discuss what it means to be talking green, lobbying brown? What is the benefit for companies in doing this? What role should an investor relations officer (IRO) play in this process?

2 Why do you think some claim that ESG funds are not just good for the world, but actually good for the wallet? Can you find facts to support or disapprove this statement?

3 Review the key aspects of the Paris Agreement. Chose any large corporation and discuss how the provisions of the Paris Agreement will affect its business. What information do you think investors would want to receive from this company in order to understand the impact of the Paris Agreement on the company's future business?

4 Discuss the role of the Board of Directors? What arguments can you provide for and against the independence of the Chair of the Board position?

5 Choose any large corporation and create a list of 10 stakeholders important for this organization's existence and success. Write down their interests and identify the conflicting stakeholders whose interests may be contradictory to each other. Propose how the company should deal with all these stakeholders. What should be communicated to them?

8

Shareholder Activism and Crisis Management

When a shareholder is unhappy with the direction the company is going in, a common response is a sale of securities. The shareholder sells their shares in the company and invests money in something else. However, in some cases, instead of selling the stock, the shareholder turns into an activist. An *activist shareholder* is one who attempts to influence the company's decision-making and bring about change on an issue or multiple issues of concern.

As discussed in Chapter 7, modern corporations are generally built on the separation of management and ownership. Thus, shareholders do not have a direct path to influence day-to-day decision-making at the corporation. However, as shown in Chapter 7, shareholders have an opportunity to voice their opinion through their representatives on the Board of Directors. Another way to effect change is by submitting *shareholder proposals* for the annual shareholder meeting. And, of course, a shareholder activist can use mass media and social media public relations and advertising tactics to influence the company's management. If the case gets bitter, shareholders use the legal system by filing or threatening to file a lawsuit.

Reasons for Activism

Declining share price and poor operational results are common reasons for shareholders to turn activist because shareholders are the ones losing money in this situation. In some cases the price of the share can get so low that it makes more sense for the shareholders to try to improve the company's performance rather than just sell the stock as the investors won't recover the losses in the case of a sell. Declining share price also creates an opportunity for an activist investor to band together with other shareholders as no shareholders want to see the price of the stock they are holding go down. Thus, activist investors have a chance to gain wider support for their shareholder proposals if they communicate with other company shareholders.

In addition to shareholders who may turn activist, there is a special group of professional activist investors. Usually an activist hedge fund would look for companies with good intrinsic value, but where there have been some management missteps causing the share price to decline. Getting caught in a scandal, misleading statements in annual reports, bad acquisitions, or any other situations like that may put a negative

Investor Relations and Financial Communication: Creating Value Through Trust and Understanding, First Edition. Alexander V. Laskin.
© 2022 John Wiley & Sons, Inc. Published 2022 by John Wiley & Sons, Inc.

pressure on the share price. Activist investors, then, would see an opportunity: by changing the management that has lost credibility or by reversing the direction the company is currently heading in they can relatively quickly restore the company's share price and post a profit.

For example, one such activist hedge fund, Third Point, describes its investment philosophy in just one sentence: "The Firm seeks to identify situations where we anticipate a catalyst will unlock value" (Third Point, 2020). One of the most famous Third Point activist campaigns was Campbell Soup. When the company expanded widely into other markets using the revenues from its main soup business, the value of the company suffered. Campbell invested billions of dollars in acquiring and internally developing new product lines, like bagged carrots, fresh refrigerated juices, nuts, and pretzels. All these expenses and the debt the company had to take on to cover the acquisitions pushed the share price below US$40 a share. This did not compare well to the price of over US$65 per share from just a few years earlier.

Third Point launched an aggressive campaign demanding to replace the entire Board of Directors, claiming that they did not provide a proper oversight of all these expansions and, as a result, hurt the company and its shareholders. Although Third Point owned only about 5% of the Campbell shares, the company expected other shareholders to join them in their shareholder proposal. They claimed that replacing the Board would lead to strategic changes at the company that could restore the share price – something that all shareholders would benefit from.

In the end, however, Third Point's proposal was able to secure the support of only 10% of the votes, meaning there would be almost certain defeat of the proposal at the shareholder meeting. Third Point then switched tactics and engaged in an expensive media campaign resulting in publications in the *Wall Street Journal*, CNBC, and other business publications. Third Point also filed a lawsuit in Camden, New Jersey, Campbell's hometown, asking the court to stop the annual shareholder meetings, claiming the company had misled investors and doubting the qualifications of the Campbell's Board of Directors. Although it was unlikely Campbell Soup would have lost in the court of law, the publicity generated by Third Point was not good for Campbell in the court of public opinion. Campbell settled with Third Point: the company agreed to expand its Board of Directors and add directors that Third Point proposed. The Board also pressured the CEO of the company to step down, Third Point had input into the selection of the new CEO, and, finally, the Board started a strategic review process of the company's overall operations. At the start of 2020, the share price was closing at US$50 a share, and Third Point reportedly sold about two million of Campbell's shares at a profit, after expressing full support for the company and its new management, and expressing confidence in Campbell Soup's "ability to continue to create value for shareholders under the leadership of its chief executive" (as cited in Walsh, 2020).

A decline in prices and revenues is a common but not the only reason for shareholder activists to target a corporation. Investors are also very interested in corporate governance issues. A common issue for shareholder activism is the *Board of Directors' composition*. Activist investors often focus on two issues: *independent directors* and the Chair of the Board. Activist investors are interested in the independence of the Board members and do not favor the Board being stacked with company insiders like the CEO, the CFO, and their friends. The Board needs to provide an objective oversight over the company and, thus, its members must be independent. As far as the position of the Chair of the Board, activist investors do not want to see the CEO of the company serving as the Board's Chair as well. This once again speaks to the independence of the Board and its ability to provide its oversight function. For example, for several years, Oracle faced a pressure from shareholders to create rules for independence of the Chair of the Board. The proposal, however, failed year after year, with Lawrence Ellison, who founded the company in 1977, keeping his control over the Chairman of the Board position.

Another common reason for shareholder activism is disclosure. Investors are looking for information that goes beyond what is required by law so that they can better understand the company's business model. If they cannot get that information, they may turn to shareholder activism. For example, climate change is an important issue that affects people around the world – floods, droughts, snowstorms, forest fires, and similar. This presents a real risk for operations at many corporations. As a result, investors demand corporations provide additional information about how they are planning for the risks triggered by *climate change*. To make their voices heard, large investors banded together into the *Climate Action 100+* coalition. At the start of 2021, the coalition included more than 500 investors with over US$52 trillion in assets under management. One of the top requirements these investors impose on the corporations they invest in is to provide enhanced corporate disclosure "to enable investors to assess the robustness of companies' business plans against a range of climate scenarios, including well below two degrees and improve investment decision-making" (Climate Action 100+, 2021).

Environmental and social issues are becoming more and more important to investors. As mentioned in Chapter 7, there are investors that specifically focus on environmental, social, and governance (ESG) issues as their strategy. The *Financial Times* reports that assets under the management of these *ESG funds* are expected to triple in the near future. ESG funds use ESG criteria as part of their investment strategy and currently represent about 15% of all assets in European funds. But if the prediction is true and over the next five years this number will grow to more than half of all funds, it will have a significant effect on the investment landscape and will put publicly traded companies under scrutiny related to their ESG actions.

If the company fails to act on its own regarding ESG concerns, investors are likely to take action. Annual general meetings in 2020 saw a record number of proposals from shareholders on issues related to ESG. These conflicts between management and shareholders can lead to proxy battles.

Proxy Battles

A *proxy statement*, or simply, proxy, is the document that a corporation prepares for the annual shareholder meeting. In this document, the company provides key information about its business and performance as well as all other information related to the items coming up for a vote at the meeting. If shareholders want to challenge a corporation on a particular issue, they can request the company to include an item for a vote in the proxy statement – this is known as a shareholder proposal, or shareholder resolution. Other shareholders will then vote on this proposal. If enough shareholders band together, they can impose their will on the company through these shareholder proposals. Thus, submitting these proposals became known as *proxy battles* or *proxy fights*.

Already today, many investors seek to change corporate behavior through proxies. Shareholder resolutions are a common form of shareholder activism. In the United States shareholder resolutions are governed by Rule 14a-8, which allows shareholders to submit proposals for inclusion in the company's proxy materials. The company must distribute the shareholder proposal at least 120 days before its annual meeting to all shareholders. In addition, the proposal is filed with the Securities and Exchange Commission's (SEC) EDGAR (Electronic Data Gathering, Analysis, and Retrieval) system – this makes it publicly available for everyone. In 1969–1970, shareholders led a campaign to stop Dow Chemical's production of napalm, which was used in the Vietnam War. Shareholders also pressured General Motors to make its cars safer for people and the environment in the 1970s.

Although not new, the number of shareholder proposals keeps growing. Investment Company Institute estimates that companies in the United States face about 20,000 proxy ballot items and that is not even counting required say-on-pay votes. *Proxy Monitor* is the organization that tracks all shareholder proposals and provides a summary for every year's proxy season, which usually lasts from March to June. Proxy Monitor focuses on the largest 250 companies by revenues. In its most recent report, it estimates that an average corporation faces 1.24 shareholder proposals. However, only 5% of proposals find enough votes from shareholders to be approved. In fact, the approval levels actually decreased in comparison with previous years. This low level of support is typically explained by corporations being more likely to engage in a dialogue with shareholders even prior to them filing a proposal or after the proposal is filed to find a compromise and a mutually beneficial solution. The dialogue replaces a proxy battle. Thus, the issue that the proposal focuses on usually gets resolved outside of the annual shareholder meeting.

The most common topic for shareholder proposals based on the most recent Proxy Monitor report is environmental sustainability: "Most of these involved greenhouse gas emissions, 'portfolio risk' from climate-change regulation, or more general sustainability concerns" (Proxy Monitor, 2017). Other popular topics include, in order of frequency, a corporation's political spending and lobbying disclosure, separation of CEO/Chair roles, voting rules, special meeting procedures, executive compensation, proxy access, and gender/diversity issues.

Most of the shareholder proposals are filed by funds and other investors who specifically focus on environment or social issues. This category also includes investments by foundations and retirement investment organizations that are affiliated with religious organizations, public-policy organizations, and universities. These shareholders filed almost half of all shareholder proposals that made it onto the corporate ballots.

Many pension funds and investment organizations for labor unions, such as the American Federation of Labor – Congress of Industrial Organizations (AFL-CIO), are also known to commonly file shareholder proposals. The same applies to large pension funds such as state and municipal funds. The California Public Employees' Retirement System (CalPERS), the largest public pension fund in the United States with over US$300 billion in assets under management, in the most recent year filed shareholder proposals at 14 companies. CalPERS states, "our engagement process involves clear communication with companies regarding our engagement objectives and is meant to be collaborative" (2021). This suggests that many of the issues were likely resolved without having to file an actual proposal. CalPERS focuses on issues such as Board diversity, executive compensation, and climate change in its shareholder proposals. Another issue important to the pension fund is proxy access. "Proxy access is a corporate governance provision giving shareowners the right to nominate director candidates to a company board for inclusion on proxy voting ballots" (CalPERS, 2021).

Many proxy battles may be avoided by having a conversation between shareholders and a company's management. This conversation may occur instead of submitting a shareholder proposal. If, after the proposal is submitted, the company and the submitting shareholder find mutually beneficial resolutions, the shareholder proposal may be withdrawn. This is generally considered a preferred outcome versus a proxy battle at the annual general meeting.

Retail Investors

Historically, shareholder activism was associated with professional investors and hedge funds. The names of large activist investors running their own hedge funds are often mentioned on the business news networks. Carl Icahn, a famous corporate raider, was involved in large acquisition and hostile takeover attempts involving some of the largest public corporations, such as Volkswagen, HP, Xerox, and Occidental Petroleum. Paul Singer, another activist investor, with over US$70 billion worth of controlled assets used his financial powers at such corporations as AT&T, Hyundai, and Barnes & Noble.

The year 2021, however, was labeled in the media as a year of revival of retail shareholders. This conclusion is largely based on the increased power that small retail shareholders can exercise if they combine their efforts and their resources. One of the best examples of retail shareholders' power was the story of GameStop. While professional hedge fund investors were short-selling the stock of GameStop, regular retail investors banded together to buy and hold these shares.

Thanks to Internet and mobile technologies it became possible for anyone to have access to information, communication, and trading. All the financial information is available online, including through the US SEC EDGAR database. Retail investors can discuss and analyze this information together – many of the GameStop retail shareholders originated on *Reddit*, more specifically on the *WallStreetBets* subreddit. All these investors have access to trading through free and easy-to-use apps like *Robinhood*. When hedge funds expected GameStop stock to go down in price even to the point of GameStop going out of business, they started short-selling the stock. Retail investors noted this short-selling and started buying the stock, sharing information about their buys on Reddit. This power of retail shareholders pushed the stock of GameStop from less than US$1 per share in 2019 to above US$450 per share in January 2021. Early reports indicated that professional hedge funds losses were in billions of dollars, while retail shareholders started talking about financial revolution, redistribution of wealth, and new fairness in the financial markets (See Figure 8.1).

Moreover, *redditors* on WallStreetBets are now spreading their influence to other stocks, such as AMC, Nokia, and Best Buy. What's interesting, however, is that the

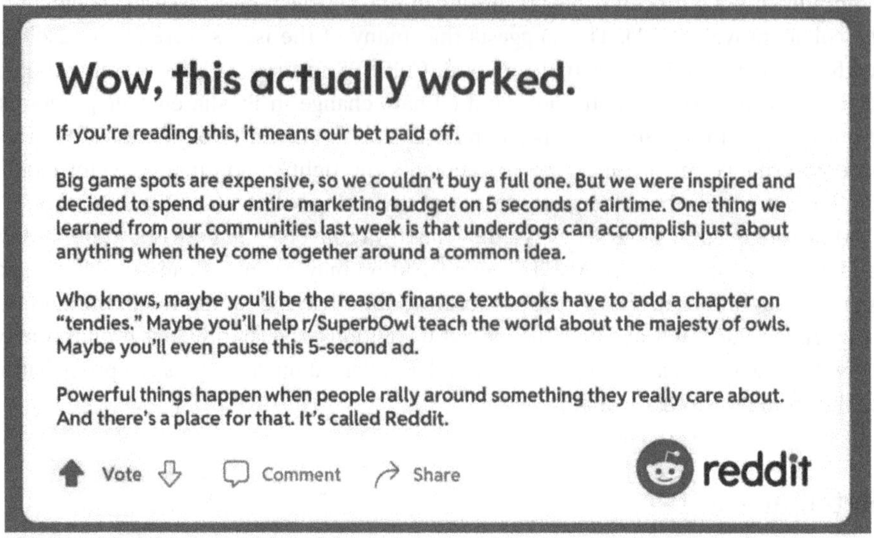

Figure 8.1 Reddit's 2021 Superbowl ad.

publicly traded companies themselves are staying silent. Short-selling hedge funds have traditionally been a nightmare for corporations, yet companies seem very cautious to join the cause and band with or even talk to the retail shareholders who seemingly come to their rescue. Yet, the ability of retail shareholders to come together using social media, discuss stocks, share insights, and coordinate their efforts makes them a force to reckon with.

Crisis Management

A *crisis* is the most stressful and difficult time for an investor relations professional. A crisis is an *unexpected, nonroutine* event that creates high levels of *uncertainty* and *threatens the existence* of an organization or its ability to carry out its mission (Ulmer et al., 2007). This definition focuses on key characteristics of a crisis.

A crisis is unexpected. It comes as a surprise. As a result, a snowstorm in the winter in Vermont can hardly be called a crisis. It should be expected, and many in Vermont are preparing and planning for it. A snowstorm in Texas on the other hand may become a crisis right away if nobody expected it and was prepared for it. Thus, crises must be out of the ordinary and violate normal expectations in order to be considered crises.

Another key characteristic of a crisis is its importance – the event should be a significant enough threat to the organization or its stakeholders to be called a crisis. Any consumer electronic company can sell defective products from time to time – that's why there is a warranty protection. A customer would return the product and it will be fixed or exchanged for a proper working one. Sometimes, companies may even have a whole line of products with subpar quality and features – phones with slow processors, cars with poor ergonomics, or laptops with not enough storage. These occurrences are rarely raised to the level of a crisis, however. On the other hand, when new Samsung phone batteries started catching fire, including on planes, forcing the Federal Aviation Administration (FAA) to ban those phones from flights in the United States, that became a crisis. Other countries followed suit, and social media and then traditional media were filled with images of Samsung phones catching fire. At one point it was not even clear if Samsung would ever recover as a phone manufacturer or if it was the end for the Samsung line of Galaxy phones.

The third key characteristic of a crisis is a short response time. The company must deal with whatever issue the crisis brings up fast – there is no chance to take a pause and postpone whatever needs to be done. It may not even be possible to consider all response options or involve all relevant parties as the urgency of the crisis may demand immediate action; inaction is often the worst possible option. If there is a fire, or flood, or snowstorm, action must be taken to save lives. The stakes in investor relations and financial communication may not always be that high, but if there is a rumor that can hurt the financial solvency of an organization, delay may harm employees, suppliers, customers, and local communities as well. Thus, fast and decisive action is required.

Finally, crises produce uncertainty. An event that is urgent, significant, and unexpected, but with a clear path of action, hardly qualifies as a crisis. It is more of an important operational process. If, on the other hand, it is unclear what to do next or how the event even occurred, this is a classic crisis scenario. Coombs (2012) suggests that because of this uncertainty component, a crisis is perception-based. The events that rise to the level of a crisis are the events that we perceive as a crisis: no perception – no crisis. When we are uncertain on how to act, when we do not know what to do in a situation, we tend to view the situation we are in as a crisis. For example, for an average person getting into a fist fight is typically a crisis situation because we do not know what to do and how to properly act in a fight, but for a professional mixed martial arts fighter, it just may be a morning warmup.

Crisis management, then, is a function of responding to this unexpected, uncertain, urgent, and important event. Researchers generally recognize three stages of crisis management: *pre-crisis*, *crisis*, and *post-crisis*. The importance of pre-crisis is highlighted by an old adage that the best crisis is the one that never happens. As discussed in Chapter 7, issue management is part of the investor relations job: investor relations and financial communication professionals are expected to actively monitor the environment and identify issues that may eventually evolve into crises. Early detection may allow the company to work on preventing the crisis from ever happening. For example, a company may suspect that an activist investor is reaching out to other shareholders in order to force a particular resolution. Learning about this early may allow the company to start reaching out proactively to shareholders as well and ensure their support in the vote. If a crisis is all but inevitable, early detection may help the company get a jumpstart on preparing a response. Following the same example, if the company learns that the activist investor has already accumulated enough votes for their proposal, the company's management may start working on the best ways to respond at the shareholder meeting once the resolution is approved and ways to proceed after the meeting.

In pre-crisis, financial communicators can also help create a *crisis response team*. Creating a crisis team helps establish a proper chain of command to ensure a fast and effective response once the crisis hits. It is also beneficial to train the people on the response team on what to do during a crisis situation – practice makes perfect!

Once in a crisis stage, all efforts must be focused on the actual response – the crisis team and all the crisis plans must be activated. An important part of the crisis stage is the actual crisis recognition – sometimes it takes an effort to recognize that what is happening is a crisis. It took some time for Samsung to recognize that phone batteries catching fire is not just a minor manufacturing defect of early products, but a full-blown crisis.

Finally, the post-crisis stage should focus on the lessons learned and evaluating the effectiveness of the response. It is also beneficial, based on the new information, to update crisis plans and perhaps the crisis team. It is also beneficial to work on restoring the reputation of the company or brand if it took a hit during the crisis. Samsung, for example, realizing that it lost a lot of public trust, opened up its technology and processes to outside auditors, relying on their independence and reputation to bolster its own – hundreds of engineers tested thousands of batteries to ensure the phones are safe to use.

Shareholder activism can be a common source of crisis in the investor relations and financial communication industry. But two additional types of crises common in the financial communication industry also deserve a special attention: hostile takeovers and bankruptcies.

Hostile Takeover

In a *hostile takeover*, one investor, the *acquirer*, gains control over all or the majority of shares of another company, the *target*, without its approval and sometimes even without its knowledge. An investor may purchase the shares on the stock market, or join forces with other shareholders to replace the Board of Directors and top management of the company. A hostile takeover may also be accomplished by a company acquiring its competitor without the approval of the target company's management. For example, when a French pharmaceutical company, Sanofi, wanted to acquire a Boston-based biotech company, Genzyme, it went to Genzyme CEO, Henri Termeer. Termeer, however, declined the offer despite the fact that Sanofi was willing to pay more for the company than its market value. Sanofi then went directly to Genzyme shareholders and offered to buy their shares of Genzyme for US$74 a share, when the market price was only around US$50, before the acquisition plans became public. This offered a very nice premium for the company's shareholders, who were set to record significant profits from going through with the deal.

Hostile takeovers are often viewed as a symbol of American capitalism – a capitalist survival of the fittest. Yet, in reality after the peak of hostile takeovers back in 1988 with 160 hostile takeover attempts on record, there was not much hostile action. A partial reason for this is the growth of the stock market. With shares in companies reaching all times highs, it is too expensive for unsolicited buyers to buy the majority of shares and take over a company.

In other words, the better the company is doing, the better the company's stock is doing, and, as a result, such a company is less likely to be the target of a hostile acquisition. With the COVID-19 epidemic, however, the stock market may be under pressure and, if the stocks start trending down, the number of hostile takeover attempts may go up. An article at the Harvard Law School Forum on Corporate Governance provides seven recommendations for companies to protect themselves from hostile takeover attempts (Liekefett & Austin, 2020):

1. Have an emergency communication response plan.
   When a hostile takeover becomes public, it can cause tensions for the company, its management, employees, suppliers, and many other stakeholders. It is important to have a communication plan ready to go so as not to be caught off-guard, and to be able to calm and reassure the affected stakeholders. A proper response in the media can have a strong effect on the public perception of the situation and can help or harm the company's position as well.

2. Review the charter and bylaws.
   Organizations operate within their bylaws and, as a result, it is important to make sure the bylaws of the company are effective in a hostile takeover situation. For example, the stipulation of who can call an extraordinary shareholder meeting, and the process for doing so, can make a big difference in a hostile takeover scenario.

3. Draft a "shelf" *poison pill.*
   A proposal for a "poison pill" that is drafted in advance and ready to be implemented immediately can be one of the most effective ways to dwarf a hostile takeover attempt. A typical "poison pill" provision allows shareholders to buy additional shares of the company with a significant discount if a company becomes a target for takeover and an unsolicited acquirer reaches a certain threshold in stock ownership. For example, Netflix has a poison pill provision, whereby if any shareholder acquires 10% of the company's stock, all other existing shareholders can purchase two shares of Netflix for the price of one. This would mean immediate profits for all the shareholders but would significantly increase the price for an entity trying to acquire Netflix by diluting the ownership of whoever accumulates a large share of Netflix stock.

4. Monitor the stock.
   Knowing what is happening with the company's stock is vital for the management team. Good investor relations officers (IROs) may be able to identify a hostile takeover attempt early by recognizing the fact that some entity is accumulating a significant amount of company stock. This early identification may allow the company to react quickly and preemptively.

5. Engage the shareholders.
   Other shareholders play a vital role during a hostile takeover. They may offer their support to the management and vote with the management, essentially protecting the company from the hostile takeover, or they may side with those who are trying to acquire the company and vote the current Board of Directors out. Thus, building and maintaining relationships with the company's shareholders is important.

6. Conduct a financial self-evaluation.
   Companies that perform well and have their stock reflect this performance rarely become the target of a hostile takeover. Thus, the management and IROs must perform and communicate this performance to the shareholders and others in the financial community. Good performance and growing stock are the best defense against hostile takeovers.

7. Retain a response team.

   As with any crisis situation, a company must maintain a crisis management plan for hostile takeovers. It should clearly identify the members of the response team and who on the team is responsible for what. Of course, the members of the team should be prepared and practice for their roles in this scenario.

Bankruptcy

Another significant event bringing a lot of anxiety and requiring a coordinated communication effort from everybody on the management team is *bankruptcy*. As discussed previously, companies can finance their development through a combination of equity and debt. In the case of equity, shareholders who own shares of the company essentially become the company's owners and, as a result, they receive an opportunity to vote on the matters related to the company's progress. The shares that represent this ownership are expected to appreciate in value as the company's business is growing. For example, one share of Amazon was trading at between US$1 and US$2 at the beginning of Amazon's journey as an online bookseller. At the start of 2021, the same one share of Amazon was traded at more than US$3,000.

Debt holders, on the other hand, do not get to be owners of the company and are not rewarded if the company is successful. Instead debt holders get repaid what they are owed. For example, a company may borrow US$1 million from a bank paying 5% interest a year on the debt. This is all the debt holder is entitled to. However, debt holders must be repaid even if the company is not doing very well. Even if the company gets liquidated, the debt must still be honored, considering whether the company has any assets to sell. Shareholders, on the other hand, may get nothing – if a company is doing poorly, its share price may go down to US$0. In the case of liquidation and sale of assets, shareholders would be the last in line to receive any compensation after the debt holders.

Thus, when times are tough and the company is having difficulties meeting its financial obligations, debt holders become an important and influential force. They require careful and patient consideration, and honest and frequent communications. A debtor may let a company extend or restructure the debt owed, but if communications fail and the company cannot repay its debt, the company becomes *insolvent*. In this case, the company may be forced to declare a bankruptcy.

Bankruptcy is a legal process to eliminate or restructure insolvent organizations taking into account the interests of the company debt holders as well as other stakeholders. Bankruptcies should try as much as possible to save the company by improving its processes and structures so that it can continue to provide its services to the society, employ and pay salaries to its staff, and meet all its financial obligations. It is, however, usually a challenge. Even before bankruptcy is officially declared, companies in this situation tend to struggle – cutting budgets, salaries, delaying payments, and laying off staff. It is common even prior to bankruptcy to experience low morale and increased employee turnover. The company may be losing customers or cutting its services in an attempt to save money. Once the bankruptcy is declared, all these processes may deepen and accelerate. It is difficult to blame employees for wanting to leave a company involved in bankruptcy proceedings.

This underscores the importance of strategic communications and open disclosure leading up to and during the bankruptcy. Employee turnover has a real cost – hiring and retraining new employees takes time and money – thus, it is important to ensure that the interests of employees are taken into account during bankruptcy. It is important to communicate often with the employees about what the company is experiencing and what is the light at the end of the tunnel. The same applies to customers and suppliers. Both of these groups of stakeholders may be apprehensive when the company is going through a bankruptcy, so, frequent and transparent communications may alleviate the apprehension and ensure continuation of the business relationship.

Svec (2021) has eight key pieces of advice for financial communicators who manage bankruptcy:

1. Show empathy to these affected.
2. Reinforce positives such as successful debt restructurings achieved.
3. Focus on the goal and the better days ahead.
4. Emphasize the social purpose of the company's products and services.
5. Avoid bunker mentality: tell your story and manage the narrative.
6. Build management credibility.
7. Focus on owned media to have a direct communication channel with key stakeholders.
8. Paint a picture of the future enterprise.

Overall, a bankruptcy declaration is a crisis scenario for an organization. It threatens the existence of the organization as a whole. Bankruptcy is not the only crisis situation, however, that financial communicators may have to respond to. Depending on the industry, location, the company itself, and many other factors, investor relations and financial communication professionals may have to react to a variety of crisis scenarios. Apple valuation, for example, lost billions of dollars in a matter of minutes when gossip circulated on social media that Apple's CEO, Steve Jobs, was admitted to an emergency room, and the share price plummeted on the stock exchange as a result. This was a crisis in itself, but later it was revealed that the rumor was fake and originated from a user-generated comment on social media – this made it a completely different type of crisis. Of course, later on it was revealed that Steve Jobs, in fact, had health problems, and that made it another type of crisis once again, and imposed additional requirements on Apple's financial communicators.

Key Terms

Acquirer
Activist shareholder
Bankruptcy
Board of Directors' composition
Chair of the Board
Climate Action 100+
Climate change
Crisis

Crisis management
Crisis response team
Debt holder
Disclosure
ESG fund
Hostile takeover
Independent director
Insolvent
Poison pill
Post-crisis
Pre-crisis
Proxy battle
Proxy Monitor
Proxy statement
Reddit
Redditors
Robinhood
Rule 14a-8
Shareholder proposal
Target
WallStreetBets

Discussion Questions and Activities

1 Why would some investors become activists instead of voting with their feet? Discuss some main reasons and find examples from recent news.

2 Discuss why environmental issues are the most common topic for the shareholder proposals. How do you expect this to change in the future?

3 Why do you think engaging in a dialogue and finding a compromise is generally considered a preferred outcome versus taking a shareholder resolution to the proxy ballot for a vote?

4 Describe the key characteristics of a crisis. What does it mean that the best crisis is the one that never happens? How can you stop a crisis from happening?

5 Access Proxy Monitor and choose any shareholder proposal to study. Describe the company, the shareholder who drafted the proposal, and the result of the vote. Analyze why the proposal was accepted or failed.

Part IV

Work

9

Main Activities and Publications in Investor Relations and Financial Communication

On a day-to-day basis, investor relations officers (IROs) produce periodic reports, respond to requests from investors and analysts, and conduct shareholder research. Strategically, the focus of all their work is on building and maintaining relationships with current and prospective shareholders as well as other financial publics. These relationships are the foundation on which understanding of the company and its business, as well as trust in the management team and its decision-making are built. Fair evaluation of the company's securities is impossible without such understanding and trust. To achieve these targets of fair valuation, understanding, trust, and relationships, investor relations and financial communication professionals engage in myriad tactical tasks. The chapter will focus on several of these responsibilities.

Disclosure

Disclosure is one of the most visible tasks of the investor relations profession because it is a regulatory mandate. In fact, some even equate disclosure with investor relations, calling investor relations professionals *disclosure officers* and citing disclosure as the main function of financial communicators. Shareholders as company outsiders do not possess direct and constant knowledge about what's going on inside the company. This makes IROs a conduit of knowledge between insiders and outsiders of the corporation. The efficient market hypothesis described in Chapter 1 calls attention to the importance of public access to information as a foundation for fair valuation – information that is not available or not understood cannot be reflected in the price, which may lead to information asymmetry and mispricing of securities, making financial markets inefficient.

The foundation of the required disclosure is *periodic reporting*. In the United States, for publicly traded companies, it is centered on *Form 10-K*, the *annual report*, and *Form 10-Q*, the *quarterly report*. As the name suggests, 10-K focuses on the results of the past year, while 10-Q discusses what happened over the most recent three months.

Form 10-K, the annual report, consists of four major parts, each of which has several subparts, called items. Part 1 includes four items that describe the business the company is in, risk factors the company is facing, property the company owns, and legal proceedings the company is involved in. A separate item is mine safety

Investor Relations and Financial Communication: Creating Value Through Trust and Understanding,
First Edition. Alexander V. Laskin.
© 2022 John Wiley & Sons, Inc. Published 2022 by John Wiley & Sons, Inc.

disclosure. Part 2 includes five items and focuses on the disclosure of the financial statements and management discussion and analysis of the company's operations and market position as well as disclosure of corporate governance mechanisms. Part 3 provides information about the company's executives and directors, and their share ownership. It also discloses details on the executive compensation. Part 4 provides appendixes and exhibits for the report.

Form 10-Q, the quarterly report, is a simplified version of the annual report. It provides quarterly financial statements and management discussion and analysis of those financial statements and the operational results. The quarterly report also requires the company to update information on the markets the company operates in, risk factors it faces, and corporate governance controls and procedures. An important difference between 10-K and 10-Q is the fact that the quarterly report's financial statements are not verified by an independent auditing company, while the annual report's financials are audited. This is one of the reasons why many investors and financial analysts tend to rely mainly on the annual report's numbers.

In addition to these periodic reports, investor relations professionals are responsible for disclosing information that may materially affect the valuation of a company as it happens. Such information is called *material information* and such reporting is called *current reporting* or *emergency reporting*. One of the ways IROs provide such disclosure is the United States Securities and Exchange Commission (SEC) *Form 8-K, current report*. The SEC explains that companies are expected to file Form 8-K in order "to announce major events that shareholders should know about" (SEC, 2012). Form 8-K does not have a standard layout and content requirements in the same way as periodic reporting forms have because its filing may be caused by a variety of reasons that would carry different informational needs. Although this form must be filed every time the issuer thinks there is a material change in the company's operations, the SEC lists several specific situations when the form must be filed without leaving it up to a company's discretion. For example, the SEC mentions bankruptcy, entry into new or termination of existing material agreements, acquisition or disposition of assets or companies, significant change in financial obligations or operational results, any changes to the securities or security holders' rights or responsibilities, and so on.

Companies usually have only four business days to file Form 8-K. Such a short turnaround is explained by the necessity for shareholders to have accurate and up-to-date information about the company. A special case for filing Form 8-K is *selective disclosure*. The CEO of a company, for example, may accidentally share some information with a financial analyst during a private meeting that is not yet publicly available to anybody else. This is a violation of Regulation FD. In order to be in compliance with the regulation, the company must file Form 8-K to disclose such information publicly. In this case, the SEC requires the company to make the disclosure promptly or, in other words, as fast as possible. Since the spirit of Regulation FD is to prevent some market participants from outperforming the market because of access to preferential information, the SEC typically expects the companies to make the 8-K disclosure before the markets open. In this case, the issuer who made an unintentional disclosure is most likely to avoid punishment as there was not an opportunity for anyone to beat the market using this information. If this is not possible, the SEC expects Form 8-K be filed within 24 hours.

The SEC constantly reviews and monitors the channels for public and nonpublic disclosure, and modifies its regulations. Although filings with the SEC are always appropriate channels of public disclosure as investors know the SEC's EDGAR (Electronic Data Gathering, Analysis, and Retrieval) system as a database of all company's public information, in 2008 the SEC added company websites as a channel of public disclosure as web usage became widespread and investors learned to expect to find information on corporate websites. In 2013, the SEC further updated its guidance on disclosure and included social media as a recognized tool for public disclosure under certain conditions.

Paid Media, Earned Media, Shared Media, and Owned Media

The web homepages of publicly traded corporations usually have a section labeled *Investors* or *For Investors* where information relevant for shareholders, investors, and financial analysts is posted. IROs are primarily responsible for managing the content of this section of the corporate website, of course working in collaboration with other corporate functions responsible for external communications. Such corporate websites are called *owned media* because the company itself is the owner of the website and has complete control over what is published there, how it is published, and when it is published.

Having complete control over the website makes it an excellent tool for setting the agenda of the conversations and promoting the topics important for the company. For example, in the investor relations section of Microsoft's website, the company draws attention to past and future events the company participates in, including providing links to event webcasts. For example, Microsoft lists a link to a recent presentation of its CEO, Satya Nadella, at the Morgan Stanley conference. The site also provides current information on the Microsoft stock price and trading volume, links to the most recent annual report and proxy statement, and has an archive of quarterly earnings. Microsoft's investor relations team also uses its website to educate investors about the corporation's products and their strengths, focusing specifically on innovation and new technology development. At the start of 2021, the investor relations page provided information about the new Transcribe app, Azure infrastructure, as well as updates for Edge and Bing. The site also discussed corporate efforts related to sustainability, diversity, and inclusion.

Facebook, similarly, has a section of its website labeled Investor Relations. The page has seven main subsections: company info, financials, annual meeting, press releases, investor events, stock information, and corporate governance. The page has direct access to Facebook's SEC filings as well as a dedicated subpage labeled *Investor Education Center.* This center provides explanation of key technologies the Facebook corporation relies on for its business, mainly *Facebook Ad Guide*, because it is important for investors to understand the corporate business model and how it makes money.

Investor relations professionals are also responsible for *shared media*. A common type of shared media is social media channels. Although social media usage for communicating with investors is not as readily accepted as websites, the SEC recognizes that social media can be used as a tool for disclosure. The SEC stipulates that such disclosure should not prioritize some investors over other investors – social media would be an appropriate disclosure vehicle only if investors know about it, know where to look for it, and have equal and unrestricted access to such social media channels. The SEC has had to address social media usage as more and more companies and their executives developed presence and began communicating on social media.

Netflix CEO, Reed Hastings, for example, famously posted on his personal Facebook page back in July 2012 that Netflix had exceeded one billion monthly viewing hours. This, of course, served as great news for many investors and led to an increase in the share price. Since the post was done on Hastings's personal page, however, it could not be considered an official announcement from the company as it was not posted on the Netflix website. The announcement was not filed with the SEC via Form 8-K either. Some argued that this is no different from a CEO telling insider information to his friends, in this case, his Facebook friends, and thus the incident is a clear violation of Regulation FD. Others argued that posting it publicly on Facebook, even to Facebook friends, is not the same as telling it to your friends in private. The SEC Division of Enforcement looked into the matter and announced potential charges in December 2012. However, in April 2013, the SEC announced that no enforcement action would follow, and that social media can serve as disclosure channels under certain conditions.

As a result, many messages to investors today are also being promoted on social media, adding an extra layer of responsibility to investor relations professionals. The SEC notes that companies must notify the investment community what social media channels they are using so that everyone knows what channels are used for disclosure. Social media communications must also be done in a way "reasonably designed to provide broad, nonexclusionary distribution of the information to the public" (SEC, 2008, p. 45862).

Equally important as speaking on social media, however, for IROs is *social media listening*. There are many communities on social media dedicated to discussing corporations, their stock, and their investment potential. It is important for IROs to monitor the social media chatter about the company itself, but also the industry and investment climate in general. Such monitoring can help with issue management and early identification of trends and potential crises. Various communities on Reddit can be relevant for IROs of certain companies and industries. In fact, one of the subreddits, WallStreetBets, had a huge influence on the stock price of GameStop as well as a few other stocks at the start of 2021 (see Chapter 8).

A dedicated community for discussing stocks is *StockTwits*. StockTwits developed based on the Twitter interface, which allows the sending of short messages organized around cashtags. *Cashtags* are similar to Twitter's *hashtags* only instead of using a hash sign they use a dollar sign followed by a stock ticker symbol; for example, $GME for GameStop. It is imperative for IROs to monitor the conversation around their company's cashtag – millions of investors participating in StockTwits may be a powerful force when it comes to stock trading, and even more powerful when it comes to generating and skewering rumors. StockTwits is not just for retail investors – financial analysts and professional investment managers also frequent this social media app.

TikTok also has millions of users interested in investing. Usually TikTok conversations related to investments use the hashtags #StockTok, #FinTok, or #Stonks; however, depending on the topic, they may use the company's ticker symbol as the hashtag or use other hashtags as well. Similarly to StockTwits, in addition to retail investors, who may be investing hundreds or thousands of dollars, the site attracts the investment professionals, who may be responsible for managing millions of dollars. For example, a professional financial analyst, Robert Ross, runs the *@TikStocks* account. In a recent video that received over a million views, he discusses how the stock of Pfizer reacted to the vaccine and how to understand future Pfizer stock movements.

More recently, the voice and chat app *Discord* started attracting conversations about stocks and investments. For example, subreddit WallStreetBest also has a large Discord community with about 600,000 members. Many other Discord servers, or communities, are appearing to discuss companies and investments in them, usually tagged with *investing* or *stocks*.

In addition to *owned media* and *social media*, investor relations professionals operate with *earned media* and *paid media*. Earned media, also called *free media*, or *publicity*, has traditionally been associated with public relations. Early public relations pioneers such as P.T. Barnum and Edward Bernays earned media attention through staging events and promoting newsworthy stories. IROs today may earn media coverage by making top executives available to the media for commenting on the company itself or larger stories related to the industry or economy in general. When a corporation is releasing its annual earnings, the CEO, CFO, or other executive may also appear on the media to comment on the results and respond to questions. Earned media coverage, similar to analyst coverage, may generate interest in the stock from new investors. Many retail investors are consumers of business media information.

Paid media, also called *advertising*, is not commonly used in investor relations but can be advantageous sometimes. The most obvious example is the publication of an advertisement announcing the annual general meeting. In many countries, it is a legal requirement; in some it is a tradition. Corporations may even take out ads, usually in business and financial media, announcing issues of stock or bonds. This may be an appropriate way to reach retail shareholders, but may help gain traction with professional investors too.

As in the case of social media, listening may be as important, or even more important, than talking. For IROs, it is important to know what the media is saying about the company. Monitoring the mass media, in the same way as monitoring social media, is a crucial responsibility for investor relations professionals. It is also essential to be able to relay any important information from the media to the executives. IROs must have access to the C-suite in order to facilitate true two-way communication between the company and the financial audiences, including business journalists. If journalists or bloggers or other influencers are working on a story about a company, it is often in the company's best interest to make the CEO or other executives participate. Otherwise, the story will still come out, but the side of the company is not going to be represented. At the very least, IROs should be working with the media to ensure the accuracy of the facts in the story. Often, investor relations departments work in close cooperation with the company's public relations or strategic communication department when it comes to earned, paid, controlled, and social media. In some cases, a specialized agency may be brought in to supplement the company's internal expertise. The agencies may have well-developed relations and a proven track record with specific journalists or publications, and may know exactly what the best course of action is in specific situations. For example, one of the leading financial communication agencies, Prosek, states on its website: "We have relationships with virtually the entire universe of top-tier journalists and particularly those who specialize in business, finance, asset management, insurance and technology". In a situation where a fast response is needed to combat misinformation or, conversely, an important story needs to be disseminated, the expense of hiring an agency may be totally worth it.

Earnings and Earning Calls

An important event for a public company is its *earnings release*, *earnings report*, or simply *earnings*. When a company submits its quarterly report or its annual report to the SEC, the company typically also issues a public media release that summarizes the key points of the filing, with a strong focus on the financial results. As discussed in Chapter 4, the final line in the financial statement of the company is its *earnings*. As a result, this media release about quarterly or annual results is often called the earnings release.

This is an important event – not just for the company, but also for the company's investors and financial analysts. This is when the actual results are compared with the predictions and the expectations. Many financial service providers maintain *earnings calendars* so that everyone on the financial markets will know about the upcoming earnings. A typical earnings calendar has the name of the company, the date when the quarter for the earnings ends, a consensus estimate of the earnings from the financial analysts covering the company, the number of financial analysts covering the company, and the previous year's earnings.

Land's End released its first quarter earnings of 2021 on March 17, 2021, with an EPS of US$0.60, while the analysts' consensus estimate was US$0.56. In other words, Land's End was able to beat the estimate by US$0.04 per share. Since investors may have strong reactions to a company *beating* or *missing* the analysts' estimates, earnings are released when the markets are closed, usually in the evening. This gives a chance for investors to process all the information and avoid knee-jerk reaction based purely on numbers. According to the National Investor Relations Institute (NIRI), the most popular day to release earnings is Thursday; the second most popular day is Wednesday.

It also gives a company's management a chance to explain the numbers and educate investors about what stands behind the numbers. As a result, earnings releases are usually accompanied by an *earnings call, earnings cast,* or *earnings conference.* Investor relations professionals are usually responsible for preparing for and managing these calls. The calls are often simulcast online and are also saved and stored on the investor relations section of a company's website, allowing investors to access them at a later date. The top company executives tend to speak at these calls, including the CEO and CFO; depending on the topics the company wishes to focus on, company experts from operations, sales, or research may also be invited to speak. The goal of the call, however, is typically to frame the most recent financial results and put them in the context of the long-term ambitions of the company and its mission. Missing the estimate may be a good thing if a company, for example, had to invest heavily in a promising new technology to be the first in a new market segment that the company strives to be in and that can start paying off in the near future. All that information can be communicated to the investors and analysts to help them better understand the story behind the numbers. A crucial part of the call is the ability of investors and analysts to ask questions and receive clarifying information from the management. Sometimes these exchanges may get tense – if the company is not doing so well or if management is withholding information, for example. It is the job of an IRO to manage both sides of the call – the investment community and the management – to ensure fair, transparent, and full disclosure of all relevant information.

At some companies, for example, if the management is not comfortable with public speaking, the presentation may be prerecorded – this gives IROs an opportunity to work with the management and train the executives on what should be communicated and how. The Q&A section is typically live, but it can also be managed – at some companies, questions must be submitted in advance, at some they can only be sent privately to an IRO who then decides what questions to announce publicly and which ones to withhold, and at yet other companies, the Q&A section is like an open-mic with open conversation between the investors, analysts, and the management.

Many companies also provide their own *earnings guidance* – a prediction of what their earnings will be next quarter and next year. Although it is a somewhat controversial practice that often generates strong arguments on both sides – whether it is appropriate to issue its own guidance or not – NIRI estimates that over 90% of corporations in the United States provide some form of earning guidance. In this case, corporate earnings can be compared with both the analysts' consensus estimate and the company's own earnings predictions. This may place an extra pressure on the company's management to achieve its own predictions. To lessen the pressure, earnings guidance is typically expressed as an *earnings range* rather than the exact number; for example, a company may say that they expect next year's EPS to be in the range of US$1.00–1.25. A few companies may avoid the numbers altogether and provide so-called *qualitative guidance* saying that they expect a good quarter and growth in EPS, for example.

Annual Shareholder Meetings and Proxy Statements

The most significant event IROs manage is the *annual shareholder meeting*, or *annual general meeting (AGM)*. The AGM is typically a large-budget event at a company's headquarters or at a large fancy hotel's conference center, where shareholders of the company can gather together to hear reports from the management and the Board of Directors, and vote on the key issues facing the corporation. The key issues requiring a vote are elections of the new Board of Directors, who would represent the shareholders between the annual meetings and perform oversight over the company's management in the best interests of all shareholders. The shareholders also vote on electing a new auditor to ensure accuracy of all the financial statements the company produces. The executive compensation must also be presented at the AGM for a shareholders' vote – this process is known as *say on pay*. The vote on executive compensation is *nonbinding*, or *advisory*, meaning that even if shareholders do not approve the compensation package for the CEO, the company can still proceed with the payments. Although nonbinding, no CEO wants to have shareholders publicly express disagreement with the proposed compensation, as it often shows lack of satisfaction with the work the CEO is doing. Finally, in addition to the required bylaw items, shareholders can propose additional items for discussion at the AGM – these are known as *shareholder proposals*. The shareholder proposals may focus on absolutely any issue related to the company – employee practices, sustainability, management diversity, the structure of the Board of Directors, or anything else.

During 2020 and 2021 many annual shareholders meetings were conducted online because of the restrictions on in-person gatherings as well as travel limitations. The so-called *virtual shareholders meetings* (*VSMs*) were praised by many for their convenience and low-cost access. Without a need to travel to a corporate headquarters' location, shareholders can simply log in into the meeting from the comfort of their home, increasing participation. Even shareholders who had never participated in an in-person shareholder meeting before were joining VSMs during these years. Climate activists also pointed out that VSMs reduce the carbon footprint of general meetings by 99%.

VSMs have their critics too. Annual shareholder meetings are already strictly controlled by corporations – VSMs give even more control over narrative and structure to the company. Many activist investors and corporate governance advocates argue for a return to in-person AGMs as quickly and safely as possible to give a better chance for marginalized shareholder voices to be heard.

Prior to the annual meeting whether it is conducted in person or online, a *proxy statement*, or simply, *proxy*, is prepared. The proxy statement is also called *Form 14A*. The goal of the proxy is to provide information to the shareholders about the matters they are expected to vote on. The proxy includes all the annual financial information as well as parts of the management discussion and analysis. Since shareholders elect the members of the Board of Directors, there is also detailed information on each candidate for the Board. The form also provides key details about the meeting with instructions on how to submit questions, how to vote, and how to attend the meeting.

Since every annual meeting is preceded by an issuance of the proxy, the time period between the publishing of the annual report and scheduled annual meetings for many corporations is known as the proxy season. In the United States, most corporations' fiscal year ends on December 31 and, as a result, most annual reports are due by March 31, three months after the end of the fiscal year. Thus, the proxy season in the United States is typically between April 1 and June 30 – the time when most companies send out proxies and conduct their annual meetings.

Some companies have their fiscal year ending on June 30. In this case, their annual reports are due on September 30, and, thus, their proxy season is between October 1 and December 31. Other companies may also run on other schedules. For example, Apple's 2020 fiscal year ended on September 26, 2020. Apple's annual meeting was scheduled for February 23, 2021, with the proxy statement filed with the SEC on January 5, 2021.

Apple's 2021 proxy started by describing Apple and its core values (Figure 9.1). Then, the section called the *proxy statement summary* listed the issues up for a vote, and provided a description of the financial and operational results for the year as well as management's reflection on these results and evaluation of the overall health of the company. A large section on Apple's corporate governance policies and procedures followed. After that, the proxy statement provided details on every candidate for the seat on the Board of Directors. Then, the same information was provided about the top executives of the company, followed by a section on the executive compensation

Annual Meeting

2021 Annual Meeting of Shareholders

Virtual Meeting Site:
www.virtualshareholdermeeting.com/AAPL2021

February 23, 2021
9:00 a.m. Pacific Time

The Record Date for the Annual Meeting is December 28, 2020. Only shareholders of record as of the close of business on this date are entitled to vote at the Annual Meeting.

Proposal	Recommendation of the Board
1. Election of Directors	FOR *each of the nominees*
2. Ratification of Appointment of Independent Registered Public Accounting Firm	FOR
3. Advisory Vote to Approve Executive Compensation	FOR
4. *Shareholder Proposal* Shareholder Proxy Access Amendments	AGAINST
5. *Shareholder Proposal* Shareholder Proposal to Improve Executive Compensation Program	AGAINST

How to Vote

You may vote online prior to the meeting by visiting proxyvote.com and entering the control number found in your Notice of Internet Availability of Proxy Materials, or, if you requested printed copies of the proxy materials, by phone or by mail. You may also vote during the Annual Meeting by visiting www.virtualshareholdermeeting.com/AAPL2021, entering the control number, and following the instructions. For more detailed information, see the section entitled "Voting Procedures" beginning on page 77.

Figure 9.1 Apple 2021 Annual meeting of shareholders proxy statement summary.
Source: Apple Inc. financial statements. Retrieved from: https://sec.report/Document/0001193125-21-001987/. Public Domain.

proposal. An interesting part of the executive compensation disclosure is a comparison of CEO pay with the average pay at the company, the *CEO pay ratio*. For Apple, CEO Tim Cook's compensation for 2020 was slightly under US$14.8 million, while the median pay at Apple was US$57,783. This resulted in a CEO pay ratio of 256 to 1.

After all these disclosures, the proxy moves on to the actual voting items. For Apple's proxy statement, these included five proposals, including two shareholder-submitted proposals that the company recommended to vote against: a proposal on proxy access and a proposal on executive compensation modification. A shareholder proposal on proxy access sought to increase the number of Board candidates proposed by the shareholders, and the proposal on the executive compensation sought to expand disclosure and consideration in establishing executive compensation beyond what is minimally required by law, specifically, taking into account social, ethical, and economic factors, as well as compensation of other executives in addition to the CEO, the *Named Executive Officers* (NEOs).

The proxy usually ends with an opportunity to vote remotely without having to attend the annual meeting – the vote can be recorded by mail or online. A shareholder is provided a unique identification code that allows the shareholder to submit votes based on the number of voting shares they have. There are many organizations that help companies prepare and conduct shareholder meetings including delivering proxy materials to all eligible shareholders and ensuring their votes are properly recorded and counted. One of the leading proxy firms, Morrow Sodali, describes its extensive list of annual meeting services for corporations as follows:

- Delivering the initial analysis of the shareholder profile.
- Drafting the solicitation plan geared to the specific requirements of the upcoming meeting, including the decision to target retail shareholders or not.
- Reviewing the preliminary proxy statement, highlighting issues that may result in "withhold" or "against" recommendations from proxy advisory firms.
- Scheduling and coordinating the distribution of the solicitation material.
- Soliciting votes from all shareholder constituencies.
- Updating clients throughout the entire process.
- Delivering the post-meeting review.

Responsiveness to Investors, One-on-One Meetings, and Relationship Building

A recent study by Alexander V. Laskin surveyed IROs at Fortune 500 companies and inquired what activity they perform most often. The research concluded that the most common investor relations activity is responding to requests they receive from various constituencies. Indeed, hardly a day goes by without a financial analyst from the sell-side or a buy-side shareholder contacting an IRO. In fact the research determined that institutional investors and financial analysts combined consume on average 70% of the IROs' time.

This finding is not surprising: investors and financial analysts want to stay up to date on every development of the company: the launch of a new product, entering new markets, or hiring a new person to the top management team. Private shareholders also submit their fair share of requests for information. In fact, some organizations have a separate department to communicate with private shareholders in order to allow IROs to have more time for financial analysts and professional investors.

The requests can be as simple as clarifying information in the most recent annual report or as complex as providing information on chemical compounds in the new batteries planned to be installed in future electric cars. IROs are not expected to be experts on everything the company is doing, but IROs should know who the experts are. It is essential for investor relations professionals to know the company's structure and develop close relationships with every department in the company in order to be able to find the information that will help investors and financial analysts better understand the corporation. An IRO should be able to take investors' requests and find answers to their questions or be able to connect them with the right people within the company. Of course, there may be situations where the information is privileged and cannot be shared. Then, it becomes the job of an IRO to explain to the investors and analysts why their questions cannot be answered. IROs works closely with other departments within the corporation – legal, production, treasury – to respond to investor requests and to identify what information can and cannot be shared.

Not everything investors ask is directly related to the finances of the company or even production facilities. Investors may be asking about the management team – their qualifications, future plans, and even their health. A strong corporate leader may be responsible for significant value added and gossip about CEO health problems may have a strong impact on the share price. IROs must work closely with the executive team to develop a strategy on how to communicate the issues of transitions in corporate leadership as well as how, if at all, to communicate about personal matters.

All things considered these information requests can be very time consuming. Spending most of the time on responding to requests from shareholders and financial analysts raises a concern about the *reactive* nature of investor relations. Indeed, if the focus of investor relations is on catching up with requests it does not leave much time for *proactive* activities and strategic planning for the benefit of the organization. In fact, controlled media communications, such as websites, mailings lists, newsletters, or other company media that might allow investor relations officers to set an agenda and proactively deliver information to the interested parties, are rarely mentioned by the IROs as the activity they are involved in. Unfortunately, IROs are often consumed by technical rather than strategic activities. Even today the overwhelming demands on IROs' time from information requests deflect attention from the symbolic nature of investor relations and take away the chance to contribute proactively to the company's value.

At the same, *responsiveness* is essential for maintaining relationships with investors and financial analysts. One of the most effective tactics IROs use for building and maintaining relationships with the financial community is *one-on-one meetings*, or simply *one-on-ones*. One-on-one meetings with investors or analysts have long been considered a cornerstone of investor relations. These one-on-ones are individual meetings, typically with an institutional investor or a sell-side financial analyst. The meetings show respect and appreciation to the investor, who gets a chance to ask questions about the company and receive direct and immediate responses. It is common to have a team of top company representatives at such meetings. In addition to the IRO, the meeting may be attended by the CEO, CFO, COO, CMO, and other executives depending on the topic of conversation and how important the investor is.

For example, if a pharmaceutical company is promoting its new chemical compound, a research scientist who developed the compound may be invited to the meeting to help investors understand the potential of the medicine. Or if a company talks about new ways to sell its products, for example, switching to a subscription model, marketing and sales leadership may be invited. Investors and analysts also cherish one-on-one meetings as these meetings provide an opportunity to get all their questions answered, while at the same time they can analyze the nonverbal cues and body language of the top management.

Research shows that involvement in one-on-one meetings depends on who manages the investor relations program. Investor relations programs managed by the corporate communication/public relations departments are not as often involved in one-on-meetings as IROs managed by finance/treasury departments or as officers from the standalone investor relation departments. One-on-ones may also be challenging from the Regulation

FD standpoint – a company cannot disclose information selectively, just to the investor participating in the one-on-one. In fact, when Reg. FD was adopted, many in the investment community predicted that the practice of one-on-ones would disappear. The numbers of one-on-one meetings did, in fact, decrease, but they are far from being extinct. Investors still value the opportunity to sit face to face with the top leadership of corporations even if no new information can be disclosed. Investors use the meetings to read nonverbal cues and get clarifications on previously released information. Of course, if some new information is accidentally released in a selective way, IROs would be responsible for filing Form 8-K as soon as possible to comply with Regulation FD.

Being responsive and available to investors and financial analysts 24/7 is an important responsibility for an IRO. It is part of building and maintaining relationships with the financial community. One of the anonymous investor relations practitioners in Laskin's (2014) study on the value of investor relations elaborates:

> Since we have invested the time and effort in building relationships … we are given the opportunity to explain our results and strategies more fully, and have a better chance to be given the benefit of the doubt in situations where investors and analysts are being asked to trust your word than if we didn't establish the relationship.

In addition, established relationships may lead to increasing the holding period and amount of ownership in the company, which can help stabilize share price volatility and thus is a part of the investor relations job. Such a holding pattern is sometimes referred to as *relational investing*, or *relationship investing*. This investing means long-term investing, investing in a large share of a company's stock, and developing a close connection to the company's management. Investor relations academics and practitioners know of the benefits of relational investing: value gaps tend to diminish, positive events and development earn higher stock gain rewards, and a down quarter isn't an automatic sell signal. Most importantly, investors listen to and trust the company's side of the story.

An academic study that analyzed relational investing noted that although the term has become quite common, there is no precise definition for this phenomenon:

> The proponents of relational investing do not define who counts as relational investor, beyond the vague requirement that the investor hold a large block for a substantial time and actively monitor the firm's performance, nor do they specify how quickly the results of the investor's monitoring should show up in a firm's performance.
>
> *(Bhagat, Black, & Blair, 2004, p. 8)*

The development of this relational approach parallels a similar approach in marketing, with its shift from transaction-oriented marketing to relationship-oriented marketing.

One study analyzed several cases of investors becoming closely involved with companies, for example, Avon, Kodak, and Lockheed. In all these cases corporate performance was improved after active involvement of shareholders in company activities. Across the literature, there is evidence that supports the claim that long-term investing can lead to improvements in corporate performance (Dobrzynsky, 1993).

The terms relational investing and relationship investing both look at the issue from the standpoint of the investment community. Analyzing the same issue from the standpoint of a corporation and the efforts of its investor relations practitioners, it can be labeled *investor relationship building*, or *investor relationship*. These terms would encompass the efforts of the investor relations professionals to recruit or develop long-term relational investors for their companies by building relationships between shareholders and the company. Thus, the term *investor relationship* becomes part of the traditional corporate function of *investor relations* but places an emphasis on the importance of developing relationships with shareholders, helping them to become *relational investors* and engaging them in *relationship investing*.

The benefits of *investor relationship building* are not limited to corporations and the investment community. In fact, relational investing has the potential to solve the common problem of investors' *rational apathy* – a situation in which investors prefer to withdraw from the company (selling the stock) if faced with problems, bad corporate practices, or unethical behavior.

Relational investors do not sell their stock in these situations. Rather, they try to communicate their dissatisfaction to the management and persuade the company to change its policies. In other words, instead of fleeing from the problem, relational investors work on solving it. These investors are often willing to lend their skills, knowledge, and expertise to the company and thus can potentially improve the company's performance and its share price. Such investors strive to gain above-average returns from their investment in *the company*, not from their investment in *the market*. This has a potential to benefit the company directly, but can also benefit the economy in general.

Sell-side and Research Coverage

An important responsibility of investor relations professionals is getting *research coverage* for the company. The buy-side may be apprehensive about investing in a corporation that does not have any financial analysts scrutinizing it and publishing research reports on its corporate development. However, the sell-side is usually interested in providing research only for larger stocks, stocks that generate lots of buy-and-sell transactions and, as a result, trade commissions for the brokers. For example, Facebook has over 15 major sell-side analysts providing coverage for its stock, including some of the largest sell-side banks: Morgan Stanley and JP Morgan Chase. This is not surprising considering Facebook's US$750 billion in market capitalization and significant daily trading volumes. However, for smaller companies, it may be a challenge to secure even one analyst to cover the company. In fact, IROs at smaller and mid-sized companies have to invest considerable efforts in reaching out to a variety of financial analysts trying to secure coverage.

The coverage serves as an outside endorsement of the company's value. It is one thing when the management is bullish about the future of the company's business; it is a different story when an independent sell-side analyst confirms all this optimism. This *third-party endorsement* is important for current shareholders and prospective investors. Some compare the work of investor relations professionals in securing financial analysts' coverage to the work of public relations professionals trying to secure media coverage for their clients and organizations.

An essential part of the analysts' coverage in addition to the research reports themselves is *analyst recommendation*, or the *investment rating*. It is common for the analysts to conclude their reports with the overarching recommendation about the stock: *Buy*, *Hold*, or *Sell*. In other words, the sell-side analysts recommend what investors should do with the shares in the company: whether they should buy the stock, sell it, or hold their position waiting for future changes. Sometimes, recommendations can be more detailed and include *Strong Buy* and *Strong Sell*, meaning the analysts are confident in their findings and they think decisive action is warranted.

These ratings raise another issue: if a company has only one sell-side analyst covering the stock, their recommendation would dominate the investors' perception whether the recommendation is positive or negative. With 10 or 20 analysts from different sell-side organizations, the corporation is not at the mercy of just one person and the coverage can be more objective and can incorporate more perspectives and approaches to investing and analysis. Thus, it is important for IROs to continually work on securing and expanding the coverage. Of course, once the coverage is secured, the work does not stop there. IROs must become close partners for those financial analysts, working with them to ensure that they have timely and accurate information about the company and its business. IROs must go beyond required disclosure and work on educating the analysts about peculiarities unique to the company that affect the company's value.

Finally, one of the most important components of the financial analysts' coverage is the *consensus estimate*. Financial analysts' recommendations about the company's stock are based on predictions of the company's future profits, typically expressed as EPS. Many stock services use the EPS prediction from each of the analysts covering the stock and average them to arrive at the consensus estimate, or the mean of all estimates. This consensus estimate number is used by investors to hold the company's management accountable – every quarter and every year, investors discuss whether the company was able to meet the consensus estimate, beat the consensus estimate, or missed the consensus estimate. Needless to say, this number has significant importance for the company and its management, and thus IROs are expected to work very closely with the analysts to help them arrive at an EPS estimate that is as accurate as possible. Many executives require IROs to know and report to them any changes in the estimates; executives may also feel pressured to deliver the consensus number the analysts arrived at. Some suggest that overly focusing on quarterly and annual estimates may lead the managers to make decisions that will help them meet the estimates but will hurt the company in the long term; for example, doing heavily discounted fire sales at the end of quarter periods or foregoing investment in research or employees. The estimate is also important for shareholders, who may react strongly if the company beats or misses the number. For example, when eBay missed its consensus estimate by just one penny, its share price plummeted 22% costing the company millions of dollars in capitalization.

The significance of analysts' opinions about the company once again highlights the importance of research coverage and, specifically, the importance of extensive and varied research coverage. In recent years, corporations that have not been successful in attracting sell-side research coverage organically have resorted to buying analyst research. This so-called *sponsored research* may raise some ethical concerns, however. Indeed, how likely is it that an analyst would conclude a negative recommendation against a stock if the company issuing the stock is paying for this research? Sponsored research may also lead to violations of Regulation FD if the analyst working directly for the company receives insider information not publicly available to anybody else. The complexities of sponsored research generate a lot of discussion among IROs, especially at smaller companies. As a result, NIRI (2020) released a six-step list of recommendations for issuers who commission research on their stock to help corporations navigate the challenges of sponsored research:

1. Issuers should engage only research firms that have adopted written ethical standards that address analyst independence and how the research firm mitigates conflicts of interest.
2. Issuers should engage only research firms that agree to produce objective and thorough research reports that fully disclose any matters that could reasonably be expected to impair their objectivity.
3. Research firms should act as "arms-length" outsiders, working with material information that is publicly available.
4. Issuers should compensate the research firm in cash – not in stock or stock warrants.
5. Issuers shall not provide any compensation to the research firm that is contingent on the content or conclusions of the research (or the resulting impact on the issuer's share price).
6. Issuers should not attempt to explicitly or implicitly influence the research, recommendations, or behavior of the research firm analysts who are preparing the sponsored research.

Roadshows, Investor Days, Conferences, and Other Special Events

Investor relations professionals also organize special events other than annual shareholder meetings. A *roadshow* is an important event for a company that is looking to go public and is an essential part of an initial public offering (IPO) and private placement, but many companies engage in roadshows on a periodic basis as well without planning an IPO. These roadshows that are not tied to the sale of new securities are called *non-deal roadshows*.

A roadshow is when a team of corporate executives travels to key financial centers of the world to meet with a variety of investors and potential investors in a short period of time. A typical roadshow could happen over a week or so and involve stops in New York, Boston, Los Angeles, London, and Singapore. The company executives may spend one day in each of these cities and have five meetings each day with large investors. These face-to-face interactions are valued by investors as they let them see the team behind the numbers and develop relationships with the executives. For example, when Alibaba was preparing to become a publicly traded company, it conducted a roadshow with stops in Boston, Baltimore, Denver, San Francisco, Los Angeles, Hong Kong, Singapore, London, and the Middle East. The roadshow kicked off at the New York Waldorf-Astoria hotel on September 8, 2014 and ended on September 18, 2014. During this time Alibaba's top executives, including the CEO, CFO, and COO, met with almost 100 of the largest global investors.

The opposite of a roadshow is an *investor day*. Instead of the company's management going to investors on a roadshow, investors are invited to the company. Investor days may be very valuable if a company wants to demonstrate new technology to investors. Tesla, for example, had an event called Battery Day. Battery Day was designed to showcase Tesla's breakthrough in battery technology, a key component for electric cars and trucks. The Battery Day was scheduled on the same day as the annual shareholder meeting, September 22, 2020, immediately following the AGM. Both events were broadcast live online and now the recorded videos are available on the Tesla website.

Often, instead of hosting investor days at headquarters or at an hotel's conference center, the investors are taken to see the actual operations of the company. These events are called *investor field trips*. A mining company, for example, may take investors and analysts into the mine – what could be better for educating the investment community about the business model of a corporation than letting everyone see the business model in action? A metallurgical company may educate investors about how special steels are made, showcasing the difference in production using an open-hearth furnace versus an electric-arc furnace.

IROs often work in close collaboration with the sell-side to engage current and potential investors through other special events such as *investor conferences*. These events allow companies, often competitors, to pitch their stock to many investors at the same time. For example, in February 2021, the Global Mining and Metals Conference allowed investors to hear directly from the executives at many different corporations such as Canada Nickel, Arizona Metals, Aurania Resources, Ceylon Graphite, Frontier Lithium, and many more, and make a decision which ones to invest in. In March 2021, Morgan Stanley, one of the largest sell-side banks, organized an investor conference focused on Technology, Media & Telecom Post-Pandemic, Future Forward. The event focused on how the companies had managed to survive and even benefit from the pandemic, and what is next to come in the technology sector. Among the speakers were top executives from the largest technology companies such as Microsoft and Facebook. This gave investors a unique opportunity to hear from the CEOs of the top global brands. Not many investors would have a chance to schedule a one-on-one meeting with Mark Zuckerberg, for example, so attending an investor conference is one of just a few opportunities to hear him speak about the future of Facebook.

Internal Activities

IROs are also charged with keeping management up to date on the shareholders of the company. IROs constantly conduct *ownership research* and provide information to the top management or other departments of the organization. The two-way flow of communication is in the very nature of investor relations: information is not traveling simply from organizations through the IRO to target publics, but investor relations professionals also deliver information from the investors, financial analysts, or brokers back to the management of their organizations.

This emphasizes an important function for investor relations: *counseling the management*. It is important for the top executives to know who owns the company, who trades the stock, and what their motivations are; shareholder research is the required component of investor relations. NIRI recommends "The company's investor relations officer ... [should] report feedback from investors and analysts." Many IROs engage in periodic *perception audits*. The goal of perception audits is to gauge how investors perceive the company and its management. Donna Stein (2018) explains that since the goal of investor relations is to educate investors on how the company translates economic value into shareholder value by communicating various investment metrics, it is important from time to time for IROs to make sure that their communications are working, and investors are getting the right messages. The information collected during perception audits is used to modify the communication strategy; it is also valued by the top executives of the company, who may consider augmenting their business strategy as well based on the investors' feedback. Thus, it is important for IROs to develop working relationships with the C-suite to be able to deliver feedback from investors to the company's leadership.

IROs may also take on the role of ethics officers. The ethical guidelines for investor relations professionals stipulate that it is not enough to act ethically and professionally: IROs must also act as advisors to others to ensure everyone at the company acts in an ethical and professional manner and "to avoid unethical, questionable, or inappropriate behavior or situations" (NIRI, 2020).

In addition to top management, IROs must build relationships with every single department within the organization – various operational departments, legal, marketing and sales, and all the others. Investors and analysts may ask about a company's technology, production processes, taxation, legal matters, or pretty much anything else they consider important for their understanding of the company. IROs must be familiar with all these issues, and, most importantly, must know where to find answers to the questions. Being in the know also allows IROs to be proactive with communications and not be blindsided by, for example, an analyst question during a public conference call.

These internal relationships are not always a given – they may require significant efforts to build and maintain. NIRI asked its members if they run into challenges developing internal cross-functional relationships. IROs responded that the most challenges they face are with relationships with the specific business line operators and the legal teams. These responses are quite typical: operations focus on production and may not always understand and appreciate the need for external communications. Legal departments often err on the side of less communication rather than more communication as any communication can potentially expose a company or its executives to lawsuits. However, for IROs it is imperative to explain the importance of communication to both operations and legal as communications are the cornerstone of building and maintaining relationships with the investment community.

It is beneficial to invite internal audiences to investor meetings. Most people outside of investor relations cannot even imagine the breadth and depth of information investors ask for. Thus, seeing and hearing it firsthand helps various internal audiences appreciate the role of the investor relations practitioner.

Targeting

An important part of the responsibilities of an IRO is investor *targeting*. Targeting refers to identifying investors who would be appropriate for the stock of the company based on their investment horizon, buying power, industry focus, and other factors, and then pitching the stock to these investors. This is a proactive part of the IRO's job.

Targeting starts with taking the base level measurement and understanding the corporation's existing shareholder base. Who owns the company's stock already, how long do they hold the stock, and what are their motivations for buying and selling? From there, IROs can identify opportunities for new investor types that would supplement and complement the existing shareholder base.

In the past much of the targeting was done by the sell-side – brokerage firms who would help companies find and meet with potential investors. But today as the role of the sell-side diminishes, more and more companies are doing the targeting themselves. In fact, a recent study done by *IR Magazine* found that 43% of IROs surveyed report increased usage of targeting tools to identify and reach out to potential investors for their companies (Byrne, 2020a). This requires IROs to take on additional responsibility and to learn new tools in order to succeed in these targeting efforts – many IROs in the survey complained about how complicated and inflexible these targeting tools are.

Transitioning targeting activities from the sell-side to IROs has also led to better relationship building between shareholders and the company. The sell-side tended to see targeting as a marketing activity, trying to "sell" the stock to investors. When the sell-side was paid by transaction fees, the banks would benefit when an investor bought the stock and when the investor sold the stock – so, for the sell-side the goal of targeting was often to generate transactions instead of finding a good match between a company and a shareholder. For IROs, however, the goal is to identify long-term owners of company stock and thus the focus is less on the "sell" and more on the establishment of long-term relationships. Successful investor targeting gives company access to additional capital, and thus maximizes the shareholder value.

These are some of the IRO's day-to-day responsibilities. Depending on the state of the company's development, its specific needs for capital, and even internal corporate structure, investor relations professionals may take on additional tasks as well. As shown in this chapter, a large part of the IRO's work is reactive – it is trying to catch up with all the requests from shareholders and analysts and demands of regulations. At the same time, it is important to create opportunities for proactive work as well – proactive activities are most likely to unlock additional value for the company stock and generate benefits for the corporation and its investors.

Key Terms

@TikStocks
Advertising
Advisory vote
AGM
Analyst recommendation
Annual report
Annual general meeting
Annual shareholder meeting
Beating the estimate
Cashtag
CEO pay ratio
Consensus estimate

Counseling the management
Current report
Current reporting
Disclosure
Disclosure officer
Discord
Earned media
Earnings
Earnings calendar
Earnings call
Earnings cast
Earnings conference
Earnings guidance
Earnings per share
Earnings range
Earnings release
Earnings report
Efficient market hypothesis
Emergency reporting
EPS
Fair valuation
Form 8-K
Form 10-K
Form 10-Q
Form 14A
Free media
Hashtag
Investment rating
Investor conference
Investor day
Investor field trip
Investor relationship
Investor relationship building
Material information
Missing the estimate
Named Executive Officer
NEO
Nonbinding vote
Nondeal roadshow
One-on-one
One-on-one meeting
Owned media
Ownership research
Paid media
Perception audit
Periodic reporting
Proactive
Proxy

Proxy season
Proxy statement
Proxy statement summary
Publicity
Qualitative guidance
Quarterly report
Rational apathy
Reactive
Relational investing
Relationship investing
Relational investor
Research coverage
Responsiveness
Roadshow
Say on pay
Selective disclosure
Shareholder proposal
Social media
Social media listening
Sponsored research
Stocktwits
Targeting
Third-party endorsement
TikTok
Virtual shareholder meeting
VTM

Discussion Questions and Activities

1 Describe the main benefits of investor relationship building. How should corporations build and maintain relationships with their shareholders?

2 Why should IROs focus their activities on the internal stakeholders within the organization? Discuss the benefits and strategies of internal communications.

3 What is investor targeting? How can IROs engage in investor targeting?

4 Choose any public company. Visit the website of the company and find the investor relations section of the website. Analyze what information is included there. Discuss why the company has the information it has on the investor relations part of the site. Propose additional information that it may be useful to include. Analyze what opportunities for two-way communication are included on the site.

5 Choose any public company. Review its social media accounts, including several of the recent posts on each account. What platforms and accounts do they use? Do they have a dedicated investor relations account? Or a dedicated corporate account? What posts would investors find relevant from the recent posts by the company? Are the accounts used for one-way spread of information or do the accounts engage in dialogue?

10

Going Public and Going Private

Many corporations start with just an idea. It may be only one or a couple of founders who imagine a new product, a new service, or a new technology. They may start in a garage, at a university campus, or somewhere else, but no matter the starting point, they want to bring their vision to life and make it real. This, of course, requires financial resources. Usually, the founders would start with their own money or a small *seed investment*. For example, Quinnipiac University organizes the Launchpad Competition every year giving a chance for student entrepreneurs to win seed money to implement their ideas.

This is pretty much all these founders can count on. At the idea stage, they would not be able to attract funding from the public as there is still no business or even a proven concept. It may even be a challenge to explain to outsiders what the company would do and how it would make money. Imagine being approached by Mark Zuckerberg in 2003 trying to persuade you that based on his early idea, FaceMash, he will build a multi-billion-dollar corporation. It is doubtful that many investors would have seen it that way. Thus, it is no surprise that the first two investors in the idea were the two founders, Mark Zuckerberg and Eduardo Saverin, who both invested US$1,000 each. This investment, nevertheless, allowed the idea to turn into reality when TheFacebook launched on February 4, 2004.

Once a prototype is built or a product is functioning or a website is running founders can start looking for outside support. The new company can now demonstrate the implementation of the idea to others, showcase early results, and explain their business model. Thus, it may be time to start looking for first investors. The early investors are often called *angel investors* and their investments are called *angel funding* or *angel investments*. In the case of Facebook, the angel investors were led by Peter Thiel, investing US$500,000 for 10.2% of the company stock. This made the total value of Facebook an estimated US$5 million. For comparison, today's market capitalization of Facebook is around US$1 trillion. Thus, this was a great investment decision for Thiel.

Although the company had shares of stock already, it was still not publicly traded – the company shares were available only to the company's insiders or professional investors. The company was in its *start-up* phase attracting professional start-up investors, often called *venture capitalists*. A regular retail investor could not buy a share of Facebook on Nasdaq as we can do today. At that stage, Facebook was a *private company* limited in its ability to raise funds or diversify its shareholder base in comparison with

Investor Relations and Financial Communication: Creating Value Through Trust and Understanding, First Edition. Alexander V. Laskin.

a *public company*. Thus, companies often come to a point when they start thinking about becoming a public corporation – or *going public*. The company grows from an idea to a start-up to an established operational company, and then its development brings it to a decision: whether it should be acquired by an already existing public corporation or whether it should become a publicly traded corporation itself. For example, Myspace, another social media network, was acquired by News Corp in 2005. In 2006, it was rumored that Yahoo was planning to acquire Facebook, offering US$1 billion for the company. In the end, Facebook declined all the acquisition offers and started on its way to become its own publicly traded corporation.

Initial Public Offering

An *initial public offering* (*IPO*) is a process that allows a company to become a publicly traded corporation. Many start-up founders dream of the day their company can start trading on a stock exchange. It is a symbol of prestige and success, and it raises the public profile of a business. In addition to reputational benefits, an IPO has direct financial benefits as well. An IPO allows a corporation to raise large sums of funds at once to further finance its growth. The Facebook IPO, for example, raised US$16 billion. This is a very significant sum of money that allowed Facebook to expand globally, invest in internal development, and acquire outside technology and competitors, such as Instagram for US$1 billion, WhatsApp for US$19 billion, and Oculus VR for US$2 billion. Although an IPO raises significant sums of cash, the ownership is spread among millions of shareholders because the shares are open to the general public. This enables the original founders to maintain control over the company. If Facebook had raised that much capital in a private transaction from just a few investors, a lot of control over the company's Board of Directors would have shifted from Mark Zuckerberg to these new investors. With an IPO this is less likely to happen.

An IPO also creates *liquidity* in shares for founders, early employees, and early investors. They can now sell their shares on a stock exchange or buy additional shares from others. An IPO allows early angel investors to *cash out* and move on to identifying another start-up or an early-stage company. And, of course, an IPO creates permanent access to the capital markets for a corporation that it can use to raise additional cash, enables clear and objective valuation for mergers and acquisitions, and even eases access to other forms of financing such as debt financing. Finally, an IPO allows the establishment of a corporate governance structure that should make a corporation more accountable and more responsive to the shareholders, benefiting everyone at the company in the long run.

Once the company has finalized its decision to start the IPO process they will start to work with an *underwriter* or a group of underwriters. The underwriters are investment banks that help companies manage all aspects of the IPO process. Among the largest investments banks who have participated in recent underwritings are Credit Suisse, JP Morgan, Merrill Lynch, Morgan Stanley, and Goldman Sachs. The key function of the underwriter is to manage the actual sale of securities, including collecting orders from potential investors and managing the market by buying and selling securities as well – this process is known as *market stabilization*. This two-step process eliminates uncertainty from the offering for the company – it knows in advance how much stock it is selling, and it also allows the company and the under-writers to set the price in advance. As a result, the company also knows how much money it is raising in advance. Of course, the underwriters will often negotiate the price with a discount, and this is how underwriters make their profit: by buying the shares from the company at a discount and then reselling them to the investors at a higher price. Underwriters also issue the first research reports on the company – this allows investors to have research coverage on the new stock.

Before the shares can be offered to the public, however, the company must register its security offering with the United States Securities and Exchange Commission (SEC), following the 1933 Securities Act. The company files *Form S-1, registration statement* under the Securities Act of 1933. The main part of S-1 is called the *prospectus*. The prospectus consists of 12 items; each item focuses on a different type of information that is required to be disclosed by the company going public.

One of the key items is determination of the price. The company's management must explain how they arrived at the price of the stock they will be selling to the public through the underwriters. The company also must specify the total number and type of shares they will be offering; for example, would these be common shares or preferred shares? The prospectus must also disclose information about the underwriters and any agreements the company has made with the underwriters, as well as any information about the legal counsel or other advisers' involvement in the IPO. This information can help investors identify any conflicts of interest that may arise for the parties involved in the process. And, of course, the prospectus has information about the corporation itself – the company must describe its operations, its financial results, management's discussion and analysis of the company business, its future prospects, risks, and all other relevant information. This is done in order to enable investors to make an informed decision about purchasing the stock, and help investors estimate the fair value of the shares. See Figure 10.1 for the cover page of the Facebook S-1.

The underwriters are directly involved in drafting the prospectus. In fact, they may be liable for providing false or misleading information in the S-1. The process of developing a prospectus is called *due diligence*. Underwriters collect and analyze detailed information about every aspect of the company's operations. They also meet with the management to go over their questions to ensure they understand the company as well as, or even better, than the founders and top managers themselves. This is essential to establish a fair price of the stock for the offering. Pricing the shares too low may mean that the company and underwriters will leave a lot of money on the table, but pricing the stock too high may limit the number of investors interested in buying the shares, and the IPO could fail. Once the registration statement is prepared and approved by everybody involved, it is filed with the SEC and is made available to the public through the EDGAR (Electronic Data Gathering, Analysis, and Retrieval) system.

In preparation for an IPO, company insiders would usually sign a *lock-up agreement*. Such an agreement prohibits company employees who own shares in the company from selling those shares immediately after the company goes public. They can sell their shares, if desired, at a later date – most often lockups are set for 180 days, but other arrangements are also possible. This lock-up agreement is often required by an underwriter to ensure that no additional shares will hit the market and influence the price of the stock. If a founder owns half of the company stock, they could significantly influence the price if they decided to sell it all at once on the day of an IPO. This could

UNITED STATES
SECURITIES AND EXCHANGE COMMISSION
Washington, D.C. 20549

Form S-1
REGISTRATION STATEMENT
Under
The Securities Act of 1933

Facebook, Inc.
(Exact name of Registrant as specified in its charter)

Delaware	7370	20-1665019
(State or other jurisdiction of incorporation or organization)	(Primary Standard Industrial Classification Code Number)	(IRS Employer Identification No.)

Facebook, Inc.
1601 Willow Road
Menlo Park, California 94025
(650) 308-7300
(Address, including zip code, and telephone number, including area code, of Registrant's principal executive offices)

David A. Ebersman
Chief Financial Officer
Facebook, Inc.
1601 Willow Road
Menlo Park, California 94025
(650) 308-7300
(Name, address, including zip code, and telephone number, including area code, of agent for service)

Please send copies of all communications to:

Gordon K. Davidson, Esq.	Theodore W. Ullyot, Esq.	William H. Hinman, Jr., Esq.
Jeffrey R. Vetter, Esq.	David W. Kling, Esq.	Daniel N. Webb, Esq.
James D. Evans, Esq.	Michael L. Johnson, Esq.	Simpson Thacher & Bartlett LLP
Fenwick & West LLP	Facebook, Inc.	2550 Hanover Street
801 California Street	1601 Willow Road	Palo Alto, California 94304
Mountain View, California 94041	Menlo Park, California 94025	(650) 251-5000
(650) 988-8500	(650) 308-7300	

Approximate date of commencement of proposed sale to the public: As soon as practicable after the effective date of this Registration Statement.

If any of the securities being registered on this Form are to be offered on a delayed or continuous basis pursuant to Rule 415 under the Securities Act, check the following box: ☐

If this Form is filed to register additional securities for an offering pursuant to Rule 462(b) under the Securities Act, check the following box and list the Securities Act registration statement number of the earlier effective registration statement for the same offering. ☐

If this Form is a post-effective amendment filed pursuant to Rule 462(c) under the Securities Act, check the following box and list the Securities Act registration statement number of the earlier effective registration statement for the same offering. ☐

If this Form is a post-effective amendment filed pursuant to Rule 462(d) under the Securities Act, check the following box and list the Securities Act registration statement number of the earlier effective registration statement for the same offering. ☐

Indicate by check mark whether the registrant is a large accelerated filer, an accelerated filer, a non-accelerated filer, or a smaller reporting company. See the definitions of "large accelerated filer," "accelerated filer" and "smaller reporting company" in Rule 12b-2 of the Exchange Act. (Check one):

Large accelerated filer ☐		Accelerated filer ☐
Non-accelerated filer ☒	(Do not check if a smaller reporting company)	Smaller reporting company ☐

CALCULATION OF REGISTRATION FEE

Title of Each Class of Securities to be Registered	Proposed Maximum Aggregate Offering Price (1)(2)	Amount of Registration Fee
Class A Common Stock, $0.000006 par value	$5,000,000,000	$573,000

(1) Estimated solely for the purpose of calculating the amount of the registration fee in accordance with Rule 457(o) of the Securities Act of 1933, as amended.
(2) Includes shares that the underwriters have the option to purchase to cover over-allotments, if any.

Figure 10.1 *Facebook Form S-1. Source*: Facebook, Inc. Financial statements. Retrieved from: https://www.sec.gov/Archives/edgar/data/1326801/000119312512034517/d287954ds1.htm. Public Domain.

jeopardize the efforts of the investment banks to place the shares they have prepurchased. In addition, it may look very bad for the investors and potential investors if the founders of the company were to sell all or large chunks of their shares immediately – this could also push the share price down, hurting the company and the underwriters.

Another important step in preparing to go public is making a decision about the stock exchange where shares will be traded. In the United States, the choice is usually between the New York State Exchange (*NYSE*) and *Nasdaq*. NYSE is the largest stock exchange, with the total value of stocks trading at the exchange exceeding US$23 trillion. Its history dates back to May 17, 1792, when New York brokers signed the

Buttonwood agreement, which established trading rules for securities transactions. It is the most prestigious exchange for corporations to be listed at, and it has its own rules and regulations limiting listing opportunities only to the largest and most profitable corporations. For smaller companies, NYSE may be inaccessible.

Nasdaq is the second largest stock exchange in the world by capitalization, with almost US$11 trillion worth of stocks trading. In addition to NYSE and Nasdaq, many European companies prefer the London Stock Exchange, while Asian companies prefer Japan Exchange Group (a combination of the Tokyo Stock Exchange and Osaka Stock Exchange) or the Shanghai Stock Exchange.

An IPO also requires significant legal counsel as all the company's documents, such as the corporation charter, or articles of incorporation, need to be updated to be in compliance with rules and regulations for publicly traded corporations. Legal counsel is also needed to establish the new corporate governance procedures required for public companies. The corporation will be required to have an auditor to audit their financial statements. A Board of Directors with independent and diverse directors, various committees, a code of ethics, and many other elements required for the corporate governance process will have to be established. The legal counsel will also work with the company and the underwriters on the timeline of the events. For example, a company cannot discuss its IPO with any potential investors or analysts before filing the S-1. This is illegal activity known as *jumping the gun* or *gun-jumping* – when the corporation starts promoting its stock before receiving the SEC's approval. In the case of gun-jumping, the SEC may order a *cooling-off period* delaying the IPO. The SEC may also impose penalties on the corporation or the underwriter. Thus, the period leading to an IPO is a very tricky time for the company's management, and especially the communication professionals, such as investor relations and public relations officers. They may still have to report their financial results and discuss business successes or failures, but the SEC will be watching closely to ensure that they do not mention IPO in any way and do not say anything that goes beyond the usual disclosure practices that could be interpreted as trying to sell or influence the future sale of securities. Some corporations prefer to withdraw completely from media appearances or even limit their marketing activities for fear of committing gun-jumping violations.

After the S-1 is approved by the SEC, the company can start promoting its securities, issuing media releases, making top management available for media appearances, and communicating with prospective investors directly. Underwriters would typically organize a nonstop series of meetings between the company's management, including the investor relations officers (IROs), and potential buy-side. This series of meetings is called a *roadshow*. A roadshow is an extensive marketing event to promote the future stock offering. The event often involves hiring private jets, limousines, plush hotels, and visiting the leading financial centers of the world over the course of a week or two. Company executives may visit New York, Boston, Chicago, Los Angeles, Tokyo, Singapore, Hong Kong, Munich, London, and similar within a 10-day period. They would spend one day in each city, where underwriters would organize meetings for them with the buy-side, who may be interested in purchasing the shares when they become public. These are usually group meetings, but for the largest investors one-on-one meetings can be arranged. Spending all day in meetings, the company's management would retire to the plane at night to move to the next destination. A roadshow is usually a very formal business-like affair, but companies often inject their own spirit into the event. The Facebook IPO, for example, that kicked off at New York's

Sheraton Hotel was described as "less of a series of boardroom meetings and more of a traveling circus, complete with sideshows and a ringmaster, and newspaper men swarming the doors" (Donnelly, 2012). In fact, instead of the usual presentation slides with financial information, Facebook went for a video with Hollywood production values complete with a soundtrack. The video went far beyond the topic of Facebook itself and talked about the future vision of interconnectedness. The presentation was described as an advertisement, a commercial, and an infomercial rather than a financial disclosure.

For many investors, however, what the company presents is less important because all this information is already available in the prospectus. What buy-side and sell-side are interested in is the question-and-answer session. They want to hear from the company's leaders, they want to understand how convinced the management is about what they are saying, how they explain their vision, and what reasons they have to believe in their future success. As a shareholder, you become a company's owner and, thus, a CEO becomes your employee. So, it is not uncommon to compare those roadshows with job interviews – investors try to understand if they would like to work with a person like that CEO or CFO. In fact, during the Facebook IPO some investors were pretty upset with the 30-minute-long infomercial, and their feedback to the underwriters prompted Facebook to stop wasting time on the video and focus on the question-and-answer session instead. The video was promptly removed from the roadshow events.

The roadshow is the last big step in the IPO process. After the roadshow, the management meets with underwriters and finalizes all the details of the IPO. If the roadshow attracts lots of investors interested in the stock, the company may see it as an opportunity to raise the share price of the offering. For example, before the roadshow Facebook initially set the IPO target at between US$28 and US$35 per share. However, when underwriters noted strong demand for the stock, Facebook increased the amount of shares available for the IPO by 25% and also raised the price per share to US$38. Some suggested that the Facebook IPO price was artificially inflated – 60 days after the IPO the stock price declined to almost US$20 per share.

Whatever final changes are made to the stock offering, underwriters and the management must update and finalize the S-1 with the SEC. This is known as the *final prospectus*. There may be important changes in the final version; thus, the whole IPO team – management, underwriters, the legal team – gets together again to make sure everything is correct and appropriate in the document. The company is then ready to be a publicly traded corporation and the date for the IPO is set. A popular tradition at many stock exchanges is that on the first day of trading a member of the company's management team gets to ring the opening or closing bell – this is when the IPO becomes real and all the efforts invested in the process finally pay off. Mark Zuckerberg rang the Nasdaq opening bell on Friday, May 18, 2012.

Companies raised over US$80 billion at NYSE alone in 2020 through the IPO process. In 2021, NYSE also had one of the largest singular IPOs in recent years. This was a non-US IPO by the South Korean company Kupang that raised US$4.6 billion. Many describe Kupang as South Korean Amazon and the total valuation of the company was estimated at US$85 billion. These examples indicate that the IPO market is still quite active, and many companies still strive to achieve an IPO as a culmination of their corporate trajectory.

Follow-on Public Offering

Although IPOs usually get all the attention, public companies can issue additional shares after an IPO as well. These are called a *subsequent offering*, or *seasoned issue*, or *follow-on public offering* (*FPO*). The process typically also involves the underwriter bank or a group of underwriters working with the publicly traded company to sell an additional offering of securities. Since the company is already public and the shares are already trading, it is usually an easier and faster process – all the legal matters are usually in place, corporate governance structures and processes are already working, disclosures are already being filed, and the stock price is already established in the stock market.

Company management, nevertheless, together with the underwriters would typically engage in roadshow activities. It is important to communicate to investors why this additional offering is needed. Investors may be wary that the reason the company is asking for money again is because it is simply running out of money and not performing well – this may create panic and force a sell-off among investors. Thus, it is important for the management to clearly communicate the reasons for and the positive aspects of the FPO. For example, a new opportunity may exist in the industry that the company can capitalize on or a potential target for acquisition may exist that may help generate good returns on the investment.

American Depositary Receipt

The US capital market draws companies from all over the world. Since this is the largest capital market in the world, it gives access to the largest financial resources, many different investors, and, as a result, lowers the cost of capital for the company. For foreign corporations, however, it may be a challenge to issue their shares in the United States. They may have shares already trading on their local stock exchange. For example, Gazprom, a large Russian natural gas corporation, has its shares trading at Moscow Exchange (MOEX). MOEX, however, is a tiny exchange and, as a result, the ability to raise capital at MOEX is very limited. In addition, large multinational investors may not have access to trading at MOEX. International investors may be wary of learning the process of how to register and transfer securities in other markets, such as Russia, which can be quite different from the United States. Finally, the securities in other markets are usually traded in local currency, which adds to the complexity and confusion; for example, one share of Gazprom is worth 219 rubles at the time of writing at MOEX.

As a result, in order to get access to multinational capital, Gazprom has to make its shares more accessible to foreign investors. One of the most popular instruments to create such access is the *American depositary receipt* (*ADR*). The foundation of the ADR is a bank that guarantees the ADR program. One of the leading ADR providers is the Bank of New York Mellon (BNY Mellon). BNY Mellon would typically secure a certain number of shares of a foreign company, for example, one million shares, and store them in a depositary in the foreign market where the corporation is headquartered and the shares are normally trading. BNY Mellon may use a local bank as a partner for this. Once the agreed-upon amount of shares is secured, the bank issues the corresponding amount of ADRs in the US market – each ADR usually represents one share (but not always!) – as a result, in this example one million ADRs would be issued on the US market.

These ADRs can be freely traded in the United States just like other US securities, using the dollar denomination and following US laws and regulations. Gazprom ADRs, for example, are trading in the United States at US\$5.80 as of the time of writing. The bank issuing the ADRs will continue to serve as the guarantor that there are still underlying shares representing those ADRs. The bank can also facilitate the process of transfer of ADRs back into shares, or shares into ADRs, to enable seamless cross-border trading in securities.

There are many ADRs being traded in the United States. Among the largest ADRs are Alibaba (ADRs traded at NYSE), Toyota (NYSE), Shell (NYSE), Sony (NYSE), AstraZeneca (Nasdaq), and many more. Of course, these companies' stock is also trading at their domestic stock exchanges (with some exceptions); for example, Sony is also trading at its "home" stock exchange in Japan – the Tokyo Stock Exchange. ADRs will be discussed further in Chapter 12.

Direct Listing

Of course, an IPO is not the only way for a company to raise capital. One of the other options is *direct listing*. During the direct listing process instead of raising new capital through an investment bank by selling newly issued shares of the company as in the IPO process, the company owners sell their already existing shares directly to the public without any investment bank involvement. For example, the founder of a start-up company may decide to sell 50% of their shares to the public on a stock exchange as part of a direct listing. A direct listing still requires the company to acquire a publicly traded status and complete the registration process with the SEC. The company also needs to have its shares listed on a stock exchange if it is looking to become a listed company. But there is no new underwritten offer of securities involved. As a result, the company itself gets no money at all. The only people who can sell the shares are those who already have shares – founders, early employees who were awarded with stock, or early investors. They can now sell their shares and make money from the transaction.

Recently, a music giant, Spotify, went down the route of direct listing successfully by turning itself into a multi-billion dollar public company trading at NYSE without going through the IPO process. Since everybody knows and understand what Spotify does, it did not really need to invest in an elaborate roadshow to explain its business. It also did not really need to raise additional money since the company generates cash flow from its millions of subscribers every single month. The company also does not anticipate any significant investment needs on the horizon. The trading was set to open at US\$132 per share – the stock was up to US\$149.01 by the end of the first day with a daily high of US\$169.50, indicating a successful direct listing and giving the company the overall valuation of over US\$26 billion. Now anybody can buy and sell shares of Spotify.

In March 2021, Roblox, a popular gaming platform, also conducted a direct listing on NYSE. The trading began on March 10 and, at the end of the first day, the Roblox share price closed at US\$69.50. This gave the company the overall market capitalization of

US$38 billion – significantly higher than its last valuation as a private company of US$29.5 billion. It is typical for a company to gain a few billion dollars in valuation during the transition from private to public status because the company significantly expands its access to investors and its investor base.

Private Listing

Another option available to companies that do not want to engage in the IPO process is a *private listing*. This is a way to raise new capital by selling shares of the company just to specific investors instead of making them available to the general public. This option is popular among many foreign companies looking to enter the US financial markets and to attract US-based investors but who may be uncomfortable with all the disclosure and reporting requirements imposed on companies that are publicly traded in the United States. These companies would typically rely on *Rule 144A* that allows the placement of securities privately with *qualified institutional buyers* (QIBs). This is a win–win situation for the companies and the professional investment community. Smaller foreign companies get access to the capital that allows them to grow and develop until they are large enough to be able to afford to become public. On the other hand, investors can gain access to new technologies and new business ideas at the early stages when they are still affordable; thus, potentially increasing their future return on investment.

In addition, the SEC can successfully claim that it has fulfilled its responsibilities because the idea behind many financial rules and regulations is the protection of small investors so that investors will not lose their life savings to fraudulent activities on the stock market. Since Rule 144A private placements are limited to QIBs only, large sophisticated investors such as banks, hedge funds, investment companies, insurance companies, and so on with millions of dollars under their control, there is less of a risk of them being deceived by financial con artists. QIBs are stock market professionals with hefty budgets, resources, and the expertise to conduct their own due diligence and ensure the legitimacy and safety of their investments – and all for the chance of a bigger pay-off in the future.

Special Purpose Acquisition Company

Finally, another alternative to an IPO is a *special purpose acquisition company (SPAC)*. A SPAC is put together with the goal of raising money in order to purchase a company that later can start trading publicly. In other words, it may look like a delayed, or a two-step, IPO. Another difference is the fact that IPOs, private placements, and direct listings are driven by the company itself, but SPACs are typically led by an investor or a group of investors (although not always). SPAC shares can be traded in the same way as shares of a corporation and when the time is right the SPAC manager may use all the cash raised from selling SPAC shares to acquire a particular company. Traditionally, a SPAC would be created in order to acquire a specific company, hence the "special purpose" in the name. For example, if there is a private company in existence, let's call it Company X, a group of investors may announce the creation of a SPAC to acquire this company. They will make the information public and invite others to buy SPAC shares in order to accumulate funds to acquire Company X. After enough money is raised, the SPAC will buy Company X, the SPAC is liquidated, and investors convert their SPAC shares to shares in Company X.

Recently, however, it is becoming more common to have a SPAC without a special target for an acquisition. Investors may announce a SPAC and start raising money before they even know what the future acquisition target is. Such a SPAC is called a *blank check company* – people give the SPAC money to do whatever the SPAC managers want to do with it. For example, recently a SPAC named Pershing Square Tontine Holdings, led by famous CEO and activist investor Bill Ackman, raised US$4 billion without ever having a particular company in mind to invest in. Why have people given their money to Mr. Ackman without any knowledge of what the money is going to be used for? As many investors commented on social media, it is their chance to get rich by aligning their interests with the interests of the rich and famous investor! Mr. Ackman himself said that although he was not sure what the target for his SPAC would be, he would choose a real "unicorn," fueling everyone's expectations even more. In the end, the target may be a family-owned business with a proven track record or a new start-up in its early stages with no track record at all but great potential; nobody knows what the final target will be and all these investments are based on nothing more than the reputation of Mr. Ackman.

Since SPACs may be based on nothing but the name of the leader, in recent years it has also become popular for celebrities to start SPACs. While willingness to invest in a SPAC created by a professional investor who has a proven track record of making money on a stock market can be explained by previous investment successes, SPACs built by celebrities often have nothing but big personalities behind them. Among the celebrities involved with SPACs are Jay-Z, Alex Rodriguez, and Serena Williams. Of course, in many cases these celebrities are not the ones running the show but rather they are the faces of those SPACs – not that different from celebrity endorsements of sneakers or cars. Recently, an article in *The New York Times* about SPACs was published in the *Style* section of the newspaper rather than the *Business* section and quoted a Wall Street professional exclaiming: "I can't believe we haven't seen a Kim Kardashian SPAC yet" (Kurutz, 2021). As the SPAC mania has reached new heights, the SEC Office of Investor Education and Advocacy has had to issue guidance to investors in March 2021 cautioning people not to make investment decisions based solely on the celebrity involved with the SPAC. Despite all the warnings, SPACs are growing in popularity and more and more investors, including retail investors, are trying them out. This, of course, may lead to a bubble collapse and lost investments, but, as always, a lucky few are destined to make it big.

Going Private

Once an organization becomes a publicly traded corporation and lists its shares on a stock exchange, it has to follow specific rules and regulations in order to maintain its public status. If the corporation fails to follow all the regulation or stops meeting the requirements of the particular exchange, shares of the company can be removed from the stock exchange – this process is known as *delisting*. NYSE and Nasdaq require the price of the company's share to be above US$4 when the company starts trading. If the price, however, declines, going below US$1, NYSE and Nasdaq can first suspend trading in the stock and then delist it if the price remains below US$1 for 30 days. The exchanges do not want to be associated with so-called *penny stocks* as they typically do not have enough trading volume, lack research coverage, and their prices can fluctuate greatly. Since an exchange lends its reputation to the stocks trading on it, stock exchanges prefer to deal with well-established high-quality stocks.

On January 3, 2012, for example, NYSE notified Kodak that its shares had been trading below US$1 for the last 30 consecutive days and, as a result, Kodak shares may be delisted from the exchange. This news, in addition to poor financial results over the past several years, finally pushed Kodak to declare bankruptcy on January 19, 2012, and the stock of what once was among the largest US corporations was delisted.

In addition to the minimum share price, exchanges typically have rules about minimum numbers of shares available for trading, overall market capitalization, average trading volume for each type of security, and number of shareholders owning the stock. Nasdaq requires listed companies to have at least 1.1 million shares publicly available for trading and the market capitalization of the company should not fall below US$8 million.

The company may also request to voluntarily delist its shares from a stock exchange. There may be many reasons for such a request. The company may go through bankruptcy or termination, the company may be merged with or acquired by another company, the company may decide to become a private company, or the company may remain a publicly traded company but not be listed on any stock exchanges. Even after being removed from the stock exchange, the company shares can still be traded off the exchange on the so-called *over-the-counter market* (*OTC*). OTC transactions are done on the bulletin boards that were created specifically to regulate the trading in stocks not listed on any stock exchanges. OTC transactions enable smaller companies to raise capital in order to expand and grow, and it gives investors a chance to invest in the firms of their choice. It is estimated that about 10,000 shares are traded on the OTC market.

OTC markets also have a structure based on the level of risk involved. *OTCQX* is the trading platform for less risky, high-quality stocks. There are fewer than 500 companies trading on OTCQX, including Roche, a pharmaceutical company, and Publicis, one of the top strategic communication conglomerates. *OTCQB* has fewer requirements in terms of financial results, corporate governance, and disclosure practices. It is designed for start-ups and is often called the *venture market*. There are about 1,000 companies trading on OTCQB. One of the key requirements of OTCQB is that the price of the stock cannot be zero – it should not fall below US$0.01. Finally, all other stocks are traded at the so-called *Pink Sheets*, or the *Pink Open Market*. This is where brokers can trade pretty much any securities, even including the ones in bankruptcy proceedings or that do not disclose information to the SEC. Trading at Pink Sheets involves the most risk, but potentially can generate significant rewards as well if an investors finds a company destined for future success.

Delisting in itself does not stop the company from being publicly traded, but a corporation can also *deregister* its public traded securities and go private. Becoming a private firm typically eliminates the requirements for periodic disclosure and many corporate governance procedures. In general, in order to deregister securities the company must have no more than 300 shareholders. All the corporation has to do is to file a *Form 15, certification and notice of termination of registration*, with the SEC. One of the key explanations cited by companies going private is the time and monetary expenses related to corporate governance and disclosure requirements – preparing financial statements, hiring an auditing company to verify the accuracy of the statements, involving legal counsel in management discussion and analysis of the results, being available for investors and financial analysts, and so on. For smaller companies, these expenses may be too burdensome.

Another reason to take the company private is to avoid corporate governance procedures and the control of shareholders and the Board of Directors. This may be very important for a company in crisis when quick decision making is important. For example, Michael Dell is often credited with saving Dell by taking it private. Dell sales and revenues were below expectations in 2012, and the share price declined reflecting poor performance. Yet, making big and strategic changes would require approval from the Board of Directors and shareholders of the company. Michael Dell decided, instead, to buy out the shareholders, offering them US$13.75 per share and US$0.13 per share as the final dividend payment. Making Dell private allowed the founder and the CEO of the company to acquire another company, EMC, for US$67 billion, which, at the time, was the largest acquisition in the technology industry. It is unlikely that the shareholders would have approved such an acquisition by a struggling corporation if Dell was still publicly traded.

As a private company, however, Dell did not need anybody's approval! The acquisition turned out to be a profitable success – five years after the buyout the value of Dell increased to US$70 billion – triple the pre-buyout valuation. On the other hand, as a private company, Dell had to finance its growth with debt, borrowing more than US$50 billion. As a result, in 2018 Michael Dell announced plans to make the company public again to attract shareholders' money and pay off some of the debt it incurred as a private entity. In December 2018 Dell became a publicly traded corporation once again with shares listed at NYSE. Its 2020 revenues exceeded US$92 billion, and the share price is over US$100 per share as of 2021. Overall, the maneuver of taking Dell private seems to have been an enormous success.

A company can also be acquired by another corporation and, as a result, cease to exist as a standalone publicly traded corporation. The shareholders in the company being liquidated may receive cash for their shares or they may receive stock in the acquiring company. For example, when T-Mobile acquired Sprint, Sprint ceased to exist as an independent company and shares of Sprint were liquidated. For each share they owned Sprint shareholders received 0.10256 of T-Mobile stock.

Key Terms

ADR
American depositary receipt
Angel funding
Angel investment
Angel investor
Blank check company
Buttonwood agreement
Cash out

Certification and notice of termination of registration
Cooling-off period
Delisting
Deregistration
Direct listing
Due diligence
EDGAR
Final prospectus
Follow-on public offering
Form 15
Form S-1
FPO
Going public
Gun-jumping
Initial public offering
IPO
Jumping the gun
Liquidity
Lock-up agreement
Market stabilization
Nasdaq
NYSE
OTC
OTCQB
OTCQX
Over-the-counter market
Penny stock
Pink Open Market
Pink Sheets
Private company
Private listing
Prospectus
Public company
QIB
Qualified institutional buyers
Registration statement
Roadshow
Rule 144A
Seasoned issue
Seed investment
SPAC
Special purpose acquisition company
Start-up
Subsequent offering
Underwriter
Venture capitalist
Venture market

Discussion Questions and Activities

1 Compare IPOs with the alternative ways to raise capital and attract investors. What are the benefits and drawbacks of each? Thinking of SPACs, specifically, why do you think they are growing in popularity recently?
2 Explain what Rule 144A is. What are the main benefits and limitations of using Rule 144A? Discuss why the United States has this rule? Would you recommend keeping it or eliminating it?
3 Why would publicly traded companies decide to go back to being private? What are the main benefits and drawbacks? What is the process of going private?
4 Review Facebook's Form S-1, which can be found in EDGAR. Discuss key components of the prospectus and explain how they could help an investor make an informed decision about the investment. Compare Facebook's predictions about its future business with the current realities of the social network.
5 Identify a company that went public in the United States last year. Find its prospectus. Analyze the information in the prospectus and try to predict based on that information how the company's stock is doing in the market. Compare your prediction with what the stock actually experienced over the past year.

11

Measurement and Evaluation of Investor Relations and Financial Communication

Measurement and evaluation is an often-debated topic in investor relations and financial communication. Yet, despite all this attention, measurement and evaluation remains an elusive target – there is still no universal acceptance or even agreement on how best to perform it. Most company managers or agency clients actually demand greater accountability and would benefit from improvements in measurement and evaluation.

Investor relations is not alone in this struggle. Management, marketing, public relations, and many other disciplines find it difficult to come up with uniformly agreed upon evaluation approaches. To make matters worse, this challenge of developing a reliable evaluation solution is occurring at the same time as an ever-growing pressure for accountability. This leaves practitioners and managers unhappy about the state of evaluation.

In the past, some practitioners have claimed that investor relations simply cannot and should not be measured, providing a whole laundry list of reasons – the effects of investor relations activities may not be observable at all, the effects may be observable but only indirectly or may demonstrate themselves years later (as with changes in reputation, for example), the effects cannot be isolated from other influences, the effects are qualitative, the effects cannot be quantified, and so on. Others have suggested that because of all of these limitations the measure should be a bottom-line measure that takes all the influences into account at once, like, for instance, *return on investment* (*ROI*). For example, Laskin (2016b) proposed an approach similar to ROI and labeled it *return on communication* (ROC). Such approaches are referred to as the *magic bullet* because they focus on finding one magic solution that can solve all the problems; however, this ignores the fact that return on investor relations itself can be defined in many different ways, some of which are out of the control of investor relations officers (IROs).

Yet, there are also practitioners who believe that the magic bullet for measuring investor relations is the share price. They claim that share price should be the main indicator of investor relations success because stock valuation is the IROs' goal according to the investor relations definition. Ragas et al. (2014) note, however, "it is difficult to establish a direct causal link between investor relations and company's share price" (p. 179). A study by Laskin (2011) also notes that "other metrics, such as earnings growth, profitability, management credibility, and others" (p. 310) drive

Investor Relations and Financial Communication: Creating Value Through Trust and Understanding, First Edition. Alexander V. Laskin.

stock prices to a larger extent than anything that IROs can do. So, it is not surprising that in a survey of National Investor Relations Institute (NIRI) members, 87% of IROs said that share price was not a valid measure of the investor relations performance as this metric is mainly out of the IROs' control.

Despite all these challenges, investor relations and financial communication activities must be measured. A typical large- and mega-cap US public company spends more than US$1 million on investor relations a year. At the very minimum, IROs are expected to demonstrate the effectiveness of these investments and demonstrate the results of their activities. Instead of looking for one magic measure, however, measuring investor relations can be achieved through a *standard operating procedures (SOP)* approach – a certain protocol, or a step-by-step guide to the measurement, conducted using a variety of interrelated metrics. Recent research has shown that many IROs believe that the best way to measure their work is with a combination of metrics, including quantitative, qualitative, and mixed-method measures. Thus, an approach that organizes, categorizes, and standardizes a variety of metrics is most likely to succeed.

Levels of Evaluation: the Model

The diverse communication metrics can, in fact, be organized into a standardized system of measurement and evaluation. This approach, labeled *Levels of Evaluation*, allows for variability of specific metrics while still presenting a unified structure of measurement. This approach also allows measurements to be taken at various stages of progression: from the actual activities of the investor relations professionals to the final bottom-line measures impacting the whole organization.

This standardized hierarchical structure can be applied across contexts and organizations in a similar way to the SOP approach. At the same time, the Levels of Evaluation model does not limit the variety of activities that can be measured. Instead, levels of evaluation define the hierarchy of levels at which any campaign should be evaluated, while the actual activities at each of these levels can vary across clients and campaigns.

The Levels of Evaluation approach consists of five hierarchical levels: each of the levels measures the effects of investor relations and financial communication efforts from the start, what IROs are actually doing, through intermediaries such as financial analyst coverage or business media reporting, to the effects on the target audiences, for example, changes in awareness, attitude, or intended behavior of investors and prospective investors; to the organizational results, for instance, changes in share price or trading volume; and, finally, to the effects of the whole economy. The initial level is labeled *Output*; the intermediary level is *Outreach*; the target audience level is *Outcome*; this business results level is *Outgrowth*; and the economy level is *Outperform*. These steps are presented in Figure 11.1: from an initial idea to the actual changes in the client's competitive environment. Each of the levels requires measurements to be taken among different publics/environments: the first level, Output, is a measure of productivity, so the measure focuses on the corporate professionals' efforts – investor relations, public relations, CFO, etc. The second level, Outreach, is a measure of how far the message was able to reach in the media, on the Internet, or among opinion leaders;

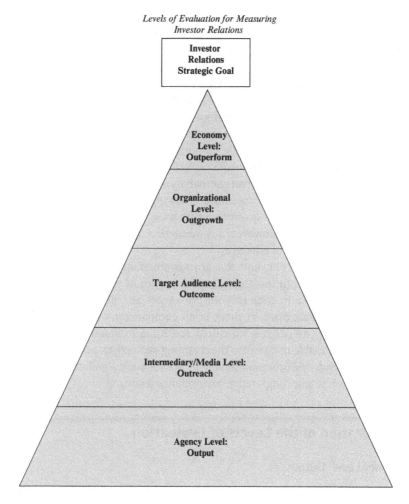

Levels of Evaluation for Measuring Investor Relations

Investor Relations Strategic Goal

Economy Level: Outperform

Organizational Level: Outgrowth

Target Audience Level: Outcome

Intermediary/Media Level: Outreach

Agency Level: Output

Figure 11.1 Levels of Evaluation model.

thus, the intermediary publics are measured. The third level, Outcome, measures outcomes among the target audiences and, as a result, the measures focus on the target audiences' awareness, knowledge, attitude, and intended behavior. The fourth level, Outgrowth, looks at the organizational results; thus, the focus is on the organization's share price or shareholder mix. Finally, the fifth level, Outperform, puts the results of all the work into the context of the overall economic environment in which the company operates, and compares the investor relations results with the performance of competitors and similar companies.

Finally, the *Levels of Evaluation* model always focuses on the organizational goal: it starts with the goal and ends with measuring how the campaign helped to achieve this goal. Although it cannot prove a definite causal relationship between measures taken at the Output level and the campaign's final results, for example, improved stock appreciation, presenting the client or the CEO with the quantitative and qualitative results for each level of evaluation can help the agency or internal department build this connection between investor relations and organizational results.

Furthermore, *Levels of Evaluation* can also serve as a financial communication development and monitoring tool; for example, having *Levels of Evaluation* as part of the campaign's pitch builds the connection between financial communication activities and organizational goals and objectives from the early planning stages, thus making IROs' work more proactive, strategic, and relevant to the organization's overall mission.

The model does not take a stand on what is the best way to measure each of the levels. Indeed, a campaign to increase analyst coverage by a small-cap company would require completely different measures than a campaign aimed at increasing retail ownership of a stock by a technology corporation. The same is true for different campaign delivery methods: social media campaigns will use different metrics at the agency or the intermediary levels than campaigns using traditional media. Yet, results for all of these campaigns can be organized following the *Levels of Evaluation* model. Some campaigns would require quantitative metrics; for others qualitative measures would be more appropriate. However, a combination of quantitative and qualitative metrics is likely to be the most effective.

Michaelson and Stacks (2011) note that any system of measurement and evaluation must allow for gauging both the absolute performance of specific programs and the comparative performance in contrast with prior years and/or competitive programs. However, without standardization there is no comparison – if every organization, every industry, every campaign is measured according to unique proprietary guide-lines, then it is impossible to compare them among each other. So, standardization is important. The *Levels of Evaluation* model allows for such standardization and thus enables both absolute and comparative performance measures.

The Application of the Levels of Evaluation

IRO/Agency Level: Output

Every financial communication campaign is based on the actions that an agency or an internal department performs in order to achieve the objectives of the campaign. Investor relations activities can include sending out news releases, preparing required filings, such as 10-K or 10-Q, organizing special events, roadshows, building relationships with finan-cial analysts, sell-side and buy-side representatives, designing online presence, and so on. Each of these activities may require significant efforts on the part of the investor relations staff and commitment of resources. Thus, the first step is to measure and demonstrate the actual work involved in all of this – in other words, the output of the production.

Thus, the focus of this level is the investor relations agency or IR department itself and what it produces – the output of their efforts. The actual metrics can vary based on the current objectives. It is possible, of course, to present clients or supervisors with an actual count of what was produced: for example, 30 news releases were written, or 50 phone calls with analysts were conducted, or 150 tweets were posted. More often, agencies use the hourly method, presenting the client with the amount of hours dedi-cated to working on their account with each hour being billed at a predetermined rate.

It is also possible to narrow down the measurement: one news release is not always equal to another. One can be 400 words while another can go over 1,000 words, thus word count produced on behalf of the client can be measured. Qualitative measures can also be incorporated; for example, some news releases can be about the quarterly results, some about the corporate structure, and some about new research and development. Specific measures should be selected to best reflect the work of the investor relations professionals.

No matter what measures are used, what is important is that the agency can present to the client what work has been done on their behalf or the investor relations department employees can present to the CEO what efforts were invested in supporting the function. This level becomes the foundation that all other levels of evaluation are built upon, because here is where the staff has the most control and, as a result, this becomes the foundation for evaluating the success of the investor relations contribution. Indeed, a campaign aimed at an increase in analyst coverage can fall short of its goal because of a lack of communications produced or because of a general economic downturn in a particular country or sector. Without looking at the actual work produced by the investor relations agency or department, evaluation won't be able to answer this question. Measuring the output can help better understand the answer to what went right and what went wrong, and what should be done next.

Intermediary/Media Level: Outreach

All the efforts investor relations professionals put into a campaign mean nothing if the outputs of their work do not go anywhere beyond their departments. The goal of many investor relations efforts is communicating a message to the target stakeholders and in order to reach these target audiences IROs usually rely on *intermediaries*: sell-side, mass media, websites, social media, opinion leaders, and so on. Thus, the second level of evaluation focuses on the intermediaries and the channels of communications to measure how far and wide the produced message was able to reach.

For example, when talking about the first level, Output, we can note that the agency produced 30 news releases on behalf of the client, but let's say only five of these releases were actually picked up and published in the financial media. Then, when measuring the intermediary level, Outreach, the agency would report that five news releases were published.

Once again, the actual measures may differ as long as they focus on the intermediaries. Instead of the number of news releases picked up, one could measure the readership of *The Financial Times* or *Barron's* where the stories were published. In addition, different media outlets have different readers – a client may be more interested in *The Wall Street Journal* than *The New York Times*. Thus, measures of circulation and measures of readership/viewership can and should be incorporated during the measurement and evaluation at the Outreach level.

The intermediary measures can apply to owned media, such as the company's website, or social media, such as Facebook or Twitter – how many people saw the message, read it, commented, and retweeted/reshared, who those people were, how far they spread the message, and whether the message reached the right audiences. And, of course, these measures apply to the research coverage about the company.

Qualitative measures may and should also be used. For example, the stories that appear in the media can be positive, negative, or neutral; they can briefly mention the client or focus on the client exclusively. A sell-side research report with a strong buy recommendation would have a very different effect on the company than a sell-side report with a strong sell recommendation. In other words, these qualitative measures can significantly enhance the relevance and accuracy of the measurements at the intermediary level.

Target Audience Level: Outcome

Having a news release on the topic important to a client prepared and published in an appropriate outlet is not sufficient, however. In order to call an effort successful, at a minimum this message should actually produce an effect on the *target audience*. Thus, the target audience level measures the effects of the campaign on stakeholders. Instead of the reach of the intermediaries, the actual stakeholders must be measured in terms of whether they have become aware of the message, understood the message, developed an intended attitude toward the message, and, in fact, now plan on acting in response to this message. In other words, what was the outcome of the investor relations efforts?

Indeed, placing a message in a business publication or having a financial analyst write a report about a stock does not guarantee that a member of the target audience, an investor, will actually receive the message. So, here, we move from measuring the intermediaries to measuring the actual target audience.

Measures of the target audience can be based on *awareness*. If our goal was to increase institutional ownership of our stock, institutional investors would be a proper target audience for our campaign, and, as a result, we would want to know if the target audience became aware of our stock at the end of the campaign.

But simply knowing about the stock is not enough – we also want to measure the *comprehension* – if the target audience understands what is unique about the stock, how we are different from our competitors, and what our investment story is. However, even knowing all this does not guarantee that members of the target audience will actually want to invest. Thus, measures of *attitude* should be used at the Outcome level – is there a perception that our stock is a good investment choice for a particular shareholder? Finally, despite knowing, understanding, and liking the stock, a member of the target audience still may not take the actual final step of investing for a variety of reasons.

Thus, another important measure is the *intent to act*. Indeed, there is little value in making sure the target audience is aware of the stock, knows all about it, and likes it, if, at the end of the day, they do not wish to buy it. Thus, when conducting a perception audit or other shareholder research, IROs should study awareness, comprehension, attitude, and the intentions of current and prospective shareholders. Even then, intending to purchase something and actually purchasing it are two very different things, but the actual purchases will be discussed at the higher level of evaluation because to measure the actual purchases we would need to go beyond the target audience measures.

Organizational Results Level: Outgrowth

As already mentioned earlier, the clients are interested in actual business results, which for IROs often means share price, trading volume, shareholder mix, and similar. Thus, the organizational results level moves away from measurement of the target audiences and focuses on measuring the organization. Instead of measuring intention to purchase among target publics we measure the actual stock movements: who purchased the stock, who sold the stock, we analyze all the stock movements, changes in the stock price, and so on. This level evaluates what actually grew out of the seeds of the campaign and what return was generated in the end.

Again, the specific metrics can vary based on the goals of the campaign – in the case of increasing the share of foreign investors, the result could be global diversification of the corporation's overall shareholder base; in the case of conducting an initial public offering (IPO), the final result most likely will be an amount raised during that IPO; and in the case of shareholder activism, it may be withdrawal of the activist's proposal.

Industry Level: Outperform

The final level of evaluation goes one step above the organization and measures the whole economic environment in which the organization operates. For example, for an automaker the sales could go up as a result of overall economic recovery or go down as a result of an economic downturn, no matter whether a specific marketing campaign was successful or unsuccessful. It is possible to have an increase in car sales simply because people have more disposable income and more consumer confidence, and thus they buy more cars across the board not just that particular car brand. Thus, this increase in sales will have nothing to do with the campaign efforts but rather is connected to the state of the economy. Sales could also be decreasing across the board in the industry because of an economic downturn or technological changes. If campaign evaluation measures were limited only to the first four stages, it would be impossible to identify the influence of factors outside of the organization's control. Thus, adding the fifth level allows communication professionals to capture this important information.

The same is true for investor relations. The overall economic forces have a very strong influence on the performance of a publicly traded corporation's stock. As a result, an outstanding IPO with excellent investor relations support could be disadvantaged by a negative economic event occurring at the same time. And, conversely, incompetent investor relations efforts may be masked by a fast-growing market lifting all stocks.

Looking at the overall economy and the company's competitors can help identify if the industry is growing or declining as a whole, which competitors are growing and which competitors are declining and why. As a result, we can see the changes in the client's market share. In this situation, a successful campaign can help make the growth larger than that of their competitors or could result in a smaller downturn in comparison with their competitors. As a result, looking at the overall economic environment during evaluation makes the measurement more valid and more reliable.

Again, the actual metrics can vary and include share price movements and trading volume versus similar companies and the industry, as well as comparisons against overall stock indicators, like the Standard and Poor's 500 (S&P 500), changes in the market share, analyst coverage for similar companies, and so on. Once again, it is important to supplement these metrics with qualitative measures and identify the reasons for changes in the economy, and how they affect the organization and its investor relations efforts.

Strategic Goal

The key advantage of the Levels of Evaluation approach is its ability to build connections between what the investor relations departments or the financial communication agencies do and the overall strategic goal of the organization. IROs cannot prove the causal connection with absolute certainty but showing how their efforts affected the results at different levels helps them make a reasonable claim and present the evidence to the C-suite.

Still, the most important part of any strategic campaign effort is focusing on the goal that advances the organizational mission. For investor relations strategic campaigns, there are four goals that IROs typically focus on: *share price, trading volume, analyst coverage*, and *shareholder mix*. The price of stock depends on a lot of factors: the company's business model, recent financial and operational results, the expectations of shareholders, the overall health of the economy, and so on. The role of investor relations in the share price is small at best, but important nevertheless. Since IROs are responsible for helping investors and analysts understand the company's value through disclosure and education, it is the job of the investor relations professionals to position the current results in the context of the larger long-term mission of the company. This is sometimes called *framing the results*, but the word framing often carries negative connotations as it may sound misleading and manipulative.

IROs work to reduce uncertainty of investors about the company. The lower the uncertainty, the lower the risk premium investors demand for buying the stock. Effective investor relations can also lead to fuller appreciation of the company's value through better understanding of its current and future business. Overall, this can lower the cost of capital and lead to fair valuation of the share price. It is still vital for investor relations professionals to clearly communicate to the C-suite that they are not responsible for share price going up or down as these changes depend primarily on the company's performance, but, for example, if the share price is going down while the company is performing exceptionally well, this may deserve careful consideration from an investor relations standpoint.

Trading volume, or *stock liquidity*, is also a common metric for investor relations. If the financial community does not know about the stock, they cannot invest in it. Thus, reaching out to investors and building awareness about the stock is an important target for IROs to increase interest in the stock and, ultimately, lead to more trading. Once again, however, it is impossible to establish a direct link between investor relations and liquidity, and this, of course, may complicate using liquidity as a metric for evaluating investor relations activities. A large mega-cap company is likely to attract more investors and more liquidity than a small company no matter how advanced and sophisticated the investor relations department is at the smaller company. Many investors have specific restrictions on the company's size or where it is listed; as a result, investing or not investing in a particular stock may not always be influenced by investor relations efforts. And, of course, underlying performance is also the foundation for liquidity – when a company performs well and has a great potential for growth, investors want to buy its stock; without performance, it is unlikely that investor relations could do much on its own. Separating performance from communications about this performance for the purpose of investor relations evaluation can prove to be a difficult task.

For mid-size and small companies, gaining and expanding on analyst coverage is also a common measure of success for investor relations. The coverage can be measured in more than one way: quantitative metrics, such as how many analysts cover the company, how many reports they produce, how often the company is mentioned, or even page volume of analysts' coverage dedicated to the company, can be supplemented with qualitative measures, such as what is the accuracy of coverage, how much it follows the company's talking points, tone and valence of coverage, and, finally, the overall recommendation given. On the other hand, many executives consider an analysts' coverage an intermediary measure and not the end goal for investor relations. In the same way as marketing should not be evaluated by media metrics and should focus, instead, on final sale numbers, investor relations should also focus on organizational results. Analysts' coverage has no value in itself but rather serves the purpose of improving share price, liquidity, and whatever other indicators are important for the organization. Financial analysts' reports are one of many communication channels available to the investor relations professionals to deliver a company message. They can be used in some situations, but in others other channels can be used instead, when appropriate. Another issue with analysts' coverage is the fact that more coverage is not always better. In fact, large mega-cap companies may struggle to accommodate 20–30 analysts following them and focusing on increasing the coverage would make no sense. At the same time, small companies may struggle to have even one or two analysts covering them because of a decrease in sell-side analysts overall, a factor completely outside of the IROs' control. They can focus instead on other intermediary measures like investor requests, website visits, and similar.

Finally, for many investor relations professionals managing the *shareholder mix* and building and maintaining *relationships* with shareholders is often considered an appropriate metric for investor relations. IROs invest significant efforts in targeted outreach to expose the stock to the right institutional and retail investors; evaluating these efforts by looking at changes in the shareholder mix is important. Perception audits and other feedback from investors are vitally important to understand if IROs are on the right track in their communications and relationship-building efforts with the financial community. Relationship quality has an effect on investors' trust and confidence in the organization's management team: in fact, whatever the numbers say may not mean much if investors do not trust the source of those numbers.

In conclusion, whether you work in a financial communication agency or in an investor relations department, accountability is important. But accountability is also hard. While organizations continually face the need for greater accountability, the actual performance measurement efforts remain unable to provide a comprehensive solution. This is especially true in investor relations. As IROs we do not have control over the share price, or the trading volume, or buy/sell decision of our shareholders. But it does not mean we have no effect on those either. The Levels of Evaluation model allows us to build our case for our clients and our supervisors in order to show them how outputs of our work from the very first level can grow through intermediaries to reaching our target audiences in order to achieve business results and performance targets contributing to the success of the corporation.

Key Words

Analyst coverage
Attitude
Awareness
Comprehension
Framing the results
Intent to act
Intermediary
Levels of Evaluation

Magic bullet
Outcome level
Outgrowth level
Outperform level
Output level
Outreach level
Relationship
Return on communication
Return on investment
ROC
ROI
Shareholder mix
Share price
SOP
Standard operating procedures
Stock liquidity
Target audience
Trading volume

Discussion Questions and Activities

1 Why is it important to measure and evaluate investor relations work?
2 What are some of the final goals or targets of investor relations activities you can think of? What are the pluses and minuses of using each of those for measurement?
3 What is SOP? Describe Levels of Evaluation as an SOP for measuring investor relations. What are the pluses and minuses of using Levels of Evaluation?
4 Discuss why it may be important to compare a company's results with those of its competitors. What additional details can such a comparison provide?
5 Identify a company that recently went public in the United States. Read about the process it engaged in going public, focusing specifically on the roadshow. Imagine you are charged with evaluating the results of this roadshow. Describe what specific measures you could use on each level of the Levels of Evaluation to measure the investor relations results of this roadshow.

Part V

Transformation

12

Globalization of the Financial Markets and Regional Distinctions

Investments Know No Boundaries

Investor relations is truly a global profession. American corporations have investors from the Middle East, African companies are trading at the London Stock Exchange (LSE), and Asian banks conduct research on the stock of Australian companies. The famous saying that money has no nationality applies completely to the world of finance; from the investor relations standpoint it can be said that investments know no boundaries. Country borders have little effect on the opportunities that investors identify, or on merger and acquisition targets that can enhance business opportunities.

Take for example, Chrysler. The company is often synonymous with the United States and its iconic cars such as Jeep Wrangler or Dodge, yet in 1998 it merged with another car manufacturer that was synonymous with Germany, Mercedes. Using stock swap the new company became DaimlerChrysler, an enormous global corporation with investors from all over the world. In 2003, DaimlerChrysler acquired part of Mitsubishi's truck and bus division, adding an iconic Japanese manufacturer to the mix. Later, after an acquisition by Fiat, Chrysler became part of another global conglomerate, FiatChrysler Automobiles, with its shares trading on the New York Stock Exchange (NYSE) and Milan's Italian Stock Exchange, Borsa Italiana. Finally, in 2021, FiatChrysler merged with Groupe PSA, maker of iconic French cars such as Peugeot and Citroen, and one of the largest French corporations traded at Euronext Paris Stock Exchange. The resultant company, Stellantis, owns and manufactures the car brands that are often viewed as representative symbols of the cultures of their countries. So, is Jeep still an iconic American brand today if it is part of Stellantis? The largest shareholder of Stellantis is a holding company that represents the interests of the Agnelli family, descendants of one of the 1899 creators of Fiat, and later contributors to the growth and development of such Italian cars as Ferrari, Lancia, and Alfa Romeo. Should Jeep now be considered an Italian car because of the company ownership? The family of Peugeot is another large shareholder of Stellantis, though, so perhaps Jeep should be viewed as a French car? Among other shareholders, there are also UBS Securities (United Bank of Switzerland), BlackRock, an investment company headquartered in New York, and Vanguard mutual funds, which many Americans use for their retirement savings.

Investor Relations and Financial Communication: Creating Value Through Trust and Understanding, First Edition. Alexander V. Laskin.
© 2022 John Wiley & Sons, Inc. Published 2022 by John Wiley & Sons, Inc.

Stellantis is not a unique example. Almost any publicly traded corporation has shareholders and investors from around the world, or has sell-side interest from foreign banks and analysts, or may be a target for merger or acquisition from any corner of the globe. Investor relations officers (IROs) have to be ready to respond 24/7 to requests from shareholders for whom it may be 10 a.m. when it is 10 p.m. in the company headquarters time zone. It is also important to understand and take into account cultural differences in communication and business practices.

As corporations become global entities, so do investors. The largest asset management company in the world is the New York-based BlackRock, yet it manages assets for clients from over 100 different countries. Even BlackRock ownership today is global – among its own largest investors are Temasek, an investment company headquartered in Singapore, and Norges Bank Investment Management, which controls the Norwegian Oil Fund.

Many of those global corporations and global investors seek the markets that can provide the most return on their investments. Smaller companies and investors often follow the big ones as well. As a result, many corporations and investors target the US equity and financial markets because these markets are the largest in the world and, as a result, provide access to the most opportunities. It is actually quite common for companies from around the world to raise capital in the United States and list their securities on the US stock exchanges.

Depositary Receipts: Global Depositary Receipts, American Depositary Receipts, and Euro-denominated Depositary Receipts

In Chapter 10, we mentioned *American depositary receipts (ADRs)*. ADRs allow a foreign corporation with shares trading at their domestic stock exchanges to raise capital in the United States. We used the example of Gazprom. Its shares are traded at the Moscow Exchange, but through ADRs issued by the Bank of New York Mellon, investors in the United States can invest in the stock of Gazprom without having to figure out how to use the exchange in Moscow or the rules of transferring and depositing securities in Russia. ADRs, as the name suggests, focus on the United States and, as a result, they are denominated in US dollars to make it easier for US investors and to mitigate the currency risks associated with securities denominated in foreign currencies. However, the concept of depositary receipts is not limited to the United States only. Samsung, for example, a large Korean technology company, used depositary receipts to list its shares at LSE.

Such depositary receipts are called *global depositary receipts (GDRs)*. LSE is the largest exchange for trading of GDRs. In fact, because of all the Russian-issued GDRs trading at LSE, it is the second largest market for Russian securities other than Moscow itself. Overall, according to LSE, it has GDRs from 44 different countries in Eastern Europe, Central Europe, Asia, and the Middle East. In theory, GDRs can be developed and listed in any country and be denominated in any currency. However, it only makes sense to launch GDRs in order to create access to developed and large capital markets with an established infrastructure. Otherwise, the issuer won't gain any benefits from developing their depositary receipt program.

In continental Europe, a special kind of depositary receipt is also used – *euro-denominated depositary receipts (EDRs)*, sometimes called *European depositary receipts*. Denominating depositary receipts in euros makes the securities more user-friendly to European investors, similarly to ADRs being denominated in US dollars for American investors.

No matter what the denomination is, however, all depositary receipts require a bank that serves as a *depositary* of shares in the company's local country and as an issuer of receipts in the country where a company seeks to be traded. The shares are removed from the market in the local country and deposited with such a bank, or sometimes its local partner. The bank should be established enough and reputable enough to have the trust of investors all over the world. The bank's name is essentially the only guarantee that the securities can be traded in one place only – people should not be able to trade at the same time the depositary receipt in one country and the share that this receipt represents in another country.

Once the share is deposited, the bank issues the depositary receipt in the country where it is intended for trading. Then, it can be traded in the same way as any other local security, including at the stock exchange where it is listed. Depositary receipts often represent shares in one-to-one proportions, but sometimes because of currency exchange rates or exchange listing requirements, one depositary receipt may be equal to 2, 5, 10, or other amounts of shares. Although investors do not even have to know the ratio of depositary receipts to underlying shares, some sophisticated investors compare the prices between shares and their depositary receipts, seeking to capitalize at arbitrage in *inter-border transactions*. If a price difference develops between the share price in the home market and the price of the depositary receipt in the foreign market, investors can convert the depositary receipt back to the original share. In this case, the bank will delete the number of depositary receipts requested and release from storage the corresponding number of underlying shares in the local market where investors will be able to sell them capitalizing on the price difference. Such transactions, of course, will already be completed in the local currency, necessitating taking the currency exchange rates into account.

All depositary receipts are divided into four large categories. *Level I depositary receipts* are the securities designed exclusively for the over-the-counter (OTC) markets. They cannot be listed on a stock exchange. They are usually focused on professional investors and often used in private placements of securities. Level I depositary receipts in the United States are often issued using *Rule 144A*, which limits their ownership to *qualified institutional buyers (QIBs)*. If the depositary receipts are designed to be traded in continental Europe as EDRs or elsewhere in the world as GDRs, these depositary receipts may also be excluded from US regulatory requirements through *Regulation S (Reg. S)*, Offshore Offers and Sales, since the US entities are not going to be trading these securities. As a result, Level I depositary receipts are sometimes called *144A/Reg S depositary receipts*.

The benefit of Level I depositary receipts is that they do not have strict financial disclosure regulations in comparison with securities that are designed to be listed on NYSE or LSE. In fact, companies can still continue to use the local accounting standards used in the home country instead of using US Generally Accepted Accounting

Principles (GAAP) or International Accounting Standards (IAS). At the same time, Level I does not give access to the investors that the companies are usually seeking as they are still limited to a few expert investors who, most likely, specialize in the particular country or a region the company is from. In fact, since international disclosure or financial reports do not have to be provided forcing investors to analyze the company using local disclosure information and local financial standards, these investors either have local offices in the company's home country or use a local subsidiary or an agent. Thus, they are likely to be able to invest in local shares directly even without the convenience of the depositary receipts. This may diminish the usefulness of 144A/Reg S depositary receipts.

Level I depositary receipts can also be *sponsored* or *unsponsored*. Unsponsored depositary receipts are not initiated by and do not have the support of the company issuing the stock. For example, a shareholder that owns a large chunk of an Ukraine company's stock may decide that they would make more money selling their shares in London versus the local market in Kiev, where the company stock is normally traded. Such an investor can hire a depositary bank such as Deutsche Bank to issue the depositary receipts representing the investor-owned shares to be traded in the United Kingdom, while the underlying shares will be deposited with the bank in Ukraine. The shareholder does not have to ask for permission for such transactions from the Ukrainian corporation that issued the shares in the first place. The *issuer* does not even have to be notified. Since Level I does not have any disclosure obligations, the Ukrainian issuer does not have to start following any disclosure rules required in the United Kingdom.

Level II depositary receipts are designed to be listed on a stock exchange. Of course, if a company is planning to list its GDRs at LSE or its ADRs at NYSE, it has to meet all the disclosure and accounting standards of the country where the exchange is located, as well as the requirements of the stock exchange. This is an expensive and time-consuming process for a company, but, in the end, it gains access to the largest and most developed financial markets in the world. Level II depositary receipts must be sponsored – the company has an obligation to follow all the requirements of both home and foreign markets. Level II depositary receipts, however, do not allow the company to issue new stock; thus, they can be issued for direct listing, for example, when existing shareholders start trading their stock on a stock exchange after the listing is completed.

Level III depositary receipts, on the other hand, are specifically designed for initial public offerings (IPOs). The company is issuing new securities and raises new capital. The process is not much different from a traditional IPO – it still involves an underwriter or a group of underwriters filing with the United States Securities and Exchange Commission (SEC) in the case of a US transaction, or with the regulatory authorities in another country, and conducting a roadshow. Level III depositary receipts must also be sponsored as the direct involvement of the company is required. Instead of the S-1 prospectus, issuer of Level III ADRs would file *Form F-1*, specifically designed for foreign issuers. For example, a large Chinese electric car maker, NIO, sold 160 million ADRs at US$6.26 each in 2018 in one of the largest IPOs of the year. At the start of 2021, NIO was traded at over US$60 per ADR.

Regional Variations in Investor Relations and Financial Communication

Although the United States has the largest equity market, many countries around the world also have their own equity markets, stock exchanges, investment regulations, and, as a result, regional variations in investor relations practices. Many countries and regions also have local professional associations of investor relations that provide resources related to their own part of the world.

The *Investor Relations Society* (IR Society) represents investor relations professionals from the United Kingdom. The membership of the IR Society includes 851 professionals, and its website provides access to the IR Society's knowledge bank with information on the role of IROs, policies and regulations, corporate communications, environmental, social, and governance issues, and similar. The society also offers its members events on a weekly basis from master classes to webinars to networking.

Similarly, *Financial Communications and Investor Relations Alliance (ARFI)* is a professional association for practitioners in the Russian Federation. ARFI focuses on four key initiatives:

1. Development and adoption of professional guidelines and standards for financial and capital markets.
2. Financial and capital markets infrastructure development.
3. Initiation of legislative proposals relating to financial and capital markets regulation.
4. Support of international activities, including establishment of contacts with international and national professional bodies.

MEIRA is the *Middle East Investor Relations Association*, with headquarters in Dubai, and serves financial communicators from such countries as UAE, Saudi Arabia, Oman, Bahrain, Qatar, Egypt, and other Middle Eastern countries. MEIRA's mission is "to promote best practice IR in the Middle East through training, education, certification and professional networking and, together with local exchanges and regulators, seek to improve the efficiency of capital markets through sound IR practices and enhancement of market infrastructure" (MEIRA, 2018). Similarly, The *Japan Investor Relations Association (JIRA)* sees its goal as "proliferation and improvement of IR activities in Japan" and being an "information center of IR activities" (n.d.).

While investor relations professional associations are good starting points to learn about and adapt to the markets in different countries and regions of the world, many of these locations also have industry publications and academic research centers focused on financial communication and investor relations. For example, research into investor relations practices in Germany notes that investor relations is still a young micro-profession with fewer than 1,500 members. The function is rarely integrated – instead, depending on the company's organizational structure, IROs perform only one of the typical investor relations functions creating five types of investor relations at German corporations: regulatory information providers; marketers of securities; financial analysts; corporate communicators; and, rarely, the actual integrated IROs who do all of the above.

Sidebar 12.1

Investor relations in Russia: the case of Bank Vozrozhdenie

The specifics of the investor relations profession in Russia are influenced by two factors: the dependence of the Russian economy on the world economy, specifically on global oil and gas prices, and the Russian government's intervention in the economy. Bank Vozrozhdenie was one of the oldest Russian banks, founded in 1991. It had one of the strongest investor relations programs and had many large institutional investors, including JP Morgan Chase and BNP Paribas. However, in 2008, the bank was affected by the deterioration of the Russian macroeconomic environment as a result of the global crisis. A sharp devaluation of the already unstable ruble also led to many of the bank's clients defaulting on their obligations. Investors worried about Vozrozhdenie's ability to survive, especially after the publication of the bank's 2008 financial statements in accordance with the International Financial Standards. The investor relations team focused on the restoration of confidence of the investment community, emphasizing the bank's large reserves and strong market position. The bank survived, but the second crisis came from the government. The Central Bank of Russia asked VTB Bank to buy Bank Vozrozhdenie. VTB Bank is 100% owned by the Russian Federation represented by the Federal Agency for State Property Management, the Ministry of Finance of the Russian Federation, and the State Corporation Deposit Insurance Agency. Vozrozdenie investors, however, were not happy with the proposed terms for the conversion of securities as the shares were significantly undervalued. The investor relations department had no response to these developments. The Bank's existence as a publicly traded corporation came to an end.

Kvashneva Snezhana Vyacheslavna
Communication Consulting Researcher, SPbSU

Scholars studying investor relations in Northern Europe (Denmark, Finland, Iceland, Norway, and Sweden) note that those countries focus on social equality, high transparency, and building and maintaining social capital. As a result, IROs have to respond to these societal demands and focus on intangible assets, corporate social responsibility, and environmental, social, and governance information in their disclosure communications. Investor relations work in the Nordic countries, as a result, involves significantly more voluntary disclosures of unregulated information than in other parts of the world.

Italy holds a special importance for its financial communication and investor relations professionals with an award founded in 1954 by Roberto Tremellion, *Oscar di Bilancio*. The award, which is given by the Italian professional association Federazione Relazioni Pubbliche Italiana (FERPI) in collaboration with the Italian Stock Exchange and Bocconi University, recognizes those who work to improve financial and nonfinancial disclosure, and who are committed to improving the quantity and quality of information. The Oscars eventually were split into several categories to recognize transparency in financial communication, quality of integrated reporting, a special Oscar for nonfinancial statement, and so on.

Volkova (2017) applied the recommendations of LSE to analyze the investor relations sections of the websites of Russian corporations. She concluded that investor relations in Russia seemed to be in its early stages as the differences between company websites were very significant, thus indicating a lack of developed standards and institutionalized best practices. In addition, out of the 100 largest Russian companies only 64 had a section for investors on their websites; in comparison almost 100% of US public companies have a section dedicated to investor relations. Another important finding was the lack of information on top executives or any other biographical details on people related to the company – all biographical information commonly provided in order to disclose conflicts of interest was often excluded in Russia. Finally, several companies, in addition to an investor relations section, had an additional section called *Disclosure*, which included information that would normally be found in the investor relations section. This can be explained by Russia's public companies law, which has a specific requirement for disclosure and a detailed description of what must be disclosed and how it must be disclosed.

Even in the countries that have historical similarities to the United States, different economic, social, and political realities may have a strong effect on the practices of investor relations and financial communication. Australia, for example, has a required *superannuation* – meaning a percentage of all earnings gets invested for retirement savings, including in the shares of Australian and foreign companies. This makes every single person an investor, an investor who cares and may one day depend on those investments. This makes the work of investor relations professionals and the communications they produce more focused on retail shareholders. Another difference is the taxation system, which favors dividends – thus, the focus on dividends rather than price growth is also unique to the Australian stock market. Finally, Westbrook (2018), having studied investor relations professionals in Australia, noted that there is a "fishbowl" effect in the country as there are just a few large publicly traded companies and a few large institutional investors, creating a situation where everybody knows everybody. He noted, however, that it also creates a tight-knit community and a collegial atmosphere for investor relations and financial communication professionals.

Key Terms

144A/Reg S depositary receipts
ADR
American depositary receipts
ARFI
Depositary
EDR
Euro-denominated depositary receipts
European depositary receipts
Financial Communications and Investor Relations Alliance
Form F-1
GDR
Global depositary receipts

Inter-border transactions
IR Society
Issuer
Japan Investor Relations Association
JIRA
Level I depositary receipts
Level II depositary receipts
Level III depositary receipts
MEIRA
Middle East Investor Relations Association
Oscar di Bilancio
QIB
Qualified institutional buyers
Regulation S
Reg. S
Rule 144A
Sponsored depositary receipts
Superannuation
Unsponsored depositary receipts

Discussion Questions and Activities

1 What does the saying "money has no nationality" mean for investor relations? Discuss the implications for the profession.
2 Explain what GDRs are. Discuss how they work.
3 Compare and contrast different levels of GDRs. Discuss the benefits and drawbacks of each level. Find examples of different levels of GDRs and compare their price with the underlying shares in the local market.
4 Identify an investor relations professional association in a country of your choice. Analyze what content the association has on its website, how it defines investor relations, and what it says about its own mission. Find information on the membership of the organization. Discuss differences and similarities between what you learn from the association's website and what you have learned from this book.
5 Identify a publicly traded company from a foreign market. Try to find contact information for their investor relations department on the website or on social media sites. Then, reach out to the IROs at that company and interview them about investor relations practices in their country.

13

The Future of Investor Relations and Financial Communication

COVID-19 Accelerates Online Processes

With the COVID-19 pandemic raging around the world, many annual shareholder meetings became virtual, roadshows were cancelled, and investor meetings moved to Zoom. Corporations also reported increased traffic to their investor relations websites and social media pages. *IR Magazine*, a leading investor relations publication, points out that among the most important information investors are looking for on the websites are the contact information for the investor relations officers (IROs), recent annual and quarterly results, and environmental, social, and governance (ESG) reporting. Also, due to the quarantine measures in many places, and as a result of having investors and financial analysts working from home, mobile traffic to websites is also on the rise; thus, it is essential for the investor relations team to make sure that the investor relations pages of the corporate website are mobile-friendly. Remote work is expected to continue for many occupations even after the pandemic is over; thus, remote communication technologies are here to stay for investor relations professionals. In the future, as a result, it is likely that controlled media communications, such as websites, will play an increased role in IROs' operations.

The online environment has also proven beneficial for increased engagement. More shareholders participated in annual meetings in 2020 than ever before. *IR Magazine* reports that, in addition to higher attendance, virtual meeting participants stayed longer, voted more often, and asked more questions. Nili and Shaner (2020) suggested that virtual shareholder meetings helped reclaim shareholder democracy! IROs will have to take these trends into account. The future may require always having a remote option available even when the meeting is conducted primarily in-person for the benefit of shareholders who cannot travel or prefer to communicate virtually.

As remote technologies develop, it is possible future annual general meetings, investor conferences, or roadshows could be conducted in *virtual reality* (*VR*). Once adoption of VR headsets becomes as widespread as smartphones and TVs, IROs will be able to seamlessly engage investors and analysts in the VR environment. This would combine the convenience of remote meetings with the face-to-face experience of in-person events. VR creates a virtual environment for users separate from the actual environment where the user is located, and thus can place a user in any place and time in the world. For example, VR can show a new mining infrastructure without actually having shareholders go into the mine. Other technologies can enhance and build upon the reality. In-person events can be supplemented with *augmented reality (AR)* and *mixed reality (MR)* layers too; for example, allowing on-demand access in real time to additional data about a company's finances while in the meeting. AR could bring an artificial object into the investor meeting like an open-hearth furnace, and MR could allow investors to interact with it to better learn its operations.

In fact, in the future, in-person events are likely to become more sparse. Yet, this will also lead to an additional appreciation of the in-person one-on-ones, small-group meetings, and roadshows. Adam Borgatti, Senior Vice President of Corporate Development and Investor Relations at Aecon, calls these in-person opportunities *touch and feel events* and proposes that those will be in significant demand. It is likely that even those in-person events will have a virtual component: investors and analysts now expect to be able to participate virtually, whether in live format or as a recording. Plus, at least for now, an ability to actually touch and feel depends significantly on the vaccination and the infection rates.

It is also likely that shareholders and financial analysts will add an extra dimension to analyzing their investments: how would that company fare in the next pandemic? Pandemic-proof businesses will command a premium, and IROs will add an extra bullet point to the investor presentations, helping investors understand how future pandemics may affect the business model of the corporation.

Technological Innovations

In addition to the increased usage of remote and online communication technologies, technological innovations will likely have an influence on every other aspect of investor relations as well. For example, IROs may have to learn how to connect with new kinds of investors: investors operating based on artificial intelligence (AI), neural networks, natural language processing, and alternative and niche data sets. The constantly growing amount of data generated and processed allows identifying the most obscure connections between share price and other performance indicators. Deep mining algorithms may find a connection between, for example, a stock price and social media reviews on Yelp, and a fund may be created to invest based on this information with millions of retail shareholders pouring their cash into such a fund. IROs will have to be at the forefront of monitoring these trends and finding and analyzing such information themselves to educate investors and to educate the company's management. Of course, IROs will also have to understand how these new investment tools work and what effect they may have on the corporate stock.

On the other hand, IROs will gain access to many new technologies themselves; this may make the lives of IROs easier in some respects, but at the same time will no doubt place additional demands on the role of IRO. The investor relations profession will undoubtedly use more data. Some professional discussions already focus on the issue of automation and AI taking jobs away from IROs and financial analysts. There is little doubt that AI is more efficient than humans at crunching the numbers; however, the relationship-building aspect and nonfinancial information may give the advantage back to humans. So, although it seems unlikely that technology will replace IROs, IROs will be able to use technology to their advantage: letting AI process quantitative data, identify investors to target, analyze trading patterns, and so on, while IROs can focus on qualitative data and producing insights based on all the data combined. And of course, and most importantly, IROs are the ones who will be acting based on those insights. Even if AI can prepare an excellent financial statement, it would still require the company executives to put their signatures on these statements.

Retail Investors

Bloomberg Intelligence reports that *retail trading* is at 10-year high with more and more individuals joining the stock trades. In fact, retail trading represents on average about 20% of all daily stock transactions. The growth in retail investments has continued for several years fueled by improved access to information, diffusion of social media, and the appearance of online brokerages that have eliminated minimum deposit requirements and even trade commission. The pandemic accelerated this trend giving people free time to discuss stocks on social media and cash from stimulus checks to invest in those stocks. Some propose that such widespread access to information and the ability to coordinate efforts on social media across millions of people shift the power balance back to the people and away from large institutions. Robinhood with 13 million accounts, Schwab also with about 13 million accounts, and Fidelity with over 30 million accounts already represent a large force of retail shareholders. This trend will no doubt continue with more and more individuals wanting to try investing on their own. This is not limited to stock investment, of course – individuals experiment with debt securities, option trading, currency instruments, and even cryptocurrencies.

Some companies have started paying attention to retail shareholders and many others will likely join in on this trend soon, too. While GameStop remained silent during early 2021 when retail shareholders pushed its stock price to unexpected heights, CarParts.com, which saw its stock go up more than 50% at the start of 2021, is now planning to host special events specifically designed for smaller shareholders. The CFO of CarParts, David Meniane, explained that after seeing how retail shareholders could move the stock price, it was important to give them a chance to talk to the management in the same way as large institutional investors are used to. Retail shareholders may generate a large part of the trading volume for corporations and, as a result, can have a significant effect on stock price fluctuations.

Many of these retail shareholders look for information and investment advice on social media. These retail investors can join forces to perform *crowdinvesting*, a phenomenon not that different from *crowdsourcing* efforts to organize knowledge on Wikipedia or *crowdfunding* efforts to support an important cause. In crowdinvesting, hundreds, thousands, perhaps millions of retail investors combine their financial and intellectual resources to attempt to outperform the market. If a company today has about five financial analysts covering its stock, in the future it will have thousands of individuals turned analysts on Reddit discussing its earnings, future potential, and the actions of the CEO. Some of them may even be financial professionals, but even the ones who have very little knowledge of investment markets may nevertheless have a captive audience in their social media peers and may have a potential to move the stock as much as Wall Street professionals.

On the plus side, thousands of people focusing their attention on the stock can actually discover price irregularities and discrepancies from the stock's intrinsic value, leading to a more efficient stock market and optimizing capital allocation. The optimistic view suggests that two heads are better than one, and thus, a thousand heads are better than a few. The pessimistic view, however, points out the madness of crowds and many popular delusions (MacKay, 1841/2011) in which individuals may react based on emotions without any substantive fundamental reason.

In any case, the increased participation of retail shareholders is likely to increase affecting share price volatility and trading volumes – once again demanding careful attention from IROs. This may be especially true for consumer-oriented companies as individuals are more likely to invest in the corporations they are familiar with. This also creates opportunities, however, from the investor relations and marketing standpoint. If Ford, for example, gives one share to everyone who purchases a Ford car, it is a surefire way to create loyalty from an individual as a shareholder and as a consumer, and lead to repeat purchases of products and shares.

At the same time, being, on average, less knowledgeable about investment processes and stocks, retail investors may act based on gossip or hints they get from social media sites such as *StockTwits*, *Seeking Alpha*, or Reddit's *WallStreetBets*. It will become a challenge for IROs to identify the sources of information and correct false information and gossip that may be spreading online. Social media will become a bigger part of the IROs' job, making it essential to monitor and, if needed, combat misinformation online or information that has been leaked without a company's authorization.

Social media today is not a big part of IROs' responsibilities, but this is likely to change. IROs will have to at the very least listen to all these conversations, carefully monitoring all the chatter related to the company on more and more social media platforms. New social media platforms, like for example the audio-based *Clubhouse*, require new tools for monitoring conversations. In the future, new tools and new service providers will emerge to provide data and insights from these data to enable IROs' decision making.

Finally, retail investors may also put pressure on companies to pay more in *dividends*. While institutional investors may consider dividend income as an afterthought, focusing instead on making money through stock price appreciation, retail investors consider dividends an important factor in their investment decision. Especially for investors who invest because of emotional or other personal connections to the stock and, as a result, are not looking to sell it due to share price increases, dividends are the only way to generate income from their investments. Changes in society and the increased focus on redistribution of wealth may add pressure for increased dividend payments. Apple, for example, was famous for never paying dividends, yet in 2020 almost 20% of all Apple's cash flow was used to pay the dividends. Despite that, at Apple's annual shareholder meeting in 2021, Apple's CEO Tim Cook faced investors' demands for additional increase in dividend payouts.

New Investment Vehicles

At the intersection of the growth in retail investing and increase in technological innovations lies an opportunity for developing new technology-based investment vehicles. One such vehicle gaining in popularity is crypto-based coins or tokens that companies can sell to potential investors. An *initial coin offering (ICO)* or *initial token offering (ITO)* may look similar to a more traditional initial public offering, when a company raises new funds to grow its business. However, ICOs and ITOs are generally not registered with the United States Securities and Exchange Commission (SEC) and there are no underwriters doing due diligence on the company. On one hand, this means significantly less expense for the company raising funds; on the other hand, it means that investors are on their own and have to research all the risks associated with such potential investments themselves, or with the help of other investors like them on social media.

Tokens can be designed to represent ownership in the company like a share of stock or they may be *utility tokens*, where instead of ownership they provide access to a product or service. *Coins* can be used simply like a currency on a native blockchain. Some tokens may be a combination of several of these approaches. To launch an ICO/ITO, a start-up company would typically create a website with details of the project and information about the offering. Such information is called a *white paper* and this can be shared on various crypto platforms and online sites, as well as on social media. At this time, potential investors can start buying the tokens or coins offered for sale, most often paying with existing *cryptocurrencies* and sometimes with traditional *fiat currencies*. Many compare the current state of crypto investments with the Wild West because of the lack of regulations and the amount of fraudulent activity – many individuals have lost all their investments in crypto tokens and coins.

Retail investors, however, are not swayed by the risks. There were more than 2,000 ICOs/ITOs in 2020 alone, with billions of dollars raised. The SEC is also looking more carefully at the ICOs/ITOs, stating that if the tokens act like securities, or in other words represent a share in the company, they may need to be registered with the SEC. For example, when Telegram, a globally popular messaging app focused on user privacy, raised almost US$1.7 billion in its ICO, the SEC intervened and demanded Telegram return the funds to investors as well as pay a civil fine.

In addition to raising money, companies may rely on blockchain in other aspects of managing their relationships with shareholders. For example, Overstock paid its dividends using blockchain-based security tokens, OSTKO. The company performed an *airdrop*, or transfer, of tokens in a proportion of 1 OSTKO for every 10 shares of Overstock. OSTKO represents Digital Voting Series A-1 Preferred Stock. OSTKO started trading at US$10 per share and reached US$65 in less than a year, making it a unique dividend that actually goes up in price.

Growing Regulations

With more and more people participating in the equities, debt, and options markets, there are more people who may not be knowledgeable enough about the risks involved in those transactions. As a result, it is likely that the SEC, other regulatory agencies, lawmakers, and regulatory agencies in other countries will focus more on protecting individual retail shareholders and introduce additional regulations. On top of that, new technologies are reshaping the investment landscape by offering new investment instruments and platforms for people to invest and discuss their investments. The SEC Division of Enforcement, for example, monitors social media activity and, if necessary, steps in to protect retail investors. On February 26, 2021, the SEC suspended trading in 15 issuers that were promoted on social media with misleading information that could have resulted in the defrauding of retail investors (Figure 13.1).

It is reasonable to expect that laws and regulations will be taking on an even more important role for investor relations professionals. Additional education and training in law for IROs and close cooperation with legal teams and outside legal counsel will be an essential part of the routine. Professional associations, such as the National Investor Relations Institute (NIRI), will have to be at the forefront of these developments, helping IROs apply the changes to their work.

Retail shareholders may not always wait for the SEC to take care of them and are also expected to take a more active role in demanding new laws and regulations to level the playing field with large institutional investors. For example, the SEC recently proposed to change Rule 13F, which requires those who hold over US$100 million in equity securities to disclose their position. The change would raise the limit for required disclosure from US$100 million to US$3.5 billion. This would have helped large investors by decreasing their reporting requirements; however, retail investors, issuers, stock exchanges, and other financial stakeholders noted that it would limit market transparency. Retail shareholders started a petition on change.org to instead make Rule 13F more transparent. By promoting the petition on Reddit and other social media platforms, the petitioners were able to collect over 12,000 signatures in less than a day. The legislature took notice, and the US House Committee on Financial Services is set to discuss the rule and its proposed reform.

Many regulatory agencies, like the SEC, for example, operate within the legal environment of one country. Yet, corporations and investors operate on a global scale. This makes them difficult to regulate. Similar to the failure of the state-based blue sky laws after the development of the telegraph, radio, and automobiles, the country-based regulations may not be sufficient in the twenty-first century.

Further regulations are also needed with the continued globalization of the markets. When a company operates halfway across the world, it makes it more difficult for investors, especially retail shareholders, to conduct due diligence and investigate the company on their own. In 2019–2020, China's Luckin Coffee conducting business in China primarily, but trading in the United States with many US investors owning Luckin stock, overstated its revenues and understated its losses. Reporting over US$311 million in fake sales pushed Luckin Coffee's share price to over US$50 a share at the start of 2020 and encouraged many investors to purchase even more stock. However, when news of the fraud came out and the SEC began its investigation, the stock collapsed to almost US$1 a share in May 2020, leaving many investors in the company

Press Release

SEC Suspends Trading in Multiple Issuers Based on Social Media and Trading Activity

FOR IMMEDIATE RELEASE

2021-35

Washington D.C., Feb. 26, 2021 — As part of its continuing effort to respond to potential attempts to exploit investors during the recent market volatility, the Securities and Exchange Commission today suspended trading in the securities of 15 companies because of questionable trading and social media activity.

Today's action follows the recent suspensions of the securities of numerous other issuers, many of which may also have been targets of apparent social media attempts to artificially inflate their stock price. The SEC continues to review market and trading data to identify other securities where the public interest and the protection of investors require trading suspensions.

"The SEC's recent suspensions of trading in nearly two dozen securities – including 15 today – are one facet of our ongoing efforts to police the market and protect investors," said Melissa Hodgman, Acting Director of the SEC's Division of Enforcement. "We proactively monitor for suspicious trading activity tied to stock promotions on social media, and act quickly to stop that trading when appropriate to safeguard the public interest. We also remind investors to exercise caution and do their diligence before investing generally, including in companies promoted on social media."

Today's order states that trading is being suspended because of questions about recent increased activity and volatility in the trading of these issuers, as well as the influence of certain social media accounts on that trading activity. The order also states that none of the issuers has filed any information with the SEC or OTC Markets, where the companies' securities are quoted, for over a year. As a result, the SEC suspended trading in the securities of: Bebida Beverage Co. (BBDA); Blue Sphere Corporation (BLSP); Ehouse Global Inc. (EHOS); Eventure Interactive Inc. (EVTI); Eyes on the Go Inc. (AXCG); Green Energy Enterprises Inc. (GYOG); Helix Wind Corp. (HLXW); International Power Group Ltd. (IPWG); Marani Brands Inc. (MRIB); MediaTechnics Corp. (MEDT); Net Talk.com Inc. (NTLK); Patten Energy Solutions Group Inc. (PTTN); PTA Holdings Inc. (PTAH); Universal Apparel & Textile Company (DKGR); and Wisdom Homes of America Inc. (WOFA).

The SEC also recently issued orders temporarily suspending trading in: Bangi Inc. (BNGI); Sylios Corp. (UNGS); Marathon Group Corp. (PDPR); Affinity Beverage Group Inc. (ABVG); All Grade Mining Inc. (HYII); and SpectraScience Inc. (SCIE). Each of these orders stated that the suspensions were due at least in part to questions about whether social media accounts have been attempting to artificially increase the companies' share price.

Under the federal securities laws, the SEC can suspend trading in a stock for 10 days and generally prohibit a broker-dealer from soliciting investors to buy or sell the stock again until certain reporting requirements are met.

The SEC's Office of Investor Education and Advocacy recently alerted investors to the significant risks of making investment decisions based on social media.

###

Figure 13.1 SEC press release suspending trading in multiple securities to protect investors. *Source*: US Securities and Exchange Commission. Retrieved from: https://www.sec.gov/news/press-release/2021-35. Public Domain.

with significant losses. Because the sales of the company are in China, yet the investors are mainly in the United States, it is difficult for investors to gauge how the company is operating, forcing them to rely on the numbers the company itself is sharing. It is reasonable to expect growing cooperation between regulatory agencies from different countries to prevent and respond to cross-border fraud and better control global corporations. Perhaps, in the more distant future global regulatory organizations and global regulatory standards will develop that will supersede national borders.

Cybersecurity

As more and more of our lives – professional and personal – is shifting online, the issue of cybersecurity is moving front and center for companies in any line of business. Malicious hacking, data breaches, data collection practices, or inept mismanagement of data can cost corporations billions of dollars. Investors and analysts are paying increased attention to companies' data practices and IROs need to become data experts in order to be able to disclose that information to the investment community. It would also be beneficial for IROs to be proactive with such disclosures, especially in companies that depend on data for their revenues, instead of waiting for shareholders to request such information.

Growing Importance of ESG

Investors will continue to realize that issues related to environmental sustainability, social responsibility, and corporate governance are not just the right thing to do, but also essential to the survival of a corporation. A recent survey of large investors conducted by Morgan Stanley Capital International (MSCI) found that climate change is viewed as one of the biggest risks of the future and the top trend impacting their investment decisions. One of the largest global investment fund managers, Vanguard, recently issued a statement about its expectation for the companies Vanguard invests in to promote executive, nonexecutive, and overall workforce diversity, equity, and inclusion. Rockefeller Asset Management in partnership with the NYU Stern Center for Sustainable Business presented a link between ESG and financial performance – companies who are better from the ESG standpoint are also better from the investment standpoint!

Sidebar 13.1

Growing importance of professional associations: the case of NIRI

The fundamentals of investor relations are a common language for practitioners regardless of the size of the company you work for or the industry you represent. There will always be sales trends, gross margins, cash flow, and capital allocation, along with earnings, investor filings, surveillance, targeting, investor days, and non-deal roadshows (NDRs) – all of which are standard practice within any investor relations program. The role has always been challenged by the outside impacts of the macro-environment, the SEC and regulatory changes, the ever-changing state of technology, and, naturally, the market. Today, there is a new wrinkle in the fold with social media and the "quant robots" actively playing a role in market movements.

Having access to the right resources is essential to a successful investor relations program and especially in staying on top of these outside influences. NIRI is one of the best resources for information, both at a national and a local level. The organization has always been, and continues to be, a beacon when it comes to very topical and relevant matters that sit outside the standard fundamentals. Areas like AI, diversity and inclusion, and ESG are topics that NIRI brought to the forefront of discussions before they were being mentioned in the mainstream media. NIRI has built a network where practitioners and service providers can easily collaborate and exchange ideas. This is in addition to a world-class advocacy program that keeps members up to date on new regulatory proposals, including the potential impact to your business or industry and how to prepare, react, or respond.

I have been a member of NIRI for nine years and proudly serve on my local chapter (NIRI Connecticut/Westchester County) board. The experience has helped me develop professionally and personally as I have built a network of trusted colleagues and friends across the country in several different industries. Being a NIRI member and relying on this organization for important information has been essential in my career as an investor relations professional.

June Vecellio-Lazaroff

NIRI Connecticut/Westchester County – Chapter President (2019–2021)

Director of Investor Relations, Pitney Bowes Inc. (2012–present)

The president of Nasdaq, Adena Friedman, states that ESG is becoming not an addition but a central point of a corporate strategy. Investors do take notice: ESG-related assets under management exceeded US\$1 trillion in 2020. Yet, IROs struggle with *ESG disclosure* as there are no universally accepted standards and procedures. While the future may bring some standardization in the area of ESG, for now the ability of IROs to educate investors on the company's ESG activities in an objective, relevant, and comprehensive manner will be of extreme importance for investors, financial analysts, and corporate management. As more and more investors are looking for companies that are socially responsible and environmentally sustainable, IROs must be at the forefront of ESG communications. It is important for IROs to take a proactive stance on ESG issues and lead investors on the disclosure rather than follow them reactively catching up on the requests for information.

Post-Information Age

The changes in the media landscape and communication technologies have also brought changes to investor relations and financial communication. The twentieth century was widely considered an *information age*, when information was the most treasured asset. Today, however, we may be entering a *post-information age*, when information is widely, publicly, and freely available to everybody and, in fact, commoditized. In fact, we may be overwhelmed by information – there is so much data that people and even machines find it difficult to process everything available and, more importantly, identify the actual meaning behind all the data. Information becomes noise; finding insights in all this information becomes similar to finding a needle in a haystack.

Investor relations professionals, whose responsibilities focus on disclosure, in other words, producing more information and adding to the noise, may have to rethink how they approach communications. Instead of producing annual reports stretching for hundreds of pages, they may instead focus on one or two key ideas, key results, or key statements. The post-information landscape also makes signaling more important – such signals may include reputation, both individual and corporate, prior track record, as well as relationships and connections. A company being recognized for its ESG by an independent ranking agency may be considered an ESG-friendly company. A company doing business with, for example, Starbucks, may be considered sustainable because Starbucks ensures its supply chain works in a sustainable manner. These signals eliminate the need for having to dig for meaning in terabytes of poorly structured data on sustainability that may exist for various companies.

Shareholder Activism

Finally, the growing numbers of retail shareholders, increased market volatility, amplified voices arguing for social justice and wealth redistribution, technological innovation, improved access to corporations, and mounting pressure on companies to demonstrate ESG commitments will continue to lead to more shareholder activism. As it is reasonable to expect more shareholder activism in terms of pure numbers, it is likely that qualitatively shareholder activism will grow, too, involving more and more issues, especially focusing on the issues of *diversity*, *equity*, and *inclusion*, which will become more and more relevant.

Key Terms

Airdrop
AR
Augmented reality
Clubhouse
Coin
Crowdfunding
Crowdinvesting
Crowdsourcing
Cryptocurrencies
DEI
Diversity
Dividend
ESG disclosure
Equity
Fiat currencies
ICO
Inclusion
Information age
Initial coin offering

Initial token offering
ITO
Mixed reality
MR
Post-information age
Retail trading
Rule 13F
Seeking Alpha
StockTwits
Token
Touch and feel events
Utility token
Virtual reality
VR
WallStreetBets
White paper

Discussion Questions and Activities

1 Discuss how the COVID-19 pandemic has affected investor relations. What changes do you expect will go away and which ones are here to stay for a long time?
2 Discuss what opportunities VR, AR, and MR create for investor relations, and for building and maintaining relationships with the financial community.
3 Since retail shareholding is growing, what should companies do, if anything, to better connect with retail shareholders? Do you expect companies will focus more on retail shareholders in the future? Why or why not?
4 Visit the SEC website. What new or proposed regulations are being discussed on the website. What do you think are the reasons behind these regulations?
5 Identify some of the largest crypto tokens. Discuss what platforms/companies they represent. Compare them with shares of corporations. What are the differences and similarities?

Bibliography

Allen, C. E. (2002). Building mountains in a flat landscape: Investor relations in the post-Enron era. *Corporate Communications: An International Journal, 7*(4), 206–211.

AMEC U.S. & Agency Leaders Chapter. (2010, October 7). Barcelona declaration of measurement principles: Validated metrics; Social media measurement. http://www.instituteforpr.org/wp-content/uploads/BarcelonaPrinciplesOct2010.pdf

AMEC U.S. & Agency Leaders Chapter. (2011, June 7). Valid metrics for PR measurement: Putting the principles into action.

AMEC U.S. & Agency Leaders Chapter. (2012, November). Measuring the true value of public relations: How an AMEC initiative changed the way PR measurement was seen. https://slideplayer.com/slide/4221461

AMEC U.S. & Agency Leaders Chapter. (2014, December). How to use the AMEC valid metrics. https://amecorg.com/amecframework

Apple. (2021). Schedule 14A. https://d18rn0p25nwr6d.cloudfront.net/CIK-0000320193/492dd75b-15df-4826-ba30-8828289290cf.pdf

Ashwell, B. (2020, December 7). A look at the fracturing US trading landscape. *IR Magazine.*

Ashwell, B. (2021, February 23). Half of IR professionals expect increase in investor meetings year on year. *IR Magazine.* https://www.irmagazine.com/shareholder-targeting-id/half-ir-professionals-expect-increase-investor-meetings-year-year

Baskin, O., Aronoff, C., & Lattimore, D. (1997). *Public relations: The profession and the practice.* Irwin/McGraw Hill.

Benton, G. J. (1986). The benefits and costs to managers of voluntary accounting disclosure. *Contemporary Accounting Research, 3*(1), 35–44.

Bhagat, S., Black, B., & Blair, M. (2004). Relational investing and firm performance. *The Journal of Financial Research, 27*(1), 1–30.

BNY Mellon. (2011). *Global trends in investor relations: Seventh edition, a survey analysis of IR practices worldwide.* BNY Mellon.

Bowen, S. A., Moon, W., & Kim, J. K. (2018). Ethics in financial communication and investor relations: Stakeholder expectations, corporate social responsibility, and principle-based analyses. In A. V. Laskin (Ed.), *Handbook of financial communication and investor relations* (pp. 71–86). Wiley-Blackwell.

Broom, G. M., & Dozier, D. M. (1990). *Using research in public relations: Applications to program management.* Prentice Hall.

Investor Relations and Financial Communication: Creating Value Through Trust and Understanding, First Edition. Alexander V. Laskin.

Budd, J. F. (1993). *CEO credibility: The management of reputation.* Turtle Publishing Company.

Business is still in trouble. (1949, May). *Fortune,* 67.

Byrne, C. (2020a, November 27). Boom in IR demand for targeting tools. *IR Magazine.* https://www.irmagazine.com/shareholder-targeting-id/boom-ir-demand-targeting-tools?MessageRunDetailID=3825760713&PostID=22580105&utm_medium=email&utm_source=rasa_io

Byrne, C. (2020b, December 2). Asset managers complain CFA's proposed ESG standards will sow confusion, not clarity. *IR Magazine.* https://www.irmagazine.com/esg/asset-managers-complain-cfas-proposed-esg-standards-will-sow-confusion-not-clarity

Byrum, K. (2018). Financial and investor relations for start-up businesses and emerging companies. In A. V. Laskin (Ed.), *Handbook of financial communication and investor relations* (pp. 157–166). Wiley-Blackwell.

Cadwalader, Wickersham & Taft, LLP. (2021, March 20). United States: House Financial Services Committee considers reform recommendations after gamestop trading event. *Mondaq.* https://www.mondaq.com/unitedstates/securities/1049124/house-financial-services-committee-considers-reform-recommendations-after-gamestop-trading-event

CalPERS (2021, May 25). Corporate engagement. https://www.calpers.ca.gov/page/investments/corporate-governance/corporate-engagements

Chambers, C. (2006, July 14). Who needs stock exchanges? MondoVisione: Worldwide Exchange Intelligence.

Chandler, C. S. (2018). More than a zero-sum game: Integrating investor and public relations to navigate conflict with activist investors. In A. V. Laskin (Ed.), *Handbook of financial communication and investor relations* (pp. 117–126). Wiley-Blackwell.

Chatlos, W. (1974). What is investor relations? In A. R. Roalman (Ed.), *Investor relations handbook* (pp. 3–19). AMACOM.

Chatlos, W. E. (1984). Investor relations. In B. Cantor (Ed.), *Experts in action: Inside public relations* (pp. 84–101). Longman.

Climate Action 100+. (2021). The three asks. https://www.climateaction100.org/approach/the-three-asks (accessed July 5, 2021).

The Coca-Cola Company. (2020). 2020 proxy statement. https://investors.coca-colacompany.com/filings-reports/proxy-statements (accessed July 5, 2021).

Colvin, G. (2016, June 1). Private desires. *Fortune, 173* (7), 52–57.

Comin, G., Ros, S., & Scotti, A. (2018). The evolution of financial communication in Italy: The case of Oscar di Bilancio. In A. V. Laskin (Ed.), *Handbook of financial communication and investor relations* (pp. 443–448). Wiley-Blackwell.

Conger, M. (2004, January/February). How a comprehensive IR program pays off. *Financial Executive,* 20, 1–4.

Coombs, T. (2012). *Ongoing crisis communication* (3rd ed.). Sage.

Copland, J. R., & O'Keefe, M. M. (2021). *Proxy Monitor 2017*: Season review. Manhattan Institute.

Cutlip, S. M. (1994). *The unseen power: Public relations. A history.* Lawrence Erlbaum Associates.

Cutlip, S. M., & Center, A. H. (1952). *Effective public relations: Pathways to public favor.* Prentice Hall.

Cutlip, S. M., Center, A. H., & Broom, G. M. (2000). *Effective public relations* (8th ed.). Prentice Hall.

Davis, K. (1973). The case for and against business assumption of social responsibilities. *Academy of Management Journal*, 16, 312–323. http://dx.doi.org/10.2307/255331

Dobrzynski, J. H. (1993, March 15). Relationship investing. *Business Week, 3309*, 68.

Donnelly, T. (2012, May 15). 3 ways Facebook changed the IPO roadshow. *Inc.*

Duhe, S. (2018). Shareholder democracy in the digital age. In A. V. Laskin (Ed.), *Handbook of financial communication and investor relations* (pp. 23–32). Wiley-Blackwell.

Edelman, Inc. (2016). Edelman trust barometer: Executive summary.

Equilar. (2013, March 13). Pay for performance disconnect cited as main shareholder concern in say on pay vote failures. https://www.equilar.com/press-releases/5-say-on-pay-vote-failures.html

Ernst & Young (1997). *Measures that matter*. Boston, MA: Ernst & Young Center for Business Innovation.

Fama, E. F. (1965). The behavior of stock-market prices. *The Journal of Business, 38*(1), 34–105.

Fama, E. F. (1970). Efficient capital markets: A review of theory and empirical work. *The Journal of Finance, 25*(2), 383–417.

Favaro, P. (2001). Beyond bean counting: The CFO's expanding role. *Strategy & Leadership, 29*(5), 4–8.

Flynn, D. (2020, September 28). Opinion: Virtual AGMs bringing increased engagement. *IRMagazine.*https://www.irmagazine.com/esg/opinion-virtual-agms-bringing-increased-engagement

Frankel, M. (2019, August 30). The 100 best Warren Buffett quotes. *The Motley Fool.*

Franklin Templeton. (2020). Templeton emerging markets small cap fund. https://www.franklintempleton.com/investor/investments-and-solutions/investment-options/mutual-funds/overview/626/templeton-emerging-markets-small-cap-fund/TEMZX

Friedman, A. (2021, March 19). Sustaining the spirit of cooperative capitalism. *Nasdaq.* https://www.linkedin.com/pulse/sustaining-spirit-cooperative-capitalism-adena-friedman

Gartenberg, C. (2018, August 13). Rise of enterprise. *The Verge.* https://www.theverge.com/2018/8/13/17644234/michael-dell-enterprise-technology-consumer-laptop-private-public-emc

Gatto, M. (1995). Sustainability: Is it a well defined concept? *Ecological Applications, 5*(4), 1181–1183.

Gelb, D. S. (2000). Managerial ownership and accounting disclosures: An empirical study. *Review of Quantitative Finance and Accounting, 15*(2), 169–185.

Gelb, D. S., & Siegel, P. (2000). Intangible assets and corporate signaling. *Review of Quantitative Finance and Accounting, 15*(4), 307–323.

Gelber, L. R. (2013). The Gelberlaw glossary: An encyclopedic dictionary of the securities industry. http://www.gelberlaw.net/Glossary.html

Global Reporting Initiative. (2020). *Consolidated set of GRI sustainability reporting standards 2020*. GRI.

Governance & Accountability Institute. (2020, October 26). G&A Institute's 2020 Research Report shows 65% of Russell 1000® published sustainability reports in 2019, up from 60% in 2018. https://www.ga-institute.com/press-releases/article/ga-institutes-2020-research-report-shows-65-of-russell-1000R-published-sustainability-reports.html (accessed July 5, 2021).

Grunig, J. E. (1984). Organizations, environments, and models of public relations. *Public Relations Research & Education, 1*(1), 6–29.

Grunig, J. E., & Hunt, T. (1984). *Managing public relations.* Holt, Rinehart and Winston.

Grunig, L. A., Grunig, J. E., & Dozier, D. M. (2002). *Excellent public relations and effective organizations.* Erlbaum.

Hall v. Geiger-Jones Co., 242 U.S. 539. (1917).

Hand, R. M., & Lev, B. (Eds.) (2003). *Intangible assets: Values, measures, and risks.* Oxford University Press.

Hays, K. (2008, September 9). Enron settlement: $7.2 billion to shareholders. *Houston Chronicle.*

Heath, R. L. (2018). Issues management in investor relations and financial communication . In A. V. Laskin (Ed.), *Handbook of financial communication and investor relations* (pp. 261–274). Wiley-Blackwell.

Higgins, R. B. (2000). *Best practices in global investor relations: The creation of shareholder value.* Quorum Books.

Hill & Knowlton (2006). *Return of reputation: Corporate reputation watch 2006.* Bisqit Design.

Hon, L. C. (1997). What have you done for me lately? Exploring effectiveness in public relations. *Journal of Public Relations Research, 9*(1), 1–30.

Hon, L. C. (1998). Demonstrating effectiveness in public relations: Goals, objectives and evaluation. *Journal of Public Relations Research, 10*(2), 103–135.

Hull, D. (2020, December 18). Elon Musk has made millionaires out of his most loyal fans. *Bloomberg.*

Human, T. (2020, October 26). Investors miss field trips under COVID-19. *IR Magazine.* https://www.irmagazine.com/corporate-access/investors-miss-field-trips-under-covid-19

Human, T. (2021, February 17). Climate change biggest issue for markets in coming years, say largest asset owners. *Corporate Secretary.*

JIRA (Japan Investor Relations Association). (.n.d.). Overview of JIRA. https://www.jira.or.jp/english

Kaplan, R. S., & Norton, D. P. (1992). The balanced scorecard: Measures that drive performance. *Harvard Business Review, 70*(1), 71–79.

Kaplan, R. S., & Norton, D. P. (1993). Putting the balanced scorecard to work. *Harvard Business Review, 71*(5), 134–142.

Kaplan, R. S., & Norton, D. P. (1996a). Using the balanced scorecard as a management system. *Harvard Business Review, 74*(1), 75–85.

Kaplan, R. S., & Norton, D. P. (1996b). *The balanced scorecard: Translating strategy into action.* Boston, MA: Harvard Business School Press.

Kaplan, R. S., & Norton, D. P. (2000). Having trouble with your strategy? Then map it. *Harvard Business Review, 78*(5), 167–176.

Kaplan, R. S., & Norton, D. P. (2001). *The strategy-focused organization: How balanced scorecard companies thrive in new business environment.* Boston, MA: Harvard Business School Press.

Kaplan, R. S., & Norton, D. P. (2004). *Strategy maps: Converting intangible assets into tangible outcomes.* Boston, MA: Harvard Business School Press.

Kaplan, R. S., & Norton, D. P. (2006). *Alignment: Using the balanced scorecard to create corporate synergies.* Boston, MA: Harvard Business School Press.

Kelly, K. S., Laskin, A. V., & Rosenstein, G. A. (2010). Investor relations: Two-way symmetrical practice. *Journal of Public Relations Research, 22*(2), 182–208.

Kim, Y. (2001). Measuring the economic value of public relations. *Journal of Public Relations Research, 13*(1), 3–26.

Kohler, K. (2018). Investor relations in Germany: Institutionalization and professional roles. In A. V. Laskin (Ed.), *Handbook of financial communication and investor relations* (pp. 429–442). Wiley-Blackwell.

Kolk, A. (2008). Sustainability, accountability and corporate governance: Exploring multinationals' reporting practices. *Business Strategy and the Environment, 17*(1), 1–15.

Koller, T. (2007, June). Valuation and IROs' important role in the equation. Paper presented at NIRI Annual Conference, Orlando, FL.

Koning Beals, R. (2020, December 9). Influential New York pension fund will drop fossil-fuel stocks, put pressure on utilities and auto makers to cut emissions. *MarketWatch.*https://www.marketwatch.com/story/influential-new-york-pension-fund-will-drop-fossil-fuel-stocks-put-pressure-on-utilities-and-auto-makers-to-cut-emissions-11607538475

Kotler, P., & Lee, N. (2005). *Corporate social responsibility: Doing the most good for your company and your cause.* Wiley.

Kurutz, S. (2021, February 27). Anyone who's anyone has a SPAC right now. *The New York Times.*

Laskin, A. V. (2006). Investor relations practices at Fortune-500 companies: An exploratory study. *Public Relations Review, 32*(1), 69–70.

Laskin, A. V. (2007). The value of investor relations: A Delphi panel investigation. *Institute for Public Relations Research Monograph.* Gainesville, FL: Institute for Public Relations.

Laskin, A. V. (2008). *Investor relations: A national study of the profession* (Doctoral dissertation). University of Florida.

Laskin, A. V. (2009). A descriptive account of the investor relations profession: A national study. *International Journal of Business Communication, 46*(2), 208–233.

Laskin, A. V. (2010a). *Managing investor relations: Strategies for effective communication.* Business Expert Press.

Laskin, A. V. (2010b). Investor relations. In R. Heath (Ed.), *The Sage handbook of public relations* (2nd ed., pp. 611–622). Sage.

Laskin, A. V. (2011). How investor relations contributes to the corporate bottom line. *Journal of Public Relations Research, 23*(3), 302–324.

Laskin, A. V. (2012a). Public relations scales: Advancing the excellence theory. *Journal of Communication Management, 16*(4), 355–370.

Laskin, A. V. (2012b). Social media and investor relations. In S. Duhe (Ed.), *New media and public relations* (2nd ed., pp. 105–114). Peter Lang Publishing.

Laskin, A. V. (2013a). Investor relations. In R. Heath (Ed.), *Encyclopedia of public relations* (2nd ed., pp. 482–486). Sage.

Laskin, A. V. (2013b). Annual financial report. In R. Heath (Ed.), *Encyclopedia of public relations* (2nd ed., pp. 27–29). Sage.

Laskin, A. V. (2013c). Financial performance and reputation. In C. Carroll (Ed.), *The handbook of communication and corporate reputation* (pp. 376–387). Wiley.

Laskin, A. V. (Ed.). (2014). Special Issue: Strategic financial communication. *International Journal of Strategic Communication, 8*(3).

Laskin, A. V. (2014). Investor relations as a public relations function: A state of the profession in the United States. *Journal of Public Relations Research, 26*(3), 200–214.

Laskin, A. V. (2015). Securities and Exchange Commission (SEC). In C. L. Cooper (Ed.), *Wiley encyclopedia of management* (Vol. 6, 3rd ed., pp. 1–3). Wiley.

Laskin, A. V. (2016a). Nonfinancial information in investor communications. *International Journal of Business Communication, 53*(4), 375–397.

Laskin, A. V. (2016b). Levels of evaluation: An agency's perspective on measurement and evaluation. *Public Relations Journal, 10*(2), 1–31.

Laskin, A. V. (2017). New media in investor relations. In S. Duhe (Ed.), *New media and public relations* (3rd ed., pp. 107–116). Peter Lang Publishing.

Laskin, A. V. (2018a). The third-person effects in the investment decision making: A case of corporate social responsibility. *Corporate Communications: An International Journal, 23*(3), 456–468.

Laskin, A. V. (2018b). The narrative strategies of winners and losers: Analyzing annual reports of publicly traded corporations. *International Journal of Business Communication, 55*(3), 338–356.

Laskin, A. V. (Ed.). (2018c). *Handbook of financial communication and investor relations.* Wiley-Blackwell.

Laskin, A. V. (2018d). Investor relations and financial communication: The evolution of the profession. In A. V. Laskin (Ed.), *Handbook of financial communication and investor relations* (pp. 3–22). Wiley-Blackwell.

Laskin, A. V. (2019). Investor relations. In B. R. Brunner (Ed.), *Public relations theory: Application and understanding* (pp. 219–232). Wiley-Blackwell.

Laskin, A. V., & Kresic, K. M. (2021). Inclusion as a component of CSR and a brand connection strategy. In D. Pompper (Ed.), *Public relations for social responsibility: Affirming DEI commitment with action* (pp. 149–163). Emerald Publishing.

Laskin, A. V., & Laskin, A. A. (2018a). Adoption of social media: A case of heads of states. In A. V. Laskin (Ed.), *Social, mobile, and emerging media around the world: Communication case studies.* Lexington Books.

Laskin, A. V., & Laskin, A. A. (2018b). Measurement and evaluation of investor relations and financial communication activities. In A. V. Laskin (Ed.), *Handbook of financial communication and investor relations* (pp. 275–282). Wiley-Blackwell.

Laskin, A. V., & Samoylenko, S. A. (2014). The investor communication strategies of newspaper corporations: A computerized content analysis. *International Journal of Strategic Communication, 8*(3), 196–214.

Lev, B. (1992). Information disclosure strategy. *California Management Review, 34*(4), 9–32.

Lev, B. (2001). *Intangibles.* Washington, DC: The Brookings Institution Press.

Lev, B. (2002).Where have all of Enron's intangibles gone? *Journal of Accounting and Public Policy, 21,* 131–135.

Lev, B. (2003). What then must we do? In R. M. Hand & B. Lev. (Eds.), *Intangible assets: Values, measures, and risks* (pp. 511–524). New York: Oxford University Press.

Lev, B. (2004). Sharpening the intangibles edge. *Harvard Business Review, 82*(6), 109–116.

Lev, B. (2005). Intangible assets: Concepts and measurements. *Encyclopedia of Social Measurement, 2,* 299–305.

Lev, B. (2012). *Winning investors over.* Boston, MA: Harvard Business Review Press.

Lev, B., Sarath, B., & Sougiannis, T. (2005). R&D reporting biases and their consequences. *Contemporary Accounting Research*, *22*(4), 977–1026.

Liekefett, K., & Austin, S. (2020, November 8). The comeback of hostile takeovers. *Harvard Law School Forum on Corporate Governance*. https://corpgov.law.harvard. edu/2020/11/08/the-comeback-of-hostile-takeovers/?MessageRunDetailID=380290860 4&PostID=21743614&utm_medium=email&utm_source=rasa_io

Likely, F., Rockland, D., & Weiner, M. (2006). *Perspectives on ROI of media relations publicity efforts*. Institute for Public Relations. http://www.instituteforpr.org/topics/ mediarelations-publicity-efforts

Lindenmann, W. K. (2003). *Guidelines for measuring the effectiveness of PR programs and activities*. Institute for Public Relations.

Linford, J. (2020, October 12). Recent trends in retail investing: What does it mean for issuers? *IR Magazine* https://www.irmagazine.com/small-cap/recent-trends-retail-investing-what-does-it-mean-issuers

Lombardo, C., & Gasparro, A. (2018, November 26). Campbell Soup, Third Point settle proxy fight. *The Wall Street Journal* https://www.wsj.com/articles/campbell-soup-third-point-settle-proxy-fight-1543254800

Loomis, C. J. (1997, October 27). Warren Buffett's wild ride at Salomon. *Fortune*. https:// fortune.com/1997/10/27/warren-buffett-salomon (accessed June 29, 2021).

Macey, J. R., & Miller, G. P. (1991). Origin of the blue sky laws. *Texas Law Review*, *70*(2), 347–397.

MacKay, C. (1841/2011). *Extraordinary popular delusions and the madness of crowds*. CreateSpace.

Mandato, J., & Devine, W. (2020, March 4). Why the CEO shouldn't also be the board chair. *Harvard Business Review*.

Manning, A., & Rockland, D. B. (2011). Understanding the Barcelona Principles. *Public Relations Strategist*, *17*(1), 30–31.

Marcus, B. W., & Wallace, S. L. (1997). *New dimensions in investor relations: Competing for capital in the 21st century*. John Wiley & Sons.

Martin, E. F., Jr. (2007). Using wave theory to maximize retail investor media communications. *International Journal of Strategic Communication*, *1*(3), 191–206.

Melgin, E., Luoma-aho, V., Hara, M., & Melgin, J. (2018). The Nordic approach to investor relations. In A. V. Laskin (Ed.), *Handbook of financial communication and investor relations* (pp. 419–428). Wiley-Blackwell.

Michaelson, D., & Gilfeather, J. (2003, January). *What you need to know to measure investor relations*. Institute for Public Relations.

Michaelson, D., & Stacks, D. W. (2011). Standardization in public relations measurement and evaluation. *Public Relations Journal*, *5*(2), 1–22.

Mikolajczak, C. (2018, April 3). Spotify shares jump in record-setting direct listing. *Reuters*. https://www.reuters.com/article/us-spotify-ipo/spotify-shares-jump-in-record-setting-direct-listing-idUSKCN1HA12B

Minow, N. (2002, May 21). Year of corporate meltdown. *CBSMarketWatch.com*.

Moffatt, I. (1994). On measuring sustainable development indicators. *International Journal of Sustainable Development and World Ecology*, *1*, 97–109.

Morrill, D. C. (1995). Origins of NIRI. The National Investor Relations Institute.

Morrill, D. C. (2007). Personal interview.

Morrison Foerster. (2017, August). The guide to social media and the securities laws.

Morrow Sodali. (2021). Proxy solicitation and shareholder meeting services.

Moscato, D. (2018). Corporate social responsibility: Coming to social and environmental impact in the global economy. In A. V. Laskin (Ed.), *Handbook of financial communication and investor relations* (pp. 245–260). Wiley-Blackwell.

Murphy, P. (1991). The limits of symmetry: A game theory approach to symmetric and asymmetrical public relations. *Public Relations Research Annual, 3,* 115–131.

National Investor Relations Institute. (2016). NIRI Earnings Process Practice Research Report. https://www.niri.org/NIRI/media/Protected-Documents_ExcludeGlobalSubs/Analytics%20Reports/Analytics_Guidance/NIRI-Earnings-Process-Practices-Report-2016.pdf

National Investor Relations Institute. (2020, March). NIRI guidelines regarding company-sponsored research.

Neu, D., Warsame H., & Pedwell K. (1998). Managing public impressions: Environmental disclosures in annual reports. *Accounting Organizations and Society, 23*(3), 265–282.

Nili, Y., & Shaner, M. W. (2020, October 21). Back to the future? Reclaiming shareholder democracy through virtual annual meetings. *Harvard Law School Forum on Corporate Governance.*

NIRI Board of Directors. (2003, March). Definition of investor relations.

Norberg, J. (2020, October 22). SEC issues record $114 million whistleblower award.

Norman, W., & MacDonald, C. (2004). Getting to the bottom of the "triple bottom line." *Business Ethics Quarterly, 12,* 243–262.

Posner, C. (2020, November 5). New initiative asks companies to disclose board racial/ethnic composition. *Cooley PubCo.*

PricewaterhouseCoopers. (2005). *The value reporting revolution: Moving beyond the earnings game.* New York, NY: Wiley.

PRSA. (2016). About public relations.

Rabouin, D., & Witherspoon, A. (2020, October 8). JPMorgan commits $30 billion to fight the racial wealth gap. *Axios.*

Ragas, M. W., & Laskin, A. V. (2014). Mixed-methods: Measurement and evaluation among investor relations officers. *Corporate Communications: An International Journal, 19*(2), 166–181.

Ragas, M. W., Laskin, A. V., & Brusch, M. (2014). Investor relations measurement: An industry survey. *Journal of Communication Management, 18*(2), 176–192.

Rao, H., & Sivakumar, K. (1999). Institutional sources of boundary-spanning structures: The establishment of investor relations departments in the Fortune 500 industrials. *Organizational Science, 10*(1), 27–42.

Rapier, G. (2020, December 26). Wall Street analysts tore down 7 competing car batteries. They found Tesla once again at the front the pack. *Business Insider.* https://www.businessinsider.com/teslas-batteries-best-cheapest-industry-ahead-competition-ubs-teardown-2020-10?fbclid=IwAR1uJ7tYLkmdZa149AppefS3NGp1Yd5Bh0kIiVMDyRteQRalU2ecGpBdsXs

Reuters. (2018, October 26). Third Point sues Campbell Soup, accusing it of misleading investors. *CNBC.* https://www.cnbc.com/2018/10/26/third-point-sues-campbell-soup-accusing-it-of-misleading-investors.html#:~:text=Activist%20investor%20Third%20Point%20sued%20Campbell%20Soup%20on%20Thursday%2C%20alleging,a%20recently%20completed%20strategic%20review.&text=It%20asked%20the%20court%20to,its%20annual%20meeting%20on%20Nov

Riding, S. (2020, October 17). ESG funds forecast to outnumber conventional funds by 2025. *Financial Times.* https://www.ft.com/content/5cd6e923-81e0-4557-8cff-a02fb5e01d42

Rivel, B., & Peebles, J. (2008, January). Ask the researchers: Insight on the questions IROs are asking. *Investor Relations Update*, pp. 18 and 21.

Robinson, E. J. (1966). *Communication and public relations.* Charles E. Merrill.

Rogers, J. A. (2012, March 6). Investor protection, market integrity and small business capital formation. *AARP.*

Rust, R. T., Lemon, K. N., & Zeithaml, V. A. (2004). Return on marketing: Using customer equity to focus marketing strategy. *Journal of Marketing, 68*(1), 109–127.

Ryan, T. M., & Jacobs, C. A. (2005). *Using investor relations to maximize equity valuation.* Wiley Finance.

Rydberg, S. (1979). *Stora Kopparberg – 1000 years of an industrial activity.* Gullers International AB.

Sanofi. (2020, June 3). Sanofi to launch "Action 2020", a worldwide employee stock purchase plan. *GlobeNewswire.*

Savage, R. H. (1972). Crucial role of investor relations. *Harvard Business Review, 48*(6), 122–130.

Schnidman, E. (2020, October 21). Understanding active investing tools and technology. *IR Magazine.* https://www.irmagazine.com/technology-social-media/understanding-active-investing-tools-and-technology (accessed June 29, 2021).

Silver, D. (2004). The IR-PR nexus. In B. M. Cole (Ed.), *The new investor relations: Experts perspective on the state of the art* (pp. 59–88). Bloomberg Press.

Smith, A. (1776/2007). *An inquiry into the nature and causes of the wealth of nations.* MetaLibri.

Sorkin, A. R. (2016, July 21). C.E.O.s meet in secret over the sorry state of public companies. *The New York Times*, p. B6.

Sorkin, A. R., Karaian, J., de la Merced, M. J., Hirsch, L., & Livni, E. (2020, December 1). Nasdaq pushes for diversity in the boardroom. *The New York Times.* https://www.nytimes.com/2020/12/01/business/dealbook/nasdaq-diversity-boards.html (accessed June 29, 2021).

Starkman, R., & Klingbail, S. (2004, March 2). Investor relations and the art of managing market expectations. *Haaretz.* www.haaretz.com/print-edition/business/investor-relations-and-the-art-of-managing-market-expectations-1.115568

Statista. (2021). Revenue per employee of selected tech companies in 2019. https://www.statista.com/statistics/217489/revenue-per-employee-of-selected-tech-companies (accessed June 29, 2021).

Stein, D. N. (2018). Perception audits: Learning investment community sentiment. In A. V. Laskin (Ed.), *Handbook of financial communication and investor relations* (pp. 283–292). Wiley-Blackwell.

Stewart, D. M. (2009). Marketing accountability: Linking marketing actions to financial results. *Journal of Business Research, 62*(6), 636–643.

Stora Enso. (n.d.). Our businesses. http://www.storaenso.com/about/businesses (accessed June 29, 2021).

Svec, V. (2021, February). The role of communications in a successful bankruptcy. *Strategies & Tactics*, p. 21.

The oldest corporation in the world. (1963, March 15). *Time, 81*(11), 98.

Third Point. (2020). Our company. https://www.thirdpoint.com/our-company (accessed June 29, 2021).

Thompson, L. M. (2002, April 9). NIRI ten point program to help restore investor confidence. *NIRI's Executive Alert*, pp 1–3.

Tonello, M. (2014, May 29). The activism of Carl Icahn and Bill Ackman. *Harvard Law School Forum on Corporate Governance*.

Trentmann, N. (2021, March 1). Companies zoom in on small shareholders amid retail trading frenzy. *The Wall Street Journal*.

Tuominen, P. (1997). Investor relations: A Nordic school approach. *Corporate Communications, 2*(1), 46–55.

Ulmer, R. R., Sellnow, T. L., & Seeger, M. W. (2007). *Effective crisis communication*. Sage.

US Securities and Exchange Commission. (2008, August 7). Commission guidance on the use of company web sites.

US Securities and Exchange Commission. (2012, August 10). Form 8-K. https://www.sec. gov/fast-answers/answersform8khtm.html

US Securities and Exchange Commission. (2013, April 2). SEC says social media OK for company announcement of investors are alerted.

US Securities and Exchange Commission. (2019, October 2). Investment Advisers Act of 1940 as amended January 3, 2019.

US Securities and Exchange Commission. (2020, November 13). SEC charges former Wells Fargo executives for misleading investors about key performance metric.

US Securities and Exchange Commission. (2021, January 21). How to read a 10-K/10-Q.

US Securities and Exchange Commission. (2021, February 4). SEC charges investment adviser and others with defrauding over 17,000 retail investors.

Uysal, N. (2018). Faith-based investor activism for corporate environmental responsibility: Catalysts for corporate change. In A. V. Laskin (Ed.), *Handbook of financial communication and investor relations* (pp. 245–260). Wiley-Blackwell.

van Elderen, W. (2011). The Dutch East India Company. *European Heritage Project*. http://european-heritage.org/netherlands/alkmaar/dutch-east-india-company

Vanguard. (2016). Vanguard 500 Index Fund Investor Shares (VFINX). https://personal. vanguard.com/us/FundsSnapshot?FundId=0040&FundIntExt=INT#tab=5

Vanguard. (2020, December). Vanguard investment stewardship insights: Diversity in the workplace. https://higherlogicdownload.s3.amazonaws.com/ GOVERNANCEPROFESSIONALS/a8892c7c-6297-4149-b9fc-378577d0b150/ UploadedImages/ISWORK_122020.pdf

Vigna, P. (2013, April 2). SEC clears Netflix's Reed Hastings; Says social media's OK for sharing. *The Wall Street Journal*. https://www.wsj.com/articles/BL-MB-46939

Volkova, O. N. (2017). Investor relations: International context, Russian practice. *Journal of Corporate Finance Research, 12*(2), 62–76.

Wallman, S. (2003). Foreword. In R. M. Hand & B. Lev. (Eds.), *Intangible assets: Values, measures, and risks (pp. v–vi)* New York: Oxford University Press.

Walsh, J. (2020, January 8). Third Point, once a Campbell Soup critic, now expresses confidence. *Courier Post*.

Watson, T. (2012). The evolution of public relations measurement and evaluation. *Public Relations Review, 38*(3), 390–398.

Watson, T., & Zerfass, A. (2011). Return on investment in public relations: A critique of concepts used by practitioners from communication and management science

perspectives. *Prism*, 8(1). http://www.prismjournal.org/fileadmin/8_1/Watson_Zerfass.
pdf

Westbrook, I. (2018). Influences and priorities in investor relations in Australia. In A. V.
Laskin (Ed.), *Handbook of financial communication and investor relations* (pp. 473–484).
Wiley-Blackwell.

Whelan, T., Atz, U., Van Holt, T., & Clark, C. (2021). ESG and financial performance:
Uncovering the relationship by aggregating evidence from 1,000 plus studies published
between 2015 – 2020.

Whitehouse, M. (2018). Financial analysts and their role in financial communication and
investor relations. In A. V. Laskin (Ed.), *Handbook of financial communication and
investor relations* (pp. 117–126). Wiley-Blackwell.

Whitten, R. L., & Coombs, W. T. (2018). Crisis communication: Insights and implications
for investor relations. In A. V. Laskin (Ed.), *Handbook of financial communication and
investor relations* (pp. 23–32). Wiley-Blackwell.

Wiesel, T., Skiera, B., & Villanueva, J. (2008). Customer equity: An integral part of
financial reporting. *Journal of Marketing*, *72*(2), 1–14.

Witkowski, W. (2020, January 7). Third Point cuts its stake in Campbell Soup by 2.1
million shares. *MarketWatch*. https://www.marketwatch.com/story/third-point-cuts-
its-stake-in-campbell-soup-by-21-million-shares-2020-01-07#:~:text=Daniel%20
Loeb's%20hedge%20fund%20Third,Exchange%20Commission%20filing%20late%20
Tuesday.&text=Following%20the%20sale%2C%20the%20hedge,company%2C%20
according%20to%20the%20filing

Wooldridge, C. R. (1906). *The Grafters of America: Who they are and how they work*.
Monarch Book Company.

World Commission on Environment and Development (1987). *Our common future*.
United Nations. http://www.un-documents.net/wced-ocf.htm (accessed July 5, 2021).

Wright, D. P. (2007). Reviewing the growth and development of scholarly, online
publishing: Forging a new frontier in public relations research. *Public Relations Journal*,
1(1), 1–15.

Young, A. (1998). *Measuring intangible investment. Towards an interim statistical
framework: Selecting the core components of intangible investment*. Paris: OECD
Secretariat.

Index

@TikStocks   139
144A/Reg S, see depositary receipts

account   31
   account assistant   31
   account coordinator   31
   account director   31
   account executive   31
   account supervisor   31
   assistant account executive   31
accredited investor, see investor,
      accredited
acquirer   128
active investing, see investing, active
activist investor, see investor, activist
activist shareholder, see investor, activist
ADR, see American depositary receipts
advertising   139
advisory vote   117
agency   31–32
agency theory   112
   agent   112
AGM, see annual general meeting
airdrop   193
aligning the incentives   112
alternative trading system   56
angel funding   40, 155
   angel investment   155
   angel investor   40, 155, 156
American depositary receipts, see depositary
      receipts
Amsterdam bourse   10
analysis   45, 75–77, see also analyst
analysis, fundamental   45
analysis, quantamental   45
   analysis, technical   45

analyst   51–52, 65–66, 87–88, 140–141,
      147–149, see also analysis
   coverage   52
   recommendation   51
annual general meeting   141–144
annual report   26, 63–75
annual shareholder meeting, see annual
      general meeting
AR, see augmented reality
ARFI, see Financial Communications and
      Investor Relations Alliance
asset   67–69
   asset turnover ratio   76
   asset, tangible   67, 83–84
   asset, intangible   67–68, 83–84, 90–91, see
      also intangibles
Association of Fundraising
      Professionals   24
ATS, see alternative trading system
attitude   170–171, 174
audit   78, 97, 101
   audit committee   116
   auditor   78, 97, 101, 117
augmented reality   190
Australian National Superannuation
      Scheme   42
awareness   171, 174, 176

balance sheet   67–70
bankruptcy   130–131
beating the estimate   140
beat the market   99
Berkshire Hathaway   46, 47, see also Buffett,
      Warren
Big Five   78
Big Four   78

Investor Relations and Financial Communication: Creating Value Through Trust and Understanding,
First Edition. Alexander V. Laskin.
© 2022 John Wiley & Sons, Inc. Published 2022 by John Wiley & Sons, Inc.

blank check company 164, see also special
    purpose acquisition company
blue chips 10
blue sky laws 11–12
blue sky securities, see blue sky securities
    under securities
Board of Directors 113–117
  board committee 115–116
  board independence 113, 115
  board composition 113
  Chair of the Board 115
bottom line 66, 76
brand 91
Brundtland Report 108
Buffett, Warren 44, 46, 47, 55, see also
    Berkshire Hathaway
business Watergate 101
Buttonwood agreement 158–159
buy-side 50–51

California Public Employees' Retirement
System 42, 110, 124
CalPERS, see California Public Employees'
    Retirement System
Calvert Social Index 44–45
capital asset 67
capitalization 62
CarParts.com 191
cash flow statement 72–73
  cash balance 72–73
  cash from financing 72–73
  cash from investments 72–73
  cash from operations 72–73
cashtag 138, see also StockTwits
cash out 156
CCO 25
CDO 30
central bank 27–28
CEO 25
celebrity CEO 87
  CEO pay ratio 103, 143
certification and notice of termination of
    registration 165–166
CFO 25
chief communication officer, see CCO
chief development officer, see CDO
chief executive officer, see CEO
chief financial officer, see CFO
chief operations officer, see COO

Climate Action 100+ 123
climate change 123
code of conduct 33–34
  NIRI's Code of Conduct 33–34
code of ethics 34
  PRSA Code of Ethics 34
Code of Hammurabi 8
COGS, see cost of goods sold
coin 193
Committee on Directors and Corporate
    Governance 114
commodization 90
common share, see share, common
competitive market position 83–84, 86, 88
comprehension 174
consensus estimate 51–52
convertible share, see share, convertible
COO 25
cooling-off period 159
Corbin Advisors 36
corporate governance 107–108, 111–118
corporate social responsibility 107–108,
    110–111
cost 65
  cost of goods sold 65
  cost of revenues 65
  cost of sales 65
counseling the management 150–151
crisis 126–132
  crisis management 127–128
  crisis response team 127
crowdinvesting 191–192
crowdsourcing 191
cryptocurrency 193
CSR, see corporate social responsibility
C-suite 7
current asset 67–69
current disclosure 26
current liabilities 69
current portion of long-term debt 69
current report 26
current reporting 26
cybersecurity 196

dark pool 56, see dark under stock exchange
under stock
debt 5, 50
  debt investor, see investor, debt
  debt holders, see investor, debt

DEI   111
delisting   164–165
depositary   161, 183
depositary receipts   161–162, 182–184
  144A/Reg S depositary receipts   183–184
  American depositary receipts   161–162
  Euro-denominated depositary
    receipts   183
  Global depositary receipts   182
  Level I   183–184
  Level II   184
  Level III   184
  sponsored   184
  unsponsored   184
deregistration   165–166
direct listing   162–163
disclosure   11, 26, 63–75, 81–84, 135–137
  disclosure officer   135
Discord   139
diversification   46
diversity   111, 114
dividend   48, 70
  dividend payout ratio   77
  dividend yield   77
DJTA, see Dow Jones Transportation Average
DJUA, see Dow Jones Utility Average
Dodd–Frank Wall Street Reform and
    Consumer Protection Act   102–103
dominant coalition   7
Dow Jones Transport, see Dow Jones
    Transportation Average
Dow Jones Transportation Average   44
Dow Jones Utilities, see Dow Jones Utility
    Average
Dow Jones Utility Average   44
due diligence   157, 163
Dutch East India Company   10

earned media   139–140
earnings   63–67
  earnings before interest, depreciation,
    taxes, and amortization   6, 66
  earnings before interest and taxes   66
  earnings before taxes   66
  earnings calendar   140
  earnings call   140–141
  earnings cast   140–141
  earnings conference   140–141
  earnings guidance   141

earnings per share   66–67, 77
earnings range   141
earnings release   140–141
earnings report   140–141
EBIT, see Earnings before interest
    and taxes
EBIDTA, see Earnings before interest,
    depreciation, taxes, and amortization
EBT, see Earnings before taxes
EDGAR, see Electronic Data Gathering,
    Analysis, and Retrieval system
EDR, see Euro-denominated depositary
    receipts under depositary receipts
efficient market hypothesis   4–5
Electronic Data Gathering, Analysis, and
    Retrieval system   55, 124, 137, 157
emergency reporting   53, 136
emerging growth company   103
employee   41–42
endowment   43, 111
Enron   21, 48, 78, 101
environmental, social, and governance,
    see ESG
EPS, see Earnings per share
equilibrium   4
equity   5
  Equity investor, see investor, equity
eras of investor relations   12–22
  communication era   12–15
  financial era   16–19
  synergy era   20–22
ESG   88, 108, 196–197
  ESG disclosure   88, 109–110
  ESG fund   110, 123

Ethics Council   34
exchange, see stock exchange
Euro-denominated depositary receipts, see
    depositary receipts
European depositary receipts, see Euro-
    denominated depositary receipts
exclusive content   99
Executive Committee   116
executive compensation   103
executive vice president   25
extra-financial information   85

fair valuation, see fair value
fair value   3–5, 8, 26–27

Falun mine   9
Federal Old-Age and Survivors Insurance
      Trust Fund   42
the Federal Reserve System   27–29
fiat currencies   193
Fidelity   191
fiduciary duty   6
finance committee   116
financial analysis, see analysis
financial analyst   17–18, 51–52, 147–149; see
      also analysis
Financial Communications and Investor
      Relations Alliance   185
financial information   63
Financial Times Stock Exchange100, 44
fixed assets   67
follow-on public offering   161
Form 8-K, see current report
Form 10-K, see annual report
Form 10-Q, see quarterly report
Form 14A, see proxy statement
Form15, see certification and notice of
      termination of registration
Form F-1, see registration statement
Form N-8A, see notification of registration
Form S-1, see registration statement
FPO, see follow-on public offering
framing the results   176
free media   139
FTSE100, see Financial Times Stock
      Exchange 100
FTSE4Good Index   44
fundraising   28–30
fundamental analysis, see analysis

GAAP, see Generally Accepted Accounting
Principles
GameStop   125–126
GDR, see Global Depositary Receipts
Generally Accepted Accounting
      Principles   77–78
Global Depositary Receipts, see depositary
      receipts
Global Reporting Initiative   109
going public   155–156
going private   164–166
goodwill   67–69
governance   88, 111–118
Graham, Benjamin   45–46

greenwashing   108–110
GRI, see Global Reporting Initiative
gross margin   65
growth investor, see investor, growth
gun-jumping, see jumping the gun

hashtag   138–139
hedge fund   42–43
hostile takeover   128–130
hot air securities, see blue sky securities

IABC, see International Association of
Business Communicators
Icahn, Carl   47, 125
ICO, see initial coin offering
IFRS, see International Financial Reporting
      Standards
IIRC, see International Integrated Reporting
      Council
impact investing   111
incentive   112
inclusion   111, 196, 198
income statement   63–67
independent director   113; see also Board of
      Directors
in-house   31
initial coin offering   193
initial public offering   40, 156–160, 184
initial token offering   193
internal director   133; see also Board of
      Directors
insider   41, 97
   Insider trading   41, 97
insolvency   130
institutional investor, see investor,
      institutional
intangibles   67, 69, 83–84, 87, 90, 91, see also
      asset, intangible under asset
intangible economy   83–84
intent to act   174
inter-border transactions   183
interest burden ratio   76
intermediary   50–51, 173
intern   31, 36
International Association of Business
      Communicators   24
International Financial Reporting
      Standards   77
International Integrated Reporting Council   109

investing   41–48
  investing, active   45–48
  investing, passive   44–45
investment adviser   98
  Investment Adviser Act of 1940, 98
  Investment Company Act of 1940, 98
investment rating   148
investor   39–50
  investor, accredited   40
  investor, activist   47
  investor, angel   40
  investor conference   149–150
  investor day   149–150
  investor, debt   50
  investor, equity   39–49
  investor field trips   150
  investor, growth   49
  investor, institutional   42–48
  investor relations definition   3–8
  Investor Relations Charter   33
  investor relationship   146–147
  investor relationship building   146–147
  investor relations officer   3
  Investor Relations Association   15
  investor relations department   17, 25
  investor, retail   41–42
  investor, value   49
  investor, venture   40
IPO, see initial public offering
IRA, see Investor Relations Association under
    investor
IRC, see Investor Relations Charter under
    investor
IRO, see investor relations officer under
    investor
IR Society   8, 185
issue management   107–108
issuer   11–12, 96
ITO, see initial token offering

Japan Investor Relations Association   185
JIRA, see Japan Investor Relations Association
JOBS Act, see Jumpstart Our Business
    Startups Act
jumping the gun   159
Jumpstart Our Business Startups Act   103–104

lead independent director   115
Level I depositary receipts, see depositary
    receipts

Level II depositary receipts, see depositary
    receipts
Level III depositary receipts, see depositary
    receipts
Levels of Evaluation   170–177
leverage ratio   76
liability   69–70
  Liability, long-term   69
  Liability, short-term   69
liquidity   156, 176
lit exchange, see stock exchange
lock-up agreement   157–158

magic bullet   169
Management Development Committee   116
Management Discussion & Analysis of
    Financial Condition and Results of
    Operations   81
market stabilization   156–157
material event   26, 97, 136
maturity date   50
material information, see material event
MD&A, see Management Discussion &
    Analysis of Financial Condition and
    Results of Operations
MEIRA, see Middle East Investor Relations
    Association
Middle East Investor Relations
    Association   185
missing the estimate   140
mixed reality   190
Morningstar Small Core Index   44
MR, see mixed reality
MSCI KLD 400 Social Index   44–45
mutual fund   16, 42, 98

Named Executive Officer   143
Nasdaq   24–25, 56, 158–159, 165
National Investor Relations Institute
    3, 24, 194
negative screening   110
NEO, see Named Executive Officer
net income   66
net profit   66
new ROE, see return on expectations
New York State Exchange   24–25, 56, 158–159
NIRI, see National Investor Relations
    Institute
noise trader, see trader, noise
nonbinding vote   103, 141–142

noncurrent asset   67–69
noncurrent liabilities   68–69
non-deal roadshow   149
nonfinancial assets, see nonfinancial
     information
nonfinancial information   81–89
non-GAAP   77–78
notification of registration   98
NYSE, see New York Stock Exchange

The Office of the Investor Advocate   102
The Office of the Whistleblower   102–103
one-on-one, see one-on-one meeting
one-on-one meeting   26, 99, 144–147
one-way communication   5–6
operating income   66
operating income ratio   76
organizational process   87
Oscar di Bilancio   186
OTC   24–25, 165
OTCQB   165
OTCQX   165
Our Common Future   108
outcome level   170–172, 174
outgrowth level   170–172, 174–175
outperform level   170–172, 175
output level   170–172, 172–173
outreach level   170–172, 173
overcorrection   3–4
over-the-counter market, see OTC
overvaluation   3–4
owned media   137–140
ownership research   150–151

paid media   137–140
Paris Agreement   110
partner   31
passive investing, see investing, passive under
     investing
PaxWorld   111
P/B, see price to book value ratio
PCAOB   101
peer   66–67
PEG, see price to earnings to growth ratio
penny stocks   164–165
perception audit   150–151
periodic reporting   26, 96–97, 135–136
Pink Open Market, see Pink Sheets
Pink Sheets   165

poison pill   129
post-crisis   127, 128
portfolio-builders   45–46
positive screening   110
post-information age   197–198
pre-crisis   127–128
preferred shares, see shares, preferred
price to book value ratio   77
price to earnings to growth ratio   77
principal   112
private company   40, 155–156, 164–166
going private   164–166
private listing   163
professional period of investor relations   12
Prosek   31, 140
prospectus   4–41, 96, 157–158
prospectus, final   160
protest divestment campaign   111
proxy   97, 123–125, 141–144
    proxy access   125
    proxy battle   123–125
    proxy fight, see proxy battle
    Proxy Monitor   124
    proxy season   142
    proxy solicitation   97
    proxy statement   97, 113, 141–144
    proxy statement summary   142
PRSA, see Public Relations Society of
     America
public company, see publicly traded company
Public Company Accounting Oversight
     Board   101
The Public Company Accounting Reform and
     Investor Protection Act   100–101
publicity   13–14, 139
Public Policy and Sustainability
     Committee   116
publicly traded company   5, 10, 141, 156–163
Public Relations Society of America   34
     Financial Communication section   24, 34

QIB, see Qualified institutional buyer
qualified institutional buyer   40, 96, 163, 183
qualitative guidance   141
quarterly report   26, 63, 96, 135, 136

R&D, see Research and development
RAP, see Russian Accounting Principles
rational apathy   147

reactive work   26, 145, 152
Reddit   125–126, 138, 192
   redditors   125–126
regional director   31
Registration statement   96, 157
Regulation Fair Disclosure, see Regulation FD
Regulation FD   98–100, 136, 138, 146
Regulation S   96
Regulation S-X   63
Reg. FD, see Regulation FD
Reg. S, see Regulation S
relational investing   146–147
relational investor   146
relationship investing   146–147
research coverage   147–149
research and development   65–66, 88
   research and development expense   65–66
responsiveness   144–147
retail investor, see retail shareholder
retail shareholder   41–42, 125–126, 139, 192
retained earnings   70
return on communication   169
return on equity   75
return on expectations   83
return on investment   169
return to shareholders   76
revenue   63–65
risk   81–83, 113, 123
risk premium   176
roadshow   149–150
Robinhood   125, 191
ROC, see Return on communication
ROE, see Return on equity
ROI, see Return on investment
rotational role   35
Rule 13F   194
Rule 144A   96, 163, 183–184
Rule 14a–8, 124
Russell Midcap Index   44
Russian Accounting Principles   77
r/WallStreetBets, see WallStreetBets

sales   63–65
   sales per employee   76
S&P, see S&P 500
S&P 500, 44
Sarbanes–Oxley Act, see The Public Company
      Accounting Reform and Investor
      Protection Act

SASB, see Sustainability Accounting
      Standards Board
say on pay   103, 124
Schedule 13D   97
Schwab   191
seasoned issue   161
SEC, see Securities and Exchange
      Commission
secondary market   5, 51, 96–97
Section   302, 101
securities   5
blue sky securities   11
   Securities Act of   1933, 96
   Securities and Exchange
      Commission   54–55, 95, 96
   Securities Exchange Act of   1934, 97
seed investment   155
Seeking Alpha   192
selling, general, and administrative
      expenses   65–66
SG&A, see Selling, general, and
      administrative expenses
selective disclosure   99–100, 136
sell-side   50–52
senior account executive   31
senior partner   31
senior vice president   31
share   5, 9, 10, 48, see also stock
share, common   48
   share, convertible   48
   share, preferred   48
   share price   3–4, 169–170
shareholder   5, 16–17, 39–49, 176–177, see
      also investor
   shareholders' equity   70
   shareholder mix   7, 176, 177
   shareholder proposal   117–118, 123–125,
      141–144
   shareholder relations department   17
   shareholding company   9–10
   shareowners   46–47
short-term liabilities   69
signaling   198
sinful stock, see stock, sinful under stock
shareholder proposals, see shareholder
      proposal under shareholder
socially responsible fund   110
social media   137–139, 172, 173, 189, 191–192
   social media listening   138

SOP, see standard operating procedure
sovereign fund   43
sovereign investment fund, see sovereign
    fund
sovereign wealth fund, see Sovereign fund
SOX, see Sarbanes–Oxley Act
SPAC, see special purpose acquisition
    company
special purpose acquisition company   163–
    164, see also blank check company
sponsored research   148–149
stakeholder   39, 50–56
Standard & Poor's   500, see S&P 500
standard operating procedure   170
start-up   155–156
stewardship theory   115
stock   5, 24, 39, 48, see also share
    stock bonus   25, 41
    stock compensation   41
    stock exchange   10, 24–25, 56, 158–159,
        160, 164–165
    lit   56
    dark   56
    stockholder   39–49, see also shareholder
    stockholders' equity, see shareholders'
        equity
    stock liquidity   156, 176
    stock, sinful   111
StockTwits   138, 192, see also cashtag
Stora Kopparberg   9–10
strategy   7, 135, 175–177
    strategic goal   175–177
    strategic investor   46–48
    strategic vision   7
subsequent offering   161
sucker list   11
superannuation fund   42
Sustainability Accounting Standards
    Board   109
sustainable development   108–110

Talent and Compensation Committee
    115–116, 117
talking green, lobbying brown   110
tangible assets, see asset, tangible under asset
target   128

targeting   151–152
target audience   171, 173, 174
tax burden ratio   75
third-party endorsement   147
TikTok   70, 138
token   193
top management   52–53, 85, 87
total-market investment   44
touch and feel events   190
trader   45
trader, noise   45
trading volume   176
True Indenture Act of   1939, 97
Truth in Securities Act   96
two-way communication   3, 5–6, 26, 139,
    150–151

underwriter   156–157
United States Securities and Exchange
    Commission, see Securities and
    Exchange Commission
utility token   193

value investor, see investor, value
Vanguard   500, 16
venture capitalist   40, see also investor,
    venture under investor
venture market   165
vice president   25
virtual meeting, see virtual shareholder
    meeting '
virtual shareholder meeting   142, 189
virtual reality   189–190
voting with your feet   47
voting with your wallet, see voting with your
    feet
VR, see virtual reality
VTM, see virtual shareholder meeting

WallStreetBets   125–126, 192, see also Reddit
whistleblower   102–103
    whistleblower protection   102–103
    whistleblower reward program   102
white paper   193
World Commission on Environment and
    Development   108